The Gendered Economy

The Gendered Economy

Work, Careers, and Success

Rita Mae Kelly

SAGE PUBLICATIONS
The International Professional Publishers
Newbury Park   London   New Delhi

For information address:

SAGE Publications, Inc.
2455 Teller Road
Newbury Park, California 91320

SAGE Publications Ltd.
6 Bonhill Street
London EC2A 4PU
United Kingdom

SAGE Publications India Pvt. Ltd.
M-32 Market
Greater Kailash I
New Delhi 110 048 India

Printed in the United States of America

Library of Congress Cataloging-in-Publication Data

Kelly, Rita Mae.
    The gendered economy : work, careers, and success / Rita Mae
Kelly.
        p.   cm.
    Includes bibliographical references and index.
    ISBN 0-8039-4215-X. — ISBN 0-8039-4216-8 (pbk.)
    1. Sex discrimination in employment—Arizona.   2. Sexual division
of labor—Arizona.   3. Sex role—Arizona.   4. Sex discrimination in
employment—United States.   5. Sexual division of labor—United
States. 6. Sex role—United States.   I. Title.
    HD6060.5.U52A65 1991
    331.4′133′09791—dc20   *72603*   91-14938
                                                              CIP

FIRST PRINTING, 1991

Sage Production Editor: Astrid Virding

Contents

Foreword

The "glass ceiling" has been explored in such diverse fields as religion, medicine, education, the public sector, and the corporate world. The research provided in *The Gendered Economy* by Dr. Rita Mae Kelly of Arizona State University together with the consensus recommendations of the participants in Arizona's Fifth Women's Town Hall add to our collective understanding of this issue at a critical time in our state's, and indeed our nation's, history.

Women and minorities will comprise the majority of entrants into the work force in the next decade. Although this trend has been predicted for some time, change has been slow and the 1990s find the world of work largely unprepared for this change, with salaries, benefits, and incentives designed for a diminishing labor pool of white, native-born males. Additionally, with more and more earning power, women will exercise more and more economic and political power as well.

By 1990 the number of women in management had increased fourfold over its level in 1970. Yet the average salary of women compared to men appeared to increase relatively little; and although sex-segregation by occupation declined, sex-segregation by industry increased. Women in 1990 remain baffled by their inconsistent and unclear progress toward gender equity and frustrated by their individual efforts to advance their own careers.

This book addresses these concerns in an interdisciplinary way, integrating and synthesizing up-to-date data and literature from management, organizational theory, psychology, sociology, political science, and law. The book is unique in that it provides a comprehensive

integration of the impact of U.S. history, the Constitution, and segmented labor markets with individual socialization, sex-role patterns,
behavioral styles, and career strategies. It addresses the relative impact
of individual decision making within the current U.S. legal, economic,
social, and institutional structures.

The book is important for the 1990s. Women—and leaders of both
sexes—are becoming increasingly concerned with the barriers women
and minorities face in attempting to advance their careers. It provides
a readable, integrative, comprehensive approach to understanding the
leverage points for removing these barriers and facilitating change and
new material on the gendered nature of the economy. It also presents
alternative frameworks for balancing the scales of justice so that women
will have an improved opportunity to gain career success in the U.S.
labor force.

This book is intended for undergraduate students in Women's Studies
and other social science courses focusing on gender issues at the
junior-senior level and for the general public. Women interested in
having successful careers as leaders or managers will benefit the most
from this book. It can be used as a text for courses on gender and society,
gender and the economy, sex roles, gender justice and public policy,
and gender, leadership, and management. Selected chapters could be
used in courses on women and the law/constitution. The discussion
questions in the Appendix will be helpful learning guides.

The book was written in response to a request of the Soroptomist
International of Phoenix, Arizona, Inc., to prepare a document to be
used as the basis for the Fifth Arizona Women's Town Hall. Arizona
holds annual meetings to discuss a topic of vital concern to women and
decision makers in the state. The last two chapters focus directly on the
gendered nature of the economy in the state of Arizona. The book is
directed at this type of audience nationally as well.

Participants in the Town Hall represent diverse ethnic, economic,
educational, and career backgrounds from throughout the state of Arizona. Their views, recommendations, and specific goals are contained
in Chapter 11, the summary and consensus document of the Town Hall.
The research and public comment contained therein is distributed to
legislators, libraries, alumnae, the media, and others interested in the
topic.

The Fifth Annual Arizona Women's Town Hall convened September
13-16, 1990. Researchers, organizers, and participants alike dedicated
themselves to a quality process through more than two years of planning

and preparation culminating in these exciting 3½ days. Reflecting the efforts of nearly 200 women from throughout the state, this document is extraordinary in its scope of research and depth of presentation. The process is a model for how university scholars and citizens can work together to advance public knowledge and the public interest.

It has been a great honor to serve as the Executive Chair of the Fifth Arizona Women's Town Hall. I would like to thank Dr. Rita Mae Kelly for a superbly authored research document. In addition, sincere appreciation is extended to the Executive Committee for countless hours of dedication, to individuals and businesses for the contributions that make a project of this scope possible, and to the participants for their hard work and consensus report that make this a document worthy of study and regard.

I strongly recommend the book to everyone who is concerned about the need for improving the status of women in the U.S. economy. It will help all readers learn more about policy options and personal choices for attaining that goal.

—DEBORAH LARKINS
Executive Chair
Arizona Women's Town Hall

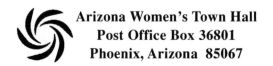

Arizona Women's Town Hall
Post Office Box 36801
Phoenix, Arizona 85067

Preface

Democracy requires knowledgeable participation of the citizenry. The difficulty of such participation, however, is great. It is time-consuming to obtain information and difficult to find quiet time and space for systematic reading of background information and relevant analytic materials. It is even more problematic for the average citizen to be able to reflect on policy-focused material and to discuss it with other citizens of diverse backgrounds in a meaningful dialogue.

The absence of community mechanisms to promote such knowledge acquisition and dialogue contributes to an apathetic citizenry and to a weakened political system. It certainly contributes to policy development that is not necessarily reflective of the broad citizenry. Non-involvement elevates the importance of the intellectual elite and policy analysts within bureaucracies and advocacy organizations. Although the role of a nation's intelligentsia, policy experts, and public servants in policymaking is vital and needs to exist, in a democratic society it is extremely important to have public fora linking university and research experts with concerned citizenry.

The Arizona Town Hall concept is an attempt to provide this link in a regularized, ongoing way. Each year in Arizona several town halls are held. Their topics are wide-ranging, encompassing transportation, crime, education, health, the economy, and the political system, among others. The basic idea of these town halls is to place the expertise of the university at the service of community. In the process it is hoped that the level of discourse over public problems will rise and that new, creative, more viable, and yet cost-effective solutions to societal problems will result. At the minimum increased understanding of the historical and philosophical bases of public problems and a broader perspective oi. 'he nature of the issues are expected.

The First Arizona Women's Town Hall was held in 1986. The Arizona Women's Town Halls have been sponsored by the Soroptimist International, Inc., of Phoenix, Arizona. As the project director for two of these, the Second Town Hall on *Women in the Arizona Political Process* (Lanham, MD: University Press of America, 1988) and this Fifth Town Hall on "Windows of Opportunity or Locked Doors: Women, Work, and Success," I have been impressed with the organization, care, and work put in by citizens to develop and make these town halls succeed. The process used by the Soroptimists illustrates the effort required.

The Soroptimists have several committees responsible for each town hall. A Research Committee, consisting of about ten to fifteen people, selects the topic, seeks a project director to be responsible for the research and writing of the document, and monitors the research progress. This committee does not interfere with the research but rather seeks to clarify for the researcher(s) the issues of concern to the citizens. A major part of this committee's responsibility is to ensure that the final research document is comprehensible and readable for the town hall participants. Because some of the citizens may have less than a high school education, this is a formidable task, and one to which university scholars often do not attend. Typically the town hall documents are written for a college-level audience but with the expectation that they will be accessible to concerned citizens with high school degrees.

Several other committees are also involved. One committee raises funds for the research. Another solicits participants and selects the final attendees at the annual three-day town hall. Another identifies and obtains keynote, luncheon, and dinner speakers, and another deals with the logistics. Of course, public relations, the media, and advertising are also important functions needing attention.

For its part the university contributes not only released-time for faculty to complete the research but typically also makes matching funds available for research assistants and secretarial support and allows free use of its library, computer and other support facilities. The project director is responsible for reshaping the research issues and questions so that up-to-date theories, methodologies, and data can be used to address and advance the topic at hand.

The result of this teamwork between the university and the community is not only a document, such as this book, but also a three-day town hall held in a conference-hotel and a consensus report (presented here as Chapter 11). The consensus report reflects the conclusions of the town hall participants on the issues raised and their recommendations to elected and appointed officials in the state. The research document along with the consensus report is then delivered to all relevant local and state officials. The Soroptimists and the town hall participants also return to their home communities and attempt to educate others on the issues and to promote nongovernmental efforts to address the problem at hand.

The greater outcome of such cooperation between universities and citizen groups is hopefully a strengthened and more participatory democracy. The process as well as any one specific research product is significant.

I have been pleased to participate in these cooperative endeavors. As an academic, I have found working with citizens helpful in focusing my research concerns. The attention of the members of the citizen Research Committee to logical argument and evidence for conclusions reached and positions stated by me substantially sharpened the presentation and analyses. The fact that many of the members and town hall participants would never consider themselves "feminists" also led to challenges concerning statements that might be considered ideological. Although all types of ideas and data were readily accepted by the committee as admissible, all material needed to be presented so that diverse ideological positions on gender, politics, the economy, and policy could deal with it logically and empirically rather than emotionally.

Citizen participation gives a different type of "peer review" than that given by one's academic colleagues. Both reviews are valuable, in my view essential, when dealing with matters of public policy. Academic review provides assurance of research quality and accuracy. Citizen review promotes clarity and relevance. In a cooperative atmosphere both contribute to a stronger and better democratic society.

—RITA MAE KELLY

Acknowledgments

This book reflects the efforts of many people, companies, and organizations. Financial support came primarily from the initiators of this project, Soroptimist International of Phoenix, Inc., which sponsored the Fifth Arizona Women's Town Hall. Arizona State University (ASU) has provided additional support. Special thanks go to Director Nancy Felipe Russo for all-around general assistance, space, and staff support from the ASU Women's Studies Program and to John Hepburn, Director of the School of Justice Studies, College of Public Programs, for facilitating my release from other duties so I could work on this project.

The number of contributors to this volume is large. Undergraduate and graduate students in the Arizona State University Justice Studies and Women's Studies programs have contributed not only to specific chapters in this Town Hall report (see credits in each chapter), but also by having completed theses and papers in classes over the years.

Steve Haugan, economist, U.S. Department of Labor, Bureau of Labor Statistics, provided us with appropriate statistics in the needed categories for 1964, Tables 3.5 and 3.6. His efforts were clearly above and beyond the call of duty and are much appreciated. Pat MacCorquodale, Associate Professor of Sociology, University of Arizona, also assisted in clarifying data in Figure 5.1. The various research assistants from the ASU School of Justice Studies and Honors College who assisted in gathering data and bibliographic references also greatly facilitated this research project: Marcia Cech-Soucy, Kimberly Fisher, Yen Li Yeh, Phoebe Morgan Stambaugh, Ria Hermann, Jody Horn, Chris Miller, and Jane Sugano.

I particularly wish to acknowledge Deborah Jean De Paoli, Kimberly A. Fischer, Marcia Cech-Soucy, and Phoebe Morgan Stambaugh who not only assisted in completing the research for portions of this book but also assisted in writing selected chapters, or portions of selected chapters.

I wish to acknowledge the assistance of Jan Lamoreaux and Julie Jones of the Women's Studies Program and Kay Korman, Gail Schroeder, and Anne El-Lissy of the School of Justice Studies for their typing, copying, and other assistance. A special note of thanks to the staff of the Auxiliary Resource Center, College of Public Programs, Marian Buckley, Fran Mularski, Tammy Stein, and Janet Soper for preparing the final manuscript in their usual outstandingly meticulous and efficient manner.

The editorial comments of Georgianne Baker, Allen Meyer, and Nancy Russo were also most important. Kimberly Fisher provided excellent assistance in facilitating the preparation of the final document.

Guidance provided by members of the Fifth Arizona Town Hall Research Committee has also been helpful. Special acknowledgments go to Mildred Bulpitt; Susan Cypert, Chair of the research committee; Janet Elsea; Jessica Funkhouser; Carol Hebert; and Deborah Larkins for their careful reviews and helpful advice throughout the project.

I also wish to acknowledge the following for granting permission to reproduce or cite specific items:

Aberdeen University Press for release of materials previously appearing in "Women, the Economy, and the U.S. Constitution," Andre-Jean Arnaud and Elizabeth Kingdom (eds.), *Women's Rights and the Rights of Man,* 1990.

Cambridge University Press for release of materials previously appearing in *Handbook of Career Theory* published in 1989.

Carolyn Desjardins, National Institute for Leadership and Development for permission to use her visual aid on morality of rights and morality of response.

Greenwood Press for permission to use data in Table 2 from Jane Bayes, "Occupational Sex Segregation and Comparable Worth," in *Comparable Worth, Pay Equity, and Public Policy,* edited by Rita Mae Kelly and Jane Bayes, 1988, page 19.

The Haworth Press, Inc. for release of material used in *Women & Politics,* Vol 10(4), 1990, and Vol 11(2), 1991.

D.C. Heath and Company for release of previously appearing figure in *Half the Human Experience: The Psychology of Women,* edited by J. S. Hyde, 1985.

National Conference of State Legislatures for release of material published in *The Fiscal Letter,* March/April 1989.

Soroptomist International of Phoenix and the Arizona Women's Town Hall Executive Committee extend sincere appreciation to the following organizations which through donations and support services have made this effort possible: All Media Communications; Arizona Public Service; Dr. Mildred Bulpitt; Communications Skills; Corroon and Black/Olliver Pilcher; Fry's Food Stores of Arizona; Gannett Foundation; Greyhound Dial Corporation; Hedlund Fabric and Supply; Honeywell, Inc.; Intergroup of Arizona; Larkins and Associates Advertising; Michael Dixon Productions; Performance Dynamics; Phoenix Camelback Hospital; Professional Data Systems; PSM Squared; Salt River Project; Security Pacific Bank; Ultrasound Diagnostic Services; University of Phoenix; US West Foundation; VSP, Inc.; Walker & Company Marketing Communications; YWCA of Maricopa County.

—RITA MAE KELLY
Project Director

1

Introduction

In the 1990s, women will become increasingly concerned with their ability to reach the very pinnacle of career success—becoming a high-level manager or a key decision maker. The number of women in management has increased fourfold since 1970. Yet Ann M. Morrison of the Center for Creative Leadership and Mary Ann Von Glinow, a professor at the University of Southern California,[1] charge that "the rate of upward movement of women and minority managers provides 'clear evidence of nothing less than the abiding racism and sexism of the corporation' " (p. 200). Women are seeking ways to move beyond the management jobs with low pay and little authority that they currently hold. The purpose of this book is to explore factors that impede or facilitate women's advancement in business and professions in the United States.

Numerous explanations have been offered for the relative absence of women in high-level positions. Generally these explanations can be classified into three groups: theories of sex and gender differences, theories based on labor market and organizational discrimination, and theories about systemic barriers. Historically most attention has been given to the sex/gender difference theories. These theories stress male and female biological differences, different reproductive roles, socialization variations, and sex differences in education, training, and work experience. The focus of such theories tends to place responsibility for success or failure on the individual.

Discrimination theories argue that the primary responsibility for the limited success of women (and minorities) lies with systematic biases of those who hold power in organizations, the economy, and the political system. Employers, supervisors, clients, and customers have bought into traditional sex-role stereotyping and discriminate against women to protect the privileged position afforded by the established gender hierarchy (or, in the case of race or ethnicity, the established racial/ethnic hierarchy). Discrimination theories imply that women and minorities will be hired, but only so long as no real change in power relations occurs.

Theories about systemic barriers concern structural patterns promoting discrimination. For example, dual labor market theory identifies primary and secondary jobs. Men tend to hold the primary or "good" jobs, which have the greatest stability and promotion potential, while women hold the secondary or "poorer" jobs, which have lower stability and lower wages.

All of these theoretical frameworks offer valid viewpoints, but each by itself offers an insufficient and distorted picture of reality. Taken individually, the picture each presents is like that of the twelve blind men describing the part of the elephant that they can touch. Each sees an important part of the reality of the elephant, but not one is able to present a comprehensive picture of the beast.

Examining the opportunities available to women in the U.S. economy is somewhat similar to examining the elephant. Describing one piece of the animal is helpful but grossly insufficient. This book seeks to provide a comprehensive overview of the place of women in the U.S. economy and the changing trends during U.S. history, with particular emphasis on the period since the mid-1960s. It also assesses the impact of sex-role ideology and socialization on gender differences in workplace aspirations, behavior, and achievements. The role that business organizations and government do and can play in incorporating women into the economic system as leaders and managers is also examined. Finally, an assessment is made of proposals offered to create an opportunity for women to play the leadership game on a level ball field.

Part I of this volume addresses the sociopolitical and cultural heritage and the economic structural constraints that shape a society and frame a human being's existence. This heritage and the institutions that enshrine it mold our belief systems and our expectations of what is possible and permissible.

Chapter 2 describes the sociopolitical heritage that has shaped U.S. cultural, legal, and institutional understandings of sex-role ideology and the role of women in the economy. It examines the impact of this ideology on gender equality in the U.S. labor force, and lays the foundation for the development of policy alternatives that will facilitate explicit strategies of empowerment for women and women's organizations. For women to become leaders and to have the highest levels of career success, national support must exist for gender equality in all aspects of citizenship and leadership. For minority women to have the same equal opportunity as white women, racial and ethnic barriers to success also need to be addressed.

In Chapter 3, the segmented nature of the U.S. labor market is detailed. As groups, men and women are positioned in different segments of the U.S. economy with women in the most vulnerable positions. The odds of increasing percentages of women becoming chief executive officers (CEOs) of Fortune 500 companies are low largely because so few women work in that part of the U.S. economy. These structural constraints of career success should not be confused with individual qualifications and/or abilities.

Part II examines socialization and career paths. Because males and females have been and are socialized differently, they are likely to have different career aspirations and follow different career paths. Career paths develop as an interaction between what the individual sees as possible and works toward and what society allows and facilitates. This interaction produces personal and organizational role conflicts for women as they enter the labor force and attempt to advance their careers.

Chapter 4 presents an overview of the impact childhood socialization can have on the attainment of skills, aspirations, and motivations appropriate for career success. Chapter 5 articulates the difficulties women have in integrating personal, political, and economic life because of the overlapping of historical sex-role and gender expectations from the private sphere to the public sphere. Chapter 6 discusses the influence of sex differences in behavioral traits and management/leadership styles on career success, particularly the attainment of high-level management and leadership positions. Chapter 7 examines the relationship of the individual to careers and to organizations.

Part III of this book calls attention to the organizational and societal supports available for women. Chapter 8 examines selected policy options that employers, businesses, and government can adopt to facilitate women's career success. Chapter 9 presents options being proposed to balance the scales of justice so that women will have a more equal chance of competing and succeeding.

Part IV presents a case study of how the gendered economy is manifested in one state, Arizona. Chapter 10 describes the legal power of women under the Arizona state constitution and statutes, details demographic characteristics and trends in the state's female labor force, and profiles influential women who are political and business leaders in the state. Chapter 11 offers the comments of a diverse group of citizens from around the state who attended the Fifth Arizona Women's Town Hall, September 13-16, 1990. This Town Hall focused on the information presented in this volume and asked the participants to offer policy recommendations to public officials to suggest ways of improving women's position in society and of increasing their chances for career success. It is hoped that these recommendations, along with the material presented, will produce a broader understanding of the factors facilitating and impeding women's efforts to have successful careers as managers and leaders. It is also hoped the material will stimulate more—and more sophisticated—discussion among the citizenry of ways of attaining greater gender equity in the United States.

Note

1. Ann M. Morrison and Mary Ann Von Glinow, "Women and Minorities in Management," *American Psychologist* 45(2) (1990): 200; partial citation of K. Bradsher, "Women Gain Numbers, Respect in Board Rooms," *Los Angeles Times,* 17 March 1988, p. 1.

PART I

The Impact of Culture and Economic Structure

Chapters 2 and 3 provide a comprehensive overview of women's historical and current position in the legal and economic systems of the United States. Both chapters highlight how the traditional roles of wife and mother have heavily influenced women's current status and position in society.

2

Sex-Role Ideology, the Constitution, and Gender Equality in the Labor Force

Americans generally believe that neither ideology nor politics ought to influence any person's career prospects. The belief, however, is belied by reality. This chapter gives an overview of the legal and political status of women in the United States relevant to professional careers and public roles. The text first highlights the constitutional prohibitions against women engaging in occupations other than wife and mother, then traces the struggles for equal access in the labor market, equal opportunity in professional training, and pay equity. This overview notes the role that affirmative action has played in advancing women to higher management in all sectors of society. Finally, some thoughts are presented on policy areas that need systematic attention in the 1990s.

Women and the Constitution

The Patriarchal Foundations

Barriers which continue to impede women's advances into upper-level positions reflect centuries-old myths about the appropriate role of women in society. Popular views of sex roles contain an assemblage of Graeco-Judeo-Christian beliefs. The Greek beliefs rest on six tenets:[1]

1. Males and females are opposite in nature; mingling of these opposite beings brings order and harmony to society.
2. The roles of males and females are opposite and complementary in accord with the design of Nature.
3. Nature divides the needs of each society into two distinct spheres: the Outdoor, or male sphere, comprising heavy labor, military activity, and deliberation over the protection and livelihood of the society; and the Indoor, or female sphere, where less strength but a greater share of love and nurturing is required.
4. The outdoor nature of man prepares him to engage in the public, political, visible, and official activities of society; woman's indoor nature relegates her to private, publicly invisible functions.
5. The public sphere, concerned with the survival of the state and the freedom of its members, is more dignified and important than the private sphere, which is concerned with the basic animal need, survival of the species.
6. Men are stronger, more courageous, superior; women are weaker, irrational, inferior.

To some extent, these tenets are still used to define the rights and prerogatives to which each sex is entitled.

Historian T. M. Marshall notes that three essential rights of citizenship have been available throughout Western history:[2]

Social rights, the right to a basic level of economic welfare and security; the right to share in the social heritage, and to live as a civilized being according to the standards prevailing in the society;
Civil rights, liberty of person; freedom of speech, thought, and faith; the right to own property and to conclude valid contracts; the right to justice;
Political rights, the right to vote and the opportunity to hold public office.

Throughout history, women have typically been granted only social rights. Women enjoyed civil and political rights indirectly through their husbands, fathers, sons, or other legally designated male protectors. Emphasis on equality, liberty, and fraternity during the French and American revolutions raised women's hopes for attaining all three rights of citizenship. These hopes were shattered by the conservative sex-role ideology of the male revolutionary leaders.[3]

The U.S. Declaration of Independence stated that men were created equal. Though many have argued that the word "man" subsumed "woman," the political and legal history of the United States conflicts with this assertion. Table 2.1 presents an overview of women and the U.S. Constitution, depicting the 200-year time line of inequality that women have faced in their efforts to participate in America's political and economic life.

The U.S. Constitution of 1789 counted white women as equal members of the population, but restricted franchise to white, propertied males. Women were not specifically mentioned in the 1789 Constitution. Fortunately, this document was relatively gender-neutral in its language, referring to citizens and persons. This wording has allowed the U.S. Supreme Court to reinterpret the Constitution in a manner more favorable to women as changes have occurred in the nation's sex-role ideology. American women were granted the right to vote in 1920.

The Bill of Rights of 1791 did not immediately impact women. Social and civil rights—the only rights for which women had legal support— were left to state rather than federal law. Unfortunately, the laws of most states functioned within the narrow framework of English common law, which afforded few rights to women. In the Southwestern states, laws based on community property ideals of Spanish traditions also afforded little legal power to women.

Laws in the United States historically have assumed the patriarchal, nuclear family to be the basic unit of society. The law has reinforced men's control over women, asserting that the well-being of the state depended upon maintaining a "unity of interests" between men and women. Indeed, the commonality of interest was believed to be so important that English common law denied women a separate legal identity once they were married. The opinion of Justice Bradley, in the well-known 1873 U.S. Supreme Court case of *Bradwell v. Illinois,* summarizes the ideology that prevailed in the United States during the 18th and 19th centuries. In this case, Bradwell was denied the right to work as a lawyer even though she had the legal training.

The civil law, as well as nature herself, has always recognized a wide difference in the respective spheres and destinies of man and woman. Man is, or should be, woman's protector and defender. . . . The constitution of the family organization, which is founded in divine ordinance, as well as in the nature of things, indicates the domestic sphere as that which properly belongs to the domain and functions of womanhood. The harmony, not to say identity, of interests and views which belong, or should belong, to the family institution is repugnant to the idea of a woman adopting a distinct and independent career from that of her husband. So firmly fixed was this sentiment in the

TABLE 2.1 Women and the Constitution: A Timeline of Inequality

1789	1791	1868	1873
U.S. Constitution No mention of women. Great Compromise included women as equal to men for counting population. Gender-neutral—refers to citizens and persons. Only in New Jersey did women have the right to vote, taken away in 1807.	Bill of Rights No immediate effect on women. State law, based on English Common Law, set women's rights (very restrictive).	14th Amendment Introduces sex-specific language into Constitution. If States denied males over 21 right to vote, then their proportional representation in U.S. Congress would be reduced. Prohibits states from "denying to any person . . . the equal protection of the laws." In effect, women not considered legal persons.	U.S. Supreme Court declares in *Slaughter-House Cases* that the Equal Protection Clause should apply only to state laws discriminating vs. blacks. In *Bradwell v. Illinois* (83 U.S. [16 Wall] 130) U.S. Supreme Court denies Myra Bradwell equal citizenship with men by denying her right to practice law, asserting basic sex differences and roles: "Man is, or should be, woman's protector and defender. The natural and proper timidity and delicacy which belongs to the female sex evidently unfits it for many of the occupations of civil life. The constitution of the family organization, which is founded in the divine ordinance, as well as in the nature of things, indicates the domestic sphere as that which properly belongs to the domain and functions of womanhood. The harmony, not to say identity, of interests and views which belong, or should belong, to the family institution is repugnant to the idea of a woman adopting a distinct and independent career from that of her husband. . . . The paramount destiny and mission of woman are to fulfill the noble and benign offices of wife and mother. This is the law of the Creator." (p. 141)

1874	1880	1908	1920
U.S. Supreme Court in *Minor v. Happersett* upheld Missouri male only voting law.	U.S. Supreme Court upheld West Virginia law restricting jury duty to men—held to 1975.	*Muller v. Oregon* special protection re working hours. Protectionist legislation justified because "history discloses the fact that woman has always been dependent upon man. . . . She is properly placed in a class by herself, and legislation designed for her protection may be sustained, even when like legislation is not necessary for men. . . ." (208 U.S. 412).	19th Amendment Women's Suffrage.
1948	**1954**	**1961**	**1963**
U.S. Supreme Court agreed Michigan state law could forbid women working as bartenders. Equal Protection Clause of 14th Amendment not violated even though the woman owned the bar. *Goesaert v. Cleary* (335 U.S. 464-466).	*Brown v. Board of Education*— beginning of civil rights litigation.	*Hoyt v. Florida* (368 U.S. 57, 61-2) reaffirmed restricting jury service to men, arguing "woman is still regarded as the center of the home and family life."	Equal Pay Act passed.
1964	**1971**	**1972**	**1973**
Title VII of the Civil Rights Act of 1964 prohibits employment discrimination on basis of sex as well as race.	14th Amendment Equal Protection Clause used for first time to prevent a state law from discriminating vs. women in *Reed v. Reed* (404 U.S. 71), enabling women to be appointed as administrators of estates.	Equal Rights Amendment passed, sent to states.	*Roe v. Wade* (410 U.S. 113) women's right to choose an abortion upheld, based on rights of privacy and integrity of the body.

(continued)

TABLE 2.1 Continued

Since 1971 over 50 cases heard by U.S. Supreme Court on sex-based challenges under Equal Protection Clause vs. sex stereotyping and discrimination stemming from it in hiring, promotions, maternity leave, disability insurance, pension rights, seniority, etc.	1987 In *Johnson v. Transportation Agency* (107 Supreme Court 1442) U.S. Supreme Court holds Title VII allows employer to adopt an Affirmative Action Plan to increase representation of women in sex-segregated jobs. In Rotary Club case (107 S.Ct. 1940) U.S. Supreme Court reaffirms California law opening membership.
1986 U.S. Supreme Court declares in *Meritor v. Vinson* sexual harassment in the workplace a violation of Title VII of the Civil Rights Act of 1964.	
1984 In *Hishon v. King & Spaulding* (467 U.S. 69) U.S. Supreme Court holds that if partnership is a privilege of employment, then firms may not discriminate on grounds of sex in hiring partners. 1st Amendment right of association no defense. In *Roberts v. Jaycees* (468 U.S. 609) Supreme Court upheld Minn. statute requiring admission of women with full voting rights. First Amendment freedom of association does not override state's right to end discrimination.	
1978 U.S. Pregnancy Discrimination Act modifies Title VII of the Civil Rights Act of 1964, prohibits employers from discriminating on the basis of pregnancy. No recognition that the workplace laws, structures, and policies are based on a male reproduction/child-bearing model.	

SOURCE: This chart was inspired by a speech given by U.S. Supreme Court Associate Justice Sandra Day O'Connor on "Women and the Constitution: A Bicentennial Perspective," in Atlanta, GA, February 11, 1988, at the Women and the Constitution Convention. Prepared by Rita Mae Kelly, Arizona State University, School of Justice Studies, Tempe, AZ 85287.

founders of the common law that it became a maxim of that system of jurisprudence that a woman had no legal existence separate from her husband, who was regarded as her head and representative in the social state.[4]

American women from Abigail Adams to the present have argued that women, as persons, are equal to men, and that women deserve separate political, economic, and legal identities. The feminist position did not gain political and occupational significance until the 20th century.

The 14th Amendment introduced sex-specific language into the U.S. Constitution for the first time in 1868, making women's position explicitly worse.[5] This Amendment stated that, if states denied males over the age of 21 the right to vote, then their proportional representation in the U.S. Congress would be reduced. Given that the 14th Amendment prohibits states from "denying to ANY person . . . the equal protection of the laws," this statement in effect denied that women were legal persons. In 1873 the U.S. Supreme Court explicitly ruled that the Equal Protection Clause applied only to state laws discriminating against blacks.[6]

This patriarchal view of women continued until recently. For example, as late as the 1960s, some states prohibited women from keeping their maiden names or from getting driver's licenses in their own names, arguing that such practices would harm the interests of the state.[7] In 1961, following previous precedent, the U.S. Supreme Court reaffirmed that jury duty could be restricted to men because a "woman is still regarded as the center of the home and family life."[8]

The argument that states had a responsibility to "protect" women from working for wages in particular capacities was politically accepted until the 1960s. For example, in the 1908 case *Muller v. Oregon,*[9] the U.S. Supreme Court justified protectionist legislation to prevent women from working as many hours as men because a "woman's physical structure and the performance of maternal functions place her at a disadvantage in the struggle for subsistence . . . History discloses the fact that woman has always been dependent upon man. . . . Legislation designed for her protection may be sustained, even when like legislation is not necessary for men."[10]

In the 1948 case *Goesaert v. Cleary,* the U.S. Supreme Court upheld a Michigan state law that forbade women from working as bartenders. In this case, Valentine Goesaert was denied the right to work at a bar which she owned after her husband had died. Reasoning that Goesaert could work as a bartender only as long as her husband was present to protect her morals, the Court ruled the state could prohibit her from such work after his death without violating the Equal Protection Clause of the 14th Amendment. The Court allowed Goesaert's gender to override her rights as a citizen, as a worker in the free labor market, and as a business owner.[11]

The Changing Legal Basis for Sex Equality

Economic and military necessity contributed to changing beliefs regarding women and work in the United States. As early as 1942, the National War Board endorsed the principle of equal pay for equal work to entice women to work for wages during World War II. Nonetheless, significant legal and ideological changes did not occur until after the rise of the civil rights and women's rights movements in the 1950s and 1960s. Employers subject to the Fair Labor Standards Act were first required to pay women and men the same wages for similar work in 1963.

The most dramatic legal change for women was the last minute inclusion of "sex" in Title VII of the Civil Rights Act of 1964. Title VII "prohibits discrimination on the basis of sex, race, color, religion, or national origin in any employment condition, including hiring, firing, promotion, transfer, compensation and admission to training programs."[12] Title VII authorized "affirmative action" as follows:

> If the court finds that the respondent has intentionally engaged in an unlawful employment practice . . . , the court may order such affirmative action as may be appropriate.[13]

Through its interpretations of Title VII, the U.S. Supreme Court has articulated two conceptual frameworks for enforcing equality in the workplace: disparate treatment and disparate impact analysis.

Disparate Treatment Doctrine

The *Disparate Treatment Doctrine* prohibits practices motivated by discriminatory intent by guaranteeing similar treatment for those who are similarly situated. Most of the Title VII cases up to 1990 have been decided using this framework. This doctrine essentially takes the labor force and economic structures as they are, together with their assumptions about job requirements, descriptions, and work hours. Hence, if a job description stated that an employee needed to be six feet tall, be able to lift 100 pounds, have been a high school wrestler, or meet other requirements that tend to fit the male physique, the courts would not be likely to find discriminatory intent. Women would not be similarly situated in seeking this job. However, if one woman met these requirements and was not considered, then discriminatory intent might be found.[14]

In the 1980s objections arose to the implicit assumption by employers and the courts that employment standards should accept masculine traits and sex-roles as the norm for job descriptions and work structures.[15] Tests for assumptions of gender neutrality and being "similarly situated" focused essentially on comparing individuals. The courts often ruled that only those women who could act like men were "similarly situated."[16]

The *EEOC v. Sears, Roebuck & Co.* case[17] provides an example of this problem. Women were not being hired for highly paid commission sales positions. Using the disparate treatment analysis, the court decided that, on the basis of the standards used, women were found to be less suited to and less interested in commission sales than men[18] and, therefore, no discrimination in hiring practices existed. The standards used, however, were such typically "masculine" traits as aggressiveness, assertiveness, competitiveness, personal dominance, and a desire to earn a large income. The tests used to screen job applicants included items that asked if the applicant had a low pitched voice, if they swore often, and if they had wrestled or played football. As Eichner[19] notes,

Disparate treatment doctrine, which prohibits practices motivated by discriminatory intent, is inherently unsuited to the task of identifying these biases because it guarantees similar treatment only for the similarly situated. Women, when they cannot or will not conform to male patterns of behavior, remain outside the scope of its protection. . . . The link that is widely thought to exist between "male" characteristics and traditionally male jobs creates a vicious cycle for many women. Because these jobs are associated with the traits and lifestyles of men, employers fail to hire women who cannot or will not adopt "male" standards of behavior. Men therefore continue to dominate these positions, which, in turn, continue to be viewed as male and adapted to men. Women, meanwhile, remain trapped in the "pink collar" ghetto of the labor market.[19]

Disparate Impact Doctrine

To address male-biased ideology in the economy and in job standards, several legal scholars have suggested examining female disadvantages rather than just sex differences. Many advocate a more sophisticated use of disparate impact doctrine. This doctrine, established in *Griggs v. Duke Power Co.* in 1971,[20] prohibits employment practices from having a discriminatory effect and establishes that "facially neutral employment practices that have significant adverse effects on protected groups may violate Title VII."[21] This doctrine goes beyond the disparate treatment doctrine by allowing courts to evaluate prohibited practices such as "male-biased job requirements [that] are 'fair in form, but discriminatory in operation.' "[22] To be successful in addressing these ideological biases the courts need to examine carefully the use of what is called the "business necessity defense." Eichner suggests a two-part test, as follows:

> They should ask first whether the challenged requirement is essential to the core function of the job. If the answer is affirmative, courts should then consider whether the selection process screens for that requirement in an unbiased manner. . . . The core function test would require courts to look beyond stereotyped notions of how the job should be performed to the basic function of the job itself.[23]

Once these tests are completed, the employer still needs to demonstrate that no other employment options of comparable business utility would have a less discriminatory impact. They also need to be most careful in accepting the idea that it would cost too much to restructure either job standards, the job environment, or job characteristics to remove impediments to women. Discrimination is not more tolerable because it is more profitable.

The Insufficiency of Title VII

In the 1970s and 1980s more women moved into the labor force, and the pressures to incorporate women into all levels of work, management, and leadership increased. As a result, it became clear that discrimination in the labor market comes in many forms.[24] Three major forms were identified: (a) pre-market types of discrimination (e.g., in socialization, education, mobility, training, and family responsibilities), (b) employment discrimination (e.g., not hiring women at all or for certain, usually less favorable, jobs only), and (c) wage and benefits discrimination (e.g., lower pay for the same or comparable job). Title VII was insufficient to deal with all of these issues.

Congressional Action

To address some of the pre-market types of discrimination, Congress passed several new laws. In 1972 the Equal Employment Opportunity Act became law; the Equal Rights Amendment cleared Congress, although it was not ratified by a sufficient number of states to become law; Title IX of the 1972 amendments to the Education Act gave women more equal educational opportunities; the Equal Credit Opportunity Act of 1974 gave women independence from husbands, fathers, and guardians in obtaining credit; the Career Education Incentive Act of 1977 sought to reduce sex stereotyping in employment; and the Women's Education Opportunity Act of 1978 sought to expand educational options. The gender bias of veterans' benefits and advantages open to males through military participation was reduced by the Defense Appropriations Act of 1976, opening the service academies to women. In 1978, the U.S. Pregnancy Discrimination Act modified Title VII of the Civil Rights Act of 1964 to prohibit employers from discriminating on the basis of pregnancy. However, there was no recognition that the workplace laws, structures, and policies are based on a male reproduction model.

Experience with differential treatment in hiring and promotion practices from the mid-1960s to the present revealed that addressing pre-market discriminatory laws and behavior, although vital, was also insufficient. Discrimination in employment and its ideological underpinnings needed to be continually confronted.

Actions of the U.S. Supreme Court: The Equal Protection Clause

A major weapon in the fight against sex discrimination became available in 1971 when the U.S. Supreme Court finally used—for the first time—the Equal Protection Clause of the 14th Amendment to prevent a state law from discriminating against women.[25] In *Reed v. Reed*,[26] this clause was used to enable women to be appointed as administrators of estates. Since 1971, over 50 cases have been heard by the U.S. Supreme Court on sex-based challenges under the Equal Protection Clause. Among other things, the clause has been effective against sex-stereotyping and discrimination stemming from discrimination in hiring, promotions, maternity leave, disability insurance, pension rights, and seniority issues.

The Reagan Era

Opposition to affirmative action became more vocal during the 1980s under the Reagan administration. Attorney General Edwin Meese attempted (unsuccessfully) to rescind Executive Order 11246, which had been issued by President Lyndon B. Johnson in 1965 and amended in 1967 by Executive Order 11375. These orders forbid sex discrimination by companies with federal contracts. Under Ronald Reagan, many departments—most notably the Justice Department—refused to set numeric goals, quotas, or timetables for the hiring and promotion of women. In addition, President Reagan appointed several conservative justices to the U.S. Supreme Court—Antonin Scalia, Anthony M. Kennedy, William A. Rehnquist—who have not always revealed support for affirmative action in general and for women in particular. Sandra Day O'Connor, though also a conservative appointed by Reagan, often has a different position than her male compatriots on women-related issues.[27]

The Reagan administration's budget cuts in social welfare programs underscored the weakness of women's economic power. During the 1970s more women had entered the labor force, but few paid attention to the source of funding for the jobs they held. With Reagan's cutbacks, the realization could not be avoided. The increase in jobs available for women—as well as for blacks—in the 1970s had come from the expansion of federal social welfare programs. "In 1980 nearly one-third of the 37 million women in the labor force worked in human services compared with only 10 percent of the men in the work force. . . . For white women, the social welfare economy accounted for 39 percent of the job gain between 1960 and 1980; for black women, an even more dramatic 58 percent."[28] Professional women were employed in this sector twice as often as men. By 1980, "70 percent of the nation's 17.3 million human service workers were women."[29] About two-thirds of this sector of the economy is dependent upon government social expenditures. Hence, the cutbacks implemented by the Reagan administration directly attacked the new jobs, roles, and status of women.

By creating jobs for women in the state social welfare economy, the federal government had placed women in a secondary, dependent, and highly vulnerable labor market. Many women had left the dependency of the patriarchal nuclear family; as many as 39% of women did not live in a joint household with a male in 1980. When the Reagan program cut back on social welfare jobs, these women in particular were put in difficult positions. Most could not have returned to the patriarchal family situation even had they wished to do so.

In the 1960s, the liberal doctrine supporting "individual freedom of choice, privacy, and equality of opportunity" dominated political discourse. Zillah R. Eisenstein[30] argues that the Reagan administration reinstated rhetorical discourse centered on the white male "head of the family" model. In the 1980s, equality was replaced with a necessary "hierarchy of difference." Some variations on this theme emerged. The New Right argued that women differ from men because they are intended for childbearing and child raising. The Reagan rhetoric again asserted that men are supposed to provide for women's and children's economic needs. Neoconservatives, on the other hand, argued that women can leave their "natural" duties to compete with men, but that they should not expect equality of results because women are different. Each of these variations contributed to the production of a rhetorical environment hostile to the pursuit of gender equality.

In the 1980s women began learning that women's liberation did not necessarily mean they were becoming free and equal with men. Just as blacks learned that a difference exists between a "freed man" and a "free man," women were learning the difference between being a "liberated woman" and a "free woman." More was needed to attain de facto equality and freedom.

Despite the executive branch's opposition to affirmative action, the courts, the business community, and the majority of the American people continued to support actions to remove disparate treatment and disparate impact on women in the labor force. For example, in 1986, in *Wygant v. Jackson Board of Education*,[31] the Court addressed the question of whether an affirmative action plan developed to facilitate the removal of sex and gender (or racial) imbalances in the work force would be legal and, if so, when? The Court affirmed such plans as constitutional and established that affirmative action plans "need not be limited to the remedying of specific instances of identified discrimination."[32] As to when such plans would be acceptable, the *Wygant* decision appears to have established the following rules:

the plan must further a compelling state purpose and be narrowly tailored. Remedying the effects of prior discrimination is at least one acceptable purpose, and to be narrowly tailored, a plan must be temporary, flexible, and necessary.[33]

The plan also should reflect target numbers that are proportionate to the relevant qualified pool and be implemented in such a way as not to unduly burden white male workers.

In the 1987 case of *Johnson v. Transportation Agency, Santa Clara County,*[34] the Court explicitly supported positive affirmative action plans for promoting women. In 1978 the Santa Clara District Board of Supervisors adopted a plan that encouraged sex to be considered a factor in promotion in those cases where women were significantly underrepresented compared to their percentage in the county labor force. Subsequently, the Transportation Agency promoted Diane Joyce to the position of road dispatcher over a male, Paul Johnson, even though Johnson had scored two more points on a qualifying examination. Johnson claimed sex discrimination and sued. The Court ruled that such positive actions on the part of employers were constitutional with a 6-3 decision. The fact that none of 238 employees in the Skilled Craft Worker category were women provided evidence of discrimination. Additionally, the affirmative action plan did not harm the interests of males or bar them from advancement.

The *Johnson* case is considered a catalyst for voluntary affirmative action.[35] The Court has determined that a statistical imbalance is all that is required for an employer to implement voluntary affirmative action measures. If the employer decides that a particular group of minorities is not adequately represented in the company, he or she may make adjustments on a voluntary basis to improve the balance. The causes for the imbalance are not at issue, only the imbalance itself is at issue. The *Johnson* holding is centered upon the premise that the use of affirmative action, even for subtle de facto discrimination, is supported and encouraged. "Most importantly, the Court in *Johnson* for the first time seems to have sanctioned the use of affirmative action to remedy the most pervasive and insidious form of discrimination—discrimination that is subtle and for which no individual, but rather society, is liable."[36]

In 1989, the U.S. Supreme Court made several rulings that appeared to threaten affirmative action. In *Martin v. Wilks,* a Birmingham, Alabama, case,[37] the Court allowed a group of white fire fighters to challenge a plan adopted in 1981 to implement affirmative action for blacks. The original lawsuit was filed against the city for discriminatory hiring and promotion practices. The white fire fighters used Title VII in 1989 to argue that they were being denied promotions because of their race. In this case, the Court ruled in favor of the white fire fighters. In the 1989 *Wards Cove Packing Co. v. Antonio* case, which involved equal opportunity issues and the disparate impact rule,[38] the Court changed the 1971 unanimous decision in *Griggs v. Duke Power Co.*[39] prohibiting employers from adopting ostensibly neutral employment practices that harmed women and minorities. In the 1989 *Wards Cove* case, the burden of proof that the "neutral" practice negatively impacted a protected class was placed on the victim. The ruling did not require employers to establish the need for such practices. In *Lorance v. A.T.&T.*,[40] tighter time limits were established for seeking legal redress against discrimination. Previously, the timing for the statute of limitations on a Title VII challenge began when a particular employment plan was applied. Under the 1989 *Lorance* ruling, the timing begins when the plan is adopted by the employer.

The extent to which this more conservative Court will erode principles of affirmative action further is unclear. Reagan's appointees appear ready to accept the traditional sex-role ideology and to see gender inequality in the labor force as the normal result of basic biological and physiological sex differences. In response to these and other Court decisions, women's rights and civil rights groups have lobbied for the Civil Rights Act of 1990.[41] This act would have reinstated the *Griggs* rule, returned to the less strict rule on determining the statute of limitations on Title VII challenges, and would have limited the time frame that people who might be adversely affected by a proposed court order can object in affirmative action cases. The act would also have made it illegal to discriminate even if legitimate motives for doing so were blended with discriminatory motives. The bill passed Congress but President George Bush's veto was sustained October 24, 1990. Thus, as of January 1991, the restrictive Court interpretations stood as the law of the land.

Wage discrimination against women has also been pervasive. Not until 1972 was the Equal Pay Act of 1963 extended to executive, administrative, and professional work, including those employed by private and public educational institutions. Additionally, Executive Order 11246, which extended affirmative action and equal employment opportunity requirements to all federal contractors receiving $50,000 or more or employing more than 50 persons, was seldom implemented until the growing momentum of the women's movement forced the government to use this order on behalf of women more frequently. The implementation of this executive order by the Department of Labor's Office of Federal Contract Compliance and the actions of the Equal Employment Opportunity Commission facilitated progress for wage justice. For example, in the 1970s, banks in Boston were forced to give cost-of-living increases to clerical workers and to post notices for administrative positions. In 1973 American Telephone and Telegraph was compelled to pay $15 million to women for previous discrimination. Although the reimbursement fell short of the actual earnings lost, the principle of recompense was established.

Pay equity requires fair and equitable payment for work performed. It is mandated by the 1963 Equal Pay Act, required by Title VII of the 1964 Civil Rights Act, and supported by both a 1980 Presidential Executive Order and a 1981 U.S. Supreme Court ruling.[42] Pay equity defends such sources of wage differences as merit, seniority, and quality or quantity of production, while prohibiting pay disparities based on sex and race.

By 1990, 46 states, all except Arkansas, Delaware, Georgia, and Idaho, had taken some action to address pay equity problems. Twenty states had adjusted their payrolls to eliminate sex or race biases, an increase from only five that had taken such actions as of 1984. In 1986, in *Bazemore et al. v. Friday et al.*,[43] the Supreme Court decided that past discriminatory practices and statistical evidence of pay inequities could be used in court. By 1990 job evaluation studies were being or had been conducted in 28 states. Three of every four states had a pay equity task force or commission. At least six states had instituted pay equity adjustments as part of a comprehensive plan to resolve sex- and race-based wage discrimination.[44]

Comparable worth policies seek to reduce the wage gap between the sexes that is unrelated to productivity and job content. They address some of the salary disparity resulting from sex-segregation in occupations that have equivalent levels of skill, ability, effort, and responsibility requirements but different pay levels. Organizational structures and procedures sustain pay inequities and are reinforced by the beliefs employers and employees have about men's and women's work.[45]

By the 1980s gender wage justice had clearly become an important political issue. The role of federal law and the legal reinterpretations of women's rights under the Constitution had been vital in encouraging states to address these issues. Again, the political foundations needed to produce legal and ideological changes are evident.

The political system is responding to the changed socioeconomic position of women in society and to evolving national beliefs regarding women and work. In 50 years, the change has been dramatic. In 1936, a Gallup poll found that 82% of those surveyed objected to married women working. At the time 26 state legislatures were considering bills to keep married women from holding jobs.[46] World War II effectively negated these views. By 1945, 36% of the nation's jobholders were women. In 1944 more than 50% of the female labor force was married. In the 1950s the proportion of women in the labor force retreated to 28% and more women became "cakewinners," leaving the "breadwinning" to the male members of their families.[47] By the late 1980s, women represented 45% of the labor force,[48] and national opinion reflected these changes.

In 1982, a Gallup poll[49] found that about one-half of both primary and secondary students thought women were equal to men in job opportunities, whereas 63% of college students felt women did not have such equal opportunities. A 1985 Harris survey of the adult population found that better than a two-to-one majority of Americans felt that "women are often discriminated against in being promoted for supervisory and executive jobs."[50] Between 1984 and 1985, the number of respondents convinced that "women often do not receive the same pay as men for doing exactly the same job" increased by 27%.[51]

The sharp jump in awareness might have been partly due to two U.S. Supreme Court cases over this one-year period, both dealing with the First Amendment rights of freedom of association. In *Hishon v. King and Spaulding,*[52] the Court held that if a partnership is a privilege of employment, then firms may not discriminate on grounds of sex in hiring partners. In *Roberts v. United States Jaycees,*[53] the Court upheld a Minnesota statute requiring women to be admitted to the Jaycees with full voting rights. The state's right to end discrimination overrode an individual's or a group's right to free association. In 1987 the Court reaffirmed this ruling in a California case involving the Rotary Club.[54] In this case the Court asserted a two-pronged test to determine whether associational rights of private clubs exempt them from state antidiscrimination laws. Essentially, the Court ruled that only close family-type relationships fell into the intimate category and that only those private groups whose purpose would be substantially impaired if forced to end discrimination were exempt from antidiscrimination laws.

The impact of these decisions on women's careers was relatively quick. A 1986 survey of women partners in accounting firms,[55] following up on a 1983 survey, found that "there were 157 women partners in 1986, more than a 125 percent increase from 69 in 1983."

The role of gender stereotyping in impeding the promotion of women and their potential to become partners of professional and business firms was the topic of the May 1989 case of *Hopkins v. Price Waterhouse*.[56] Ann Hopkins sued Price Waterhouse on the grounds that her rights were violated under Title VII of the Civil Rights Act of 1964. The U.S. Supreme Court concluded that the firm had not discouraged sex-biased evaluations and that it had used sex stereotyped assumptions about women to reject Hopkins as a partner. The Court's decision affirmed that, even in a "mixed-motives" case in which both valid and invalid reasons for nonpromotion exist, the Court will find a defendant guilty of sex discrimination. The decision clearly makes it easier for women and minorities to win in such promotion cases if a woman or other plaintiff proves discriminatory attitudes are present.

Conclusion

This brief overview demonstrates that the U.S. Constitution and U.S. Supreme Court decisions have reflected various sex-role ideologies. This chapter also reveals the great ideological change that has taken place in the United States among its populace at large and in its laws. This review reveals the necessity of proactively monitoring the courts and appointees to them as well as electing officials favorable to gender equality in the labor force. It also highlights the crucial role of public policy in stimulating and solidifying social change.

Social change typically stems from a variety of forces. Governmental policies are often reactive, attempting to control or channel these changes so that they impact existing societal structures and mores as little as possible. From a feminist perspective, such reactive policy-making is not only insufficient and shortsighted, but also a barrier to the goal of women becoming free and equal, and fully incorporated into society.

A major part of a proactive strategy would deal with explicit means for empowering women, that is, for increasing the accountability of decision makers and policy systems to women's organizations, women leaders, and women voters. All too often, research and policies have been designed to incorporate women into the public realm of work and politics by changing women to fit an extant model. From this assimilationist perspective the question all too often is, "How can we change the talents, motivations, abilities, and bodies of women to fit existing societal structures and needs?" Women do not have to become neuters or male clones to enter the labor force; rather, the economy can adapt to attract women and utilize the skills and abilities of women as well as minorities.

Notes

1. T. H. Marshall, *Class, Citizenship, and Social Development* (Garden City, NY: Doubleday, 1964), 71-72.

2. Marshall, *Class, Citizenship, and Social Development,* 71-72.

3. In France women leaders working for equality were guillotined. In 1792 French law gave the franchise to all adult males except servants. French women were not enfranchised until 1945. See Rita Mae Kelly and Mary Boutilier, *The Making of Political Women* (Chicago: Nelson-Hall, 1978), 36.

4. *Bradwell v. Illinois,* 83 U.S. (16 Wall) 130 (1873).

5. The 14th Amendment, Section 1 [Citizenship Defined; Privileges of Citizens.]: "All persons born or naturalized in the United States and subject to the jurisdiction thereof, are citizens of the United States and of the State wherein they reside. No State shall make or enforce any law which shall abridge the privileges or immunities of citizens of the United States; nor shall any State deprive any person of life, liberty, or property, without due process of law; nor deny to any person within its jurisdiction the equal protection of the laws."

The 14th Amendment, Section 2 [Appointment of Representatives.]: "But when the right to vote at any election for the choice of electors for President and Vice President of the United States, Representatives in Congress, the executive and judicial officers of a State, or the members of the Legislature thereof, is denied to any of the male inhabitants of such State, being twenty-one years of age, and citizens of the United States, or in any way abridged, except for participation in rebellion, or other crime, the basis of representation therein shall be reduced in the proportion which the number of such male citizens shall bear to the whole number of male citizens twenty-one years of age in such State."

6. Slaughter-House Cases, 83 U.S. (16 Wall.) 36, 21 L. Ed. 394 (1873).

7. Kirsten Amundsen, *The Silenced Majority* (Englewood Cliffs, NJ: Prentice-Hall, 1971), 130.

8. *Hoyt v. Florida,* 368 U.S. 57, 61-2 (1961).

9. *Muller v. Oregon,* 208 U.S. 412 (1908).

10. *Muller v. Oregon,* 208 U.S. 412 (1908).

11. *Goesaert v. Cleary,* 335 U.S. 464-466 (1948).

12. Title VII Civil Rights Act of 1964, 3701 et seq., as amended, 42 U.S.C.A. 2000e et seq. See also G. N. Powell, *Women & Men in Management* (Newbury Park, CA: Sage, 1988), 209.

13. N. Glazer, "The Affirmative Action Stalemate," *The Public Interest* 90 (Winter 1988): 101.

14. *EEOC v. Sears, Roebuck and Co.* 628 F. Supp. 1264 N.D. Ill. (1986).

15. For example, Maxine Eichner, "Getting Women Work that Isn't Women's Work: Challenging Gender Biases in the Workplace under Title VII," *Yale Law Journal* 97 (June 1988): 1404; Robin West, "Jurisprudence and Gender," *University of Chicago Law Review* 55 (Winter 1988): 1-72.

16. W. Williams, "The Equality Crisis: Some Reflections on Culture, Courts, and Feminism," *Women's Rights Law Reporter* 7 (1982): 175.

17. *EEOC v. Sears, Roebuck and Co.,* 628 F. Supp. 1264, N.D. Ill. (1986).

18. *EEOC v. Sears.;* see also Eichner, "Getting Women Work."

19. Eichner, "Getting Women Work," 1400, 1404, *passim.*

20. *Griggs v. Duke Power Co.,* 401 U.S. 424 (1971).

21. Eichner, "Getting Women Work," 1408.

22. Eichner, "Getting Women Work," 1408.

23. Eichner, "Getting Women Work," 1413.

24. Gunther Schmid, "Equal Opportunity Policy: A Comparative Perspective," *International Journal of Manpower,* 5(3) (1984): 15-25.

25. Justice Sandra Day O'Connor, "Women and the Constitution: A Bicentennial Perspective," *Women & Politics,* 10 (Summer 1990): 5-16.

26. *Reed v. Reed,* 404 U.S. 71 (1971).

27. Karen O'Connor and Jeffrey A. Siegel, "Justice Sandra Day O'Connor and the Supreme Court's Reaction to its First Female Member," *Women & Politics,* 10 (Summer 1990): 95-104.

28. Steven P. Erie, Martin Rein, and Barbara Wiget, "Women and the Reagan Revolution: Thermidor for the Social Welfare Economy," in *Families, Politics, and Public Policy,* ed. Irene Diamond (New York: Longman, 1983), 103.

29. Erie, Rein, and Wiget, "Women and the Reagan Revolution," 103.

30. Zillah R. Eisenstein, *The Female Body and the Law* (Berkeley: University of California Press, 1988), 117-151.

31. *Wygant v. Jackson Board of Education,* 54 LW 4480 (1986).

32. *Wygant v. Jackson Board of Education,* 54 LW 4480 (1986).

33. *Wygant v. Jackson Board of Education,* 54 LW 4480 (1986).

34. *Johnson v. Transportation Agency, Santa Clara County,* 107 S. Ct. 1442 (1987).

35. Martha Minow, "The Supreme Court, 1986 Term Leading Cases: Affirmative Action—Gender Preferences," *Harvard Law Review* 101(1) (November 1987): 300-310.

36. Minow, "The Supreme Court," 305.

37. *Martin v. Wilks,* U.S., 109 S. Ct. 2180 (1989). See also, S. Wermiel, "Workers Hurt by Affirmative Action Suit," *Wall Street Journal,* 13 June 1989, A3, A12.

38. *Wards Cove Packing Co. v. Antonio,* U.S., 109 S. Ct. 2115 (1989).

39. *Griggs v. Duke Power Co.,* 401 U.S. 424 (1971).

40. *Lorance v. A.T.& T.,* U.S., 109 S. Ct. 2261 (1989).

41. The Civil Rights Act of 1990 (Senate 2104; House of Representatives 4000). The House bill 4000 was incorporated into the Senate bill 2104, which passed Congress but

was vetoed by President George Bush on October 22, 1990. The Senate sustained the veto on October 24, 1990.

42. Rita Mae Kelly and Jane Bayes, "Conclusion," in *Comparable Worth, Pay Equity, and Public Policy,* eds. Rita Mae Kelly and Jane Bayes (Westport, CT: Greenwood, 1988), 239-246.

43. *Bazemore et al. v. Friday et al.* 478 U.S. 385 (1986).

44. See *Pay Equity Activity in the Public Sector, 1979-1989.* Washington, DC: National Committee on Pay Equity, 1989; *1990 Press Kit Update*, National Committee on Pay Equity, Washington, DC: National Committee on Pay Equity, 1990.

45. William J. Bielby and James N. Baron, "Men and Women at Work: Sex Segregation and Statistical Discrimination," *American Journal of Sociology* 91 (January 1986): 759-799.

46. *The Gallup Poll Public Opinion, 1935-1971, Vol. 1* (New York: Random House, 1972). The question, "Should a married woman earn money if she has a husband capable of supporting her?" was from a November 15, 1936, poll.

47. For more discussion and statistics, see Bureau of the Census, *Money Income and Poverty Status of Families and Persons in the United States,* Current Population Reports, Series P-60, No. 127 (Washington DC: Government Printing Office, August 1981); and Nancy McGlen and Karen O'Connor, *Women's Rights: The Struggle for Equality in the Nineteenth and Twentieth Centuries, Part II* (New York: Praeger, 1983).

48. Bureau of the Census, 5.

49. *The Gallup Report,* August 1982, Report #203, 23-30.

50. *Harris Poll,* 19 August 1985, #67, 2-3.

51. *Harris Poll,* 2-3.

52. *Hishon v. King and Spaulding,* 467 U.S. 69 (1984).

53. *Roberts v. United States Jaycees,* 468 U.S. 609 (1984).

54. *Board of Directors of Rotary International v. Rotary Club of Duarte,* 107 S. Ct. (1940); 468 U.S. 609 (1987).

55. Karen L. Hooks and Shirley J. Cheramy, "Women Accountants—Current Status and Future Prospects," *CPA Journal* 58(5) (May 1988): 18-27.

56. *Hopkins v. Price Waterhouse,* 618 F Supp. 1109 (1989).

3

Women, the Economy, and Careers

In the 21st century women will play an increasingly significant role in the development of American business strategies and in the economy as a whole. In 1988, 45% of the U.S. labor force and 39.3% of all executive, administrative, and managerial persons were women.[1] These figures illustrate the remarkable change in the U.S. economy since 1900, when women constituted only 4% of the labor force and virtually no managers were women. This rapid expansion of women in the work force has been called "the greatest change in society since the invention of the wheel."[2]

In the 1980s women penetrated lower and middle levels of management in both the public and private sectors of the economy and became more visible in leadership positions in voluntary noneconomic groups (e.g., religious groups) as well. Table 3.1 presents the percentages of women employed full-time in 1988 in various managerial occupations. In 1988, 10.8% of all women workers were in management, up from 5% in 1947.[3] In 1988, 13.6% of all male full-time workers were employed as executive, administrative, or managerial personnel.[4]

By 1990, significant numbers of women had become concerned with not just equal opportunity and access to entry- and middle-level leadership positions, but also with breaking through the "glass ceiling" to upper-level management positions.[5] Although the percentage of corporate managers who are women increased from 24% in 1978 to 37% in 1988, few of these women entered queues that would enable them to move to even higher levels. For example, in 1983, *Business Horizons* reported that a great many of these female managers were older, not

28

TABLE 3.1 Employed Civilians in Executive, Administrative, and Managerial Occupations: Percentage Who Were Women in 1988

	Total Employed (in thousands)	Percentage Women
Total, 16 years and over	114,968	45.0
Executive, administrative, and managerial	14,216	39.3
Officials and administrators, public administration	472	44.5
Financial managers	502	42.4
Personnel and labor relations managers	130	49.1
Purchasing managers	99	24.4
Managers, marketing, advertising, and public relations	482	32.0
Administrators, education and related fields	562	48.9
Managers, medicine and health	163	61.3
Managers, properties and real estate	433	44.8
Management-related occupations	3,772	50.6
Accountants and auditors	1,329	49.6
Underwriters and other financial officers	741	50.7
Management analysts	199	33.0
Personnel, training, and labor relations specialists	390	58.9
Buyers, wholesale and retail trade, except farm products	233	50.4
Inspectors and compliance officers, except construction	194	26.8

SOURCE: Employed civilians by detailed occupation, sex, race, and Hispanic origin, 1983-88. U.S. Department of Labor, Bureau of Labor Statistics (1989). *Handbook of Labor Statistics* (Washington, DC: Government Printing Office, 1989), p. 90, Table 18.

well-educated, and in dead-end positions (being corporate secretary or treasurer).[6] A study of the executives listed in *Standard and Poor's Register*[7] in 1987 found that women constituted only 16% of all presidents and 13% of executive vice presidents. Although the percentage of vice presidents was 37.5%, up from the 1982 level, women still "comprise[d] only 5-6 percent of newly appointed executives."

When one considers minority status with gender the situation is even more bleak. According to Juanita Cox-Burton,

In 1979, a survey of 1,708 senior executives [within Fortune 1000 companies], three were black, two were Asian, two were Hispanic, eight were female; none were women of color. Six years later, in 1985, a survey of 1,362 senior executives found four blacks, six Asians, three Hispanics, and 29 women; none were women of color. . . . For white males, on average, 1 out of every 21 who enters a major corporation makes it to officer level within that corporation. For white females, the statistics are 1 out of every 136. For men of color, the ratio is 1 out of every 42. For women of color, there are no ratios, because in mid-1986, when we conducted the survey, we could not locate a woman of color at officer level within a major corporation.[8]

Changes have occurred since 1986, but not many. In the public sector the situation is only marginally better.

This chapter provides a description of the proportion of women holding high-level managerial and leadership positions in the United States. An adapted model of segmented labor market theory is used to organize the material. This model helps identify areas of the economy and society successfully penetrated by women. Segmented labor market theory has previously been used to analyze between-industry and be-tween-firm differences in earnings among all workers.[9] It has not, to my knowledge, been used as a broad framework for exploring gender differences in achieving career success. As the following discussion reveals, however, the gendered nature of the U.S. segmented labor market directly impacts women's probability of attaining equality with men as managers and leaders in the nation as a whole. Although segmented labor market theory does not provide sufficient guidance for detailed analyses of the factors contributing to women's career success or failure, it does facilitate grasping the overall gendered picture of the U.S. economy needed for these other analyses to occur. The analysis in this chapter examines the perpetuation of sex-segregation in the U.S. labor force and highlights factors that inhibit women attempting to follow male models of career advancement. To follow such models, women would minimally need to work in a comparable occupation, industry, and/or labor market segment as the men in the model.

The chapter also reveals how gender is used as an organizing force in the economy. Applying segmented labor market theory to the place of women in the economy reveals that gender is strongly related to the structure of occupations and industrial sectors. As Joan Scott notes,[10] most discourse historically has proceeded as though economic structure is ungendered, based on universal classifications and gender-neutral categories.

Scott documented the historical inaccuracy of this assumption.[11] Politically active seamstresses organized producer cooperatives and formulated alternatives to socialist and capitalist work forms. In the political debate, male tailors had insisted that all work be performed in the shop, claiming that work at home corrupted the order and emotional fabric of family life. Economic deterioration and deskilling were equated with a move from the male model (work in shops) to a female model (work at home). In their efforts to gain suffrage and equality with men, seamstresses emphasized their similarity to men. Seamstresses and tailors were wage earners doing identical or comparable work. The women viewed themselves as equal producers and citizens. The male tailors, however, based their identity—and superiority—on the location of work and on their possession of particular skills. Wage earning itself and comparability of the nature of work was not sufficient for attaining political and economic equality.

Studies such as Scott's show that the political and social meaning of gender and work are highly interrelated. In the following assessment of interactions between gender assumptions and the segmentation of the U.S. labor market, it will become clear that this relationship between gender and work remains strong and that genderized work continues to substantially affect the structure of the labor market.

The Segmented Labor Market

In 1988, Jane Bayes[12] utilized segmented labor market theory to help explain the continual gaps between male and female salaries. In developing her model, Bayes combined elements of the dual labor market theory[13] and the dependencia theory.[14] The dual labor market theory suggests that two distinct segments of the market determine pricing and allocation of labor. In the first segment, or external market, economic supply and demand make this determination, but in the second, or internal market, this determination is made by administrative rules and procedures.[15]

Internal market jobs tend to have high wages, good fringe benefits, advancement potential, and job stability. In Figure 3.1, these are called primary occupations. Only a few points of entry allow workers to obtain these jobs. Advancement occurs through job clusters called "mobility chains."[16] Only at the entry point does significant competition exist.

> Thereafter workers within the firm fill jobs higher in the organizations as they advance along the mobility chains. The upper tier of the primary sector consists of professional, managerial, technical, and administrative jobs. Elaborate administrative procedures are absent, pay is higher and control tends to be through an internalized professional code. Upper-tier jobs emphasize a generalized body of theoretical knowledge and principals rather than specific

LABOR MARKETS

TYPES OF EMPLOYER

Core Economy Firms - 500-800 Firms
Over 1/2 of GNP
Employs 45% of U.S. workers in mining/mfg.
Examples: heavy industry, large banks, mfg., chemicals, drugs, autos, metals, aircraft, petroleum

Periphery Economy Firms - 14,000 + Firms
About 1/4 of GNP
Highly competitive, entrepreneurial
Examples: textile mfg., restaurants, real estate, smaller computer firms, law firms, retail and service firms, geographically dispersed

Public Sector - Government/Nonprofits
About 1/4 of GNP
Noncompetitive, budget-driven

Voluntary Sector - Mostly connected with the public sector
Religious Institutions Prevalent

	Primary	Intermediate	Secondary
Core Economy Firms	**1** Chemists Engineers Top Managers Bankers Corporate Lawyers Corporate Accountants etc. **MALE DOMINATED**	**2** Skilled Craft Workers Sales Personnel Insurance Claims Adj. Computer Analysts Middle Managers	**3** Maintenance Workers Clerical Staff Assembly Workers
Periphery Economy Firms	**4** Lawyers Doctors Managers Administrators in some hospitals, large chains Social Scientists MORE WOMEN HERE THAN 1 AND 2	**5** Bank Tellers Computer Programmers Middle Managers Nurses	**6** Fast-food Workers Operatives Word Processors
Public Sector	**7** Elected Officials High Level Administrators Top Staff Appointed Judges	**8** Mid-range Civil Servants Teachers Librarians Nurses HIGH PROPORTIONS OF	**9** Clerical Staff Maintenance Part-time WOMEN ARE IN 8 AND 9
Voluntary Sector	**10** Clergy CEO of Red Cross Fundraisers	**11** Volunteer Planners Coordinators	**12** Daily and Incidental Workers

Figure 3.1. Types of Segmented Labor Markets

SOURCE: Expanded from Jane Bayes, "Occupational Sex Segregation and Comparable Worth," in *Comparable Worth, Pay Equity, and Public Policy*, eds. Rita Mae Kelly and Jane Bayes (Westport, CT: Greenwood Press, 1988), p. 40.

32

skills. The lower tier of the primary sector includes clerical, sales and skilled craftspersons. In this tier, training is specific to special skills and occurs primarily on the job. In contrast, secondary-market jobs have low wages, few fringe benefits, higher labor turnover, little chances for advancement or training, and often are supervised in arbitrary, personal, and unroutinized ways. Entry into secondary labor markets is characterized less by a queuing process than is entry into primary markets.[17]

In Figure 3.1, the dual-labor market theory is expanded to three components—the primary level, reflecting the very best jobs; the intermediate level, reflecting less desirable jobs; and the secondary level, reflecting the least desirable jobs.

The dependencia version of the segmented labor market theory developed as an effort to understand multinational corporations and the global economy. It posits that three major sectors exist: a core, a periphery, and a public sector. To this I have added a voluntary sector (see Figure 3.1).

A major reason for focusing on segmented labor markets can be seen in Table 3.2. This table shows that the proportion of female sex-segregated industries almost doubled between 1972 and 1981, and that little change occurred between 1981 and 1988. The percentage of industries where 70% to 100% of the employees were female rose from 6% in 1972 to its present level of 10%. During this same period the number of male sex-segregated industries declined from 53% to 40%. Increasingly more men are working with women, but simultaneously, increasingly large numbers of women are working primarily with other women.

This pattern is seen more strikingly in the data on the sex-segregation of occupations. From 1970 to 1988, the percentage of male-segregated occupations declined from 67% to 43%; yet female sex-segregated occupations rose from 15% to 22% (see Table 3.3).

As Table 3.4 shows, sex-segregation by major occupational group is still great, with women being disproportionately employed in the administrative-support-clerical, household, and other service categories. Women are disproportionately absent from the protective service, craft, transportation, and handler-laborers categories. Sex segregation by both industry and occupation requires attention to the segmented nature of the U.S. labor market and its gender linkage.

A brief overview of the location of the power elite in the United States by its function and sex composition also illustrates the connection between one's sex and the segmented power structure. A 1981 study

TABLE 3.2 Changes in Number of Sex-Segregated Industries, 1972, 1981, and 1988

	1972		1981		1988	
	No.	%	No.	%	No.	%
Number of female sex-segregated industries[a]	11	6	21	11	26	10
Number of integrated industries[b]	76	41	85	45	123	50
Number of male sex-segregated industries[c]	103	53	84	44	99	40
	190	100	190	100	248	100

SOURCE: Data derived from U.S. Bureau of Labor Statistics Bulletin 2096 (1982), Table B-21; *Handbook of Labor Statistics* (1989), Table 19, pp. 104-107.
NOTE: a. 70-100% female employees; b. 31-69% female employees; c. 0-30% female employees.

TABLE 3.3 Occupations Classified by Degree of Sex Segregation (Percentages)

	1970	1980	1988
Male Sex-Segregated[a]	67	58	43
Sex Integrated[b]	15	27	34
Female Sex-Segregated[c]	15	16	22

SOURCES: The 1970-80 data were derived from Rytina (1982) as reported in Jane Bayes, "Occupational Sex Segregation and Comparable Worth," in *Comparable Worth, Pay Equity, and Public Policy*, eds. Rita Mae Kelly and Janes Bayes (Westport, CT: Greenwood Press, 1988), p. 21, for 250 two- and three-digit occupations with total employment of 50,000 or more, as classified by the U.S. Census Bureau using 1981 annual averages. The 1988 data were calculated for the 344 occupations listed in the U.S. Department of Labor, Bureau of Labor Statistics, *Handbook of Labor Statistics* (Washington, DC: Government Printing Office, 1989), pp. 90-95.
NOTE: a. Occupations that are 0—30% female; b. Occupations that are 31—69% female; c. Occupations that are 70—100% female.

of the most power-oriented organizational structures in the United States—military, corporate, and political—found that only 22 out of 2292 top leaders were women.[18] A 1982 study compared males and females in leadership positions in 12 sectors of society,[19] finding that the proportion of women in top positions had doubled between 1970 and 1980, from 1.9% to 4.1%. The increases were uneven and still minor. In 1970 only two sectors—the foundations (7.4%) and the civic and the cultural (16.0%)—had more than 5% of women in top positions. In 1980, sectors with more than 5% were the foundations (14.7%), the universities (10.6%), the civic and cultural (9.0%), the government (7.7%), and the mass media (6.8%).

Segmented labor market theory helps examine the placement of women in various industries and occupations from a broader perspective. Taking the industry perspective first, we can consider as core

TABLE 3.4 Percentage of Women in Major Occupational Groups, 1970, 1980, and 1988

Group	1970[a]	1980	1988
Executive administrative, managerial	18.5	30.5	39.3
Professional specialty	44.3	49.1	49.8
Technical	34.4	43.8	47.9
Sales	41.3	48.7	48.9
Administrative support/clerical	73.2	77.1	80.1
Household	96.3	95.3	96.3
Protective services	6.6	11.8	14.4
Other Services	61.2	57.0	65.1
Craft	7.3	7.8	8.7
Machine operators	39.7	40.7	40.8
Transportation	4.2	7.8	9.0
Handlers/laborers	17.5	19.8	17.2
Total labor force	38.0	43.0	45.0

SOURCES: 1970/1980 data derived from Rytina and Bianchi (1984), table 2, Jane Bayes, "Occupational Sex Segregation and Comparable Worth," in *Comparable Worth, Pay Equity, and Public Policy*, eds. Rita Mae Kelly and Jane Bayes (Westport, CT: Greenwood Press, 1988), p. 19. Reprinted by permission. 1988 data derived from U.S. Bureau of Labor Statistics (1989) pp. 104-107.
NOTE: a. The 1980 census reclassified occupations extensively. In this table, 1970 data have been adjusted to the 1980 code. See N. F. Rytina and S. M. Bianchi, "Occupational Reclassification and Changes in Distribution by Gender," *Monthly Labor Review*, 107(3) (1984), pp. 11-17.

industries those firms that have sufficient business and demands for their goods and services, profit, and cash flow that they are able to employ workers on a full-time, year-round basis at a higher level than other industries.

In Table 3.5, the 11 major industries in the United States have been regrouped according to whether they fall above or below the national mean for stable or unstable employment (defined in terms of the percentage of workers in that industry employed on a year-round, full-time basis). Industries whose employment falls below the mean of full-time, year-round employment are grouped as "competitive" industries. Industries whose employment is above the mean of all industries are "monopoly" industries. A third category of "public administration" is included. The data indicate striking differences in the percentage of U.S. workers who are employed full-time, year-round between the competitive and monopoly industries. For example, in 1988 the mean percentage of workers with stable employment in the competitive industries was 48.1%; in monopoly industries it was 74.9%. These three sectors are detailed by sex in Table 3.6.

TABLE 3.5 Stability of Employment by Industry

	1960	1964	1968	1972	1976	1980	1984	1988
Mean for All Industries	53.7	55.0	57.9	57.1	54.3	56.1	58.2	61.3
Competitive Industries								
Agriculture	38.9	37.7	46.1	48.6	46.1	50.8	33.9	39.8
Construction	41.8	48.8	55.2	52.8	44.4	47.4	48.1	54.9
Retail Trade	42.5	41.8	42.6	38.9	38.0	38.0	40.2	42.6
Services[a]	44.5	43.0	45.1	46.1	35.6	44.1	52.3	55.2
Forestry/Fishermen	—	44.0	50.6	38.0	44.6	34.2	54.0	—
Mean	41.9	43.1	47.9	44.9	41.7	42.9	45.7	48.1
Monopoly Industries								
Mining	65.2	67.5	70.8	70.9	66.9	68.8	65.7	74.1
Manufacturing	64.3	67.7	69.5	67.5	65.8	66.9	71.1	75.9
Transportation; public								
utilities; communication	71.7	75.4	73.2	72.7	70.7	71.2	75.5	76.4
Wholesale trade	66.2	70.8	70.9	71.4	67.2	71.2	71.7	74.1
Finance; insurance; real estate	66.1	68.2	67.7	68.0	66.1	69.0	70.2	73.8
Mean	66.7	69.9	70.4	70.1	67.3	69.4	70.8	74.9
Public Administration	73.0	79.8	76.7	76.0	73.7	72.6	75.1	79.0

SOURCE: Developed from data in U.S. Bureau of Labor Statistics (1983), *Handbook of Labor Statistics*, Bulletin No. 2175, Table 48 and unpublished tabulations from Current Population Survey, Matrix 80040, Table 4 (1985; 1989).
NOTE: a. Excluding: (1) finance, insurance, real estate; (2) forestry/fisheries

The data in Table 3.6 show that women are disproportionately employed in the less stable, more competitive industries. In 1988, two of every three employed women worked in this less stable, more competitive sector whereas only one of every two males did (columns c and e).

Table 3.6 also reveals that the proportion of employed persons who are women has increased in all sectors (column b); the percentage of employed persons who are men is decreasing in all sectors (column d). In the competitive industries, the percentage of women rose from 42.2% in 1964 to 50.8% in 1988. In the monopoly sector, it rose from 25.4% in 1964 to 36.0% in 1988. In public administration, it increased from 27.8% in 1964 to 42.7% in 1988.

Comparing the proportion of females in each sector relative to all employed women (column c), the data show a slight increase of 1.2 percentage points from 1964 to 1988 in the competitive industries and a slight decrease of 1.4 percentage points in the monopoly industries. The percentage of employed men working in the less stable sector increased significantly during the Reagan era (from 46.4% in 1980 to

TABLE 3.6 Sectors of the U.S. Economy Detailed by Sex by Election Years 1964-1988

Sector	Year	(a) %Total Workforce Employed in Sector	(b) %Sector Workforce Who Are Female	(c) %All Employed Females Working in Sector	(d) %Sector Workforce Who Are Male	(e) %All Employed Males Working in Sector
Competitive	1964	52.8	42.2	64.6	57.8	46.4
	1968	52.8	42.3	61.8	57.7	47.8
	1972	54.0	45.5	64.6	54.5	47.3
	1976	63.0	47.9	66.9	52.1	44.5
	1980	65.1	51.5	66.9	48.5	46.4
	1984	57.2	50.8	65.6	49.2	50.8
	1988	58.3	50.8	65.8	49.2	52.2
Monopoly	1964	41.8	25.4	31.0	74.6	47.6
	1968	45.6	28.2	35.6	71.8	52.7
	1972	40.7	27.8	30.5	72.2	46.8
	1976	38.2	30.3	30.4	69.7	42.9
	1980	39.6	33.4	31.3	66.6	45.7
	1984	38.3	35.0	30.4	65.0	44.4
	1988	37.0	36.0	29.6	64.0	43.2
Public Administration	1964	5.2	27.8	4.2	72.2	5.7
	1968	6.1	30.7	5.2	69.2	6.6
	1972	5.3	29.7	4.2	70.3	6.1
	1976	5.2	31.9	4.4	68.1	5.7
	1980	5.3	35.8	4.8	64.2	6.4
	1984	4.5	40.2	4.2	59.8	4.8
	1988	4.7	42.7	4.5	57.3	4.9

SOURCES: U.S. Bureau of Labor Statistics, unpublished tabulations from 1964 *Current Population Survey*, Table 16; unpublished 1968 *Current Population Survey*, Table 16; the 1982 *Handbook of Labor Statistics*, Bulletin No. 2096, Table 13-21; the 1989 *Handbook of Labor Statistics*, Bulletin No. 2340, Table 19.
NOTE: Columns c and e answer the question: Of all the females(c)/males(e) employed in the labor force, what percentage is employed in each sector?

52.2% in 1988), reflecting the greater vulnerability of all U.S. workers to unemployment and poverty in the last eight years. As Lance de Haven-Smith notes,

a larger and larger proportion of the labor force is employed in the competitive sector where wages are set through the market, and the incidence of poverty necessarily increases. Policies that prop up the monopoly sector, even though they benefit big business and organized labor, tend to lower wages and to higher rates of poverty and unemployment.[20]

"Core" and "periphery" are also defined by the types of firms of which they are composed. Although considerable overlap with the industry segmentation exists, some differences in categorization occur. For example, textile manufacturing would be classified as core if industry groupings are used and as peripheral if such characteristics of the firm as size, international scope, and administered versus competitive pricing are used.

When viewing the U.S. economy from a firm rather than an industry perspective, the "core" consists of the 500 to 800 very large multinational corporations that contribute more than half of the total gross national product (GNP). Typically the top few (four or more) firms dominate more than half of their respective markets. These core firms are highly bureaucratic, "operating usually on an international basis with a high division of labor, and administered pricing systems where complicated international accounting procedures, transfer payments, and a variety of other factors prevent the operation of competitive markets in production and finance."[21]

The "periphery" consists of the 14,000-plus firms that contribute about one-fourth of the GNP. This highly competitive labor market provides the training ground for new entrepreneurs. The majority of these firms are small, labor intensive, and geographically dispersed. Examples include restaurants, many hospitals, law firms, retail and service firms.[22]

The "public sector," containing both the governmental and non-profit private sectors, accounts for about 25% of the GNP. The government's mode of operations is not typically competitive but rests rather on budget-based finance and politics.[23] Although most of this sector consists of the various governmental operations, substantial nonprofit operations have come into existence as well, as a consequence of the privatization movement in the 1980s.

Within these various segments of the economy and society, human beings attain employment and opportunities to exercise leadership. To understand the difficulties facing women and minorities in achieving the highest level positions it is necessary to understand how these various labor markets function and the extent to which they are actually competitive. As already noted, jobs within each of the cells in Figure 3.1 tend to be highly correlated with female- and male-dominated occupations and industries.

Approximately 45% of all U.S. workers in manufacturing and mining are employed by the top 500 to 800 firms in the core economy. Jobs in the core industries typically deal with heavy industry, manufacturing, large banks, insurance organizations, aircraft, petroleum, metals, electronics, automobiles, pharmaceuticals, and chemicals. Jobs in the core economy, particularly in Cell 1 of Figure 3.1, have higher entry level, advanced education, or certification requirements. They also provide employees with the highest pay, the greatest job security, on-the-job training, benefits, and opportunities for advancement with the least external competition once an individual is hired. Most of these occupations are heavily male-dominated with the highest median weekly earnings for men employed full-time.[24] Examples of these occupations would be engineers, physicians, educational and health administrators, bank officers and financial managers, airline pilots, certain lawyers, economists, chemists, physicists, and other technical professions.

Relatively few women have been able to penetrate into the upper echelons of this labor market. A survey by the Administrative Management Society of Fortune 500 found that in these larger corporations only 10% of the managers were female, even though women constituted 69% of all white-collar workers.[25] Prior to 1970 the main reason was lack of access to and attainment of educational credentials. For example, in 1965 only about 5% of the enrollees in law, medicine, and architectural schools were female and the percentage of women engineers was almost nonexistent. By 1986, 32% of such enrollment was female,[26] showing progress toward eliminating that barrier but highlighting other, less obvious obstacles. In 1988, 7.3% of all engineers, 20% of all physicians, 19% of lawyers, and 15% of all architects were women.[27]

The wave of women into the physical sciences still has not been substantial. In the late 1980s there were 800 to 1000 high energy physicists in the entire world; women comprised only 3% of that total (24-30 individuals). More women have entered engineering fields; nevertheless, in 1988 females constituted only 13% of the engineering graduates. Northrup[28] also notes that about half of the women who do have engineering and science degrees choose to work in academic institutions, because the more flexible work hours of academe allow greater likelihood of combining professional and family responsibilities. Mobility and location preferences also reduce the number of women scientists and engineers available to the core economy firms.

One primary indicator of women's progress is the number of women on the boards of directors of corporations and businesses. In 1987, 405 women held 576 directorships on the board of directors of the top Fortune 1000 corporations. Since 1969, the percentage of Fortune 1000 companies including women on the board rose from 13 to 45%. Usually, however, women sit alone on these boards. Only 116 corporations have more than one woman director. The financial, manufacturing, and retail sectors have the largest number of female directors. Among the Fortune 1000 companies, however, fewer than 5% of the directorships are filled by women. Those they do hold are in peripheral rather than mainstream companies. Moreover, women are seldom directors within their own companies.[29]

The likelihood of the proportion of female directors increasing sharply in the immediate future is low. The eligible pool for becoming a director typically comes from chief executive officers and presidents of comparable companies. Very few women hold such positions or are in the queue to attain them.[30]

Almost no companies founded or directed by women are on the Fortune 500 list. In 1985 the company founded by the designer Liz Claiborne moved to Fortune 500 with revenues of $556 million.[31] To my knowledge, this is the only company founded by a woman to be so recognized. In 1985 the only female head of a Fortune 500 company was Katharine Graham, CEO of the Washington Post, whose company's net worth surpassed $1 billion. In 1990, three women were CEOs of Fortune 1000 companies: Katharine Graham, Linda Wochner of WORNACO Group, and Marion Sandle of the Golden West Financial Corporation.[32]

In 1987 Forbes, Piercy, and Hayes concluded "women will hold not more than 2 percent of the top jobs at major corporations in the near future. However, even 10 or 20 females in top positions within *Fortune* 1000 firms will be a radical breakthrough."[33]

A substantial barrier to women attaining high-level leadership positions in the core economy stems from the multinational nature of many of these firms. In 1989 only 3% of all expatriate managers of multinational corporations were women.[34] Barriers to their promotion included dual-career marriages, gender-based prejudices of foreigners, and general patriarchal stereotypes and prejudices. Women have progressed most rapidly in areas such as foreign exchange trading and financial hedging. In such fields the profit/loss results are clear and immediate and difficult to quarrel with, helping make the job market more open and competitive.

In Cell 2 (Figure 3.1) of the "core" economy, an intermediate labor market exists that tends to have medium to high entry barriers, relatively high pay, good benefits, and steady employment. Included here are such occupations as skilled precision, repair, and craft workers (in 1988 only 8.7% were female); sales personnel in large corporations (in 1988, 33% of wholesale sales personnel, sales supervisors, and proprietors were women); and computer programmers (33% of whom were female).[35] Unions are more active in organizing the workers in Cell 2 and also in Cell 3. The workers in Cell 1 tend to rely on professional associations for work and pay standards.

In 1981, only 9 of the 20 top paying jobs for females fell into Cell 2.[36] These occupations in 1988 included operators, systems researchers and analysts (39.6% female), computer systems analysts and scientists (29.5% female), lawyers (19.3% female), social scientists (47.6% female), engineers (7.3% female), natural scientists (24.1% female), personnel and labor relations workers (58.9% female), and computer programmers (32.2% female).[37] Although a higher percentage of females hold jobs in Cell 2 than in Cell 1, still relatively few women are employed in these positions. Given that men and women in the same occupations are employed by different firms or industries and that they receive different wages,[38] it appears that this segment of the core economy not only admits few women, but also allows fewer women to enter the pipeline for promotions to the highest levels. Some large corporations, such as IBM, Traveler's Corporation, Mobil Corporation, and the Equitable Financial Companies, made efforts in the 1980s to advance and retain women.[39] In 1989, American Express was one of the core corporations that did have a female senior vice president, Joan E. Spero.

This segmented labor market theory draws attention to the fact that within the core economy women tend to fall into either "pink ghettos" or "velvet ghettos." Wage discrimination occurs in part because highly schooled females are concentrated in professions in the peripheral sector, whereas in the core economy women are disproportionately located in clerical and support occupations. Table 3.7 illustrates this fact. Although in 1988 half of all professionals were women, only 19.2% of these specialties in high demand in the core economy (architects, engineers, mathematical and computer scientists, natural scientists, social scientists, urban planners, and lawyers) were women. In contrast, women constituted 62.4% of the professional specialties in higher demand in the peripheral sector: physicians; dentists; registered

TABLE 3.7 Numbers of Women in Professional Specialties Relevant to Core and Peripheral Segments of the Economy: 1988 Data

	Total Employed (in thousands)	Total Female (in thousands)	% Female
Core Sector Oriented Specialties			
Architects	143	20.9	14.6
Engineers	1,805	131.8	7.3
Mathematical and computer scientists	732	244.5	33.4
Natural scientists	395	95.2	24.1
Social scientists and urban planners	343	163.3	47.6
Lawyers	724	139.7	19.3
Subtotal	4,142	795.4	19.2
Percentage of all employed	3.6%		
Percentage of all females employed			1.5%
Peripheral-Sector Oriented Specialties			
Physicians	541	108.2	20.0
Dentists	152	14.1	9.3
Registered nurses	1,559	1,474.8	94.6
Pharmacists	168	53.6	31.9
Dieticians	74	63.6	86.0
Therapists	298	217.5	73.0
Teachers (college and university)	700	269.5	38.5
Teachers (other)	3,773	2,750.5	72.9
Counselors	206	127.3	61.8
Librarians, archivists, curators	219	180.9	82.6
Social, recreation, and religious	1,052	485.0	46.1
Writers, artists, entertainers, athletes	1,855	866.3	46.7
Subtotal	10,597	6,611.3	62.4
Percentage of all employed	9.2%		
Percentage of all females employed			12.8%

SOURCE: Data derived from U.S. Bureau of Labor Statistics, *Handbook of Labor Statistics* (Washington, DC: Government Printing Office, 1989), pp. 90-95.

nurses; pharmacists; dieticians; therapists; college and university teachers; other teachers; counselors; librarians; social, recreation and religious workers; writers; artists; entertainers; and athletes.

Given that in 1988 about the same percentages of women and men were managers or executives (22.2% of the 51,735,600 employed women; 25.5% of the 63,232,400 employed men), it is clear that the broad occupational categories are less important in determining elite and societal status than one's core or peripheral position within the segmented labor market.

Prospective female managers also confront a "velvet ghetto." When women do advance in management and leadership positions, they do so primarily in subordinate, nonlinear, supportive positions, for example, in personnel departments, accounting, management information systems, and public relations. In 1987, for example, only 24.6% of women at the vice presidential level in the *Standard and Poor Registrar* were in production/operations, marketing, finance, and legal areas— the functional backgrounds of a majority of top executives.[40]

Employers' discriminatory tastes and perceptions of the preferences of their clients combine to keep both women and minorities from key, visible line positions.[41] Employers have tended not to hire women for jobs preferred by men. Given the legal and political drive for equal opportunity and affirmative action, the response of employers, especially in the core economy, has been to place women in administrative, staff support positions.

Conditions in the 1980s that facilitated women's advancement to higher positions in the primary and intermediate labor markets of the core economy included the general economic shift to services and the restructurings, leveraged buyouts, and spinoffs that have disrupted traditional male business traditions and cultures.[42] The Women's Movement and the gender gap during presidential and national elections also contributed substantially.[43]

Cell 3 (Figure 3.1) of the core economy refers to jobs that are highly vulnerable, have high turnover, relatively low pay, little job security, and poor or nonexistent benefits. Many of these jobs have been moved to Third World countries or been made defunct by technology. For example, computerized phone systems have replaced telephone operators; robotized manufacturing is replacing machinery operators.

The Peripheral Economy

The peripheral sector encompasses "retail trade businesses, subcontractors of the core economy firms, many finance, insurance, and real estate companies, construction firms, local transportation, local public utility firms, and much of the service industry that includes business and repair services, personal services, and professional services that are not provided by the public sector."[44] Most of the occupations found in the core economy firms also are found in the peripheral sector. However, since peripheral sector firms are more vitally affected by business cycle trends, competition among firms and workers is often intense. Occupations that would be typical of Cell 4 of Figure 3.1 include high-paying professional, technical, and managerial occupations and self-employed professionals, such as doctors, lawyers, and professional consultants. Female professionals and high-level managers tend to work in this segment or in Cells 7 and 8 of the public sector.[45]

Although this segment of the economy has been more receptive to women, many of the same patterns found in the "core" economy are found here as well. For example, in the communications industry the "velvet ghetto" gets played out slightly differently, although it also reflects a common pattern. Women enter the public relations field and management information systems in technical rather than management areas. Hence, although women now constitute 49% of the total membership of the nation's two largest professional organizations for communications, they earn on the average $5,500 less than their male counterparts and hold relatively few of the managerial positions.[46]

A study of 1,000 members of the International Communications Association revealed that 66% of the women did not feel they were moving up the corporate ladders as quickly as their male peers.[47] About half of the women thought they were receiving comparable pay. In actuality, 91% of the men were paid more than $35,000 annually, whereas only 65% of the women were. Contributing to the pay gap is the gender difference in position and location in the industry. Few women choose careers in hardware technology and work in plants in the telecommunications industry.[48]

Women have tended to fare better in industries pressured by technological change, corporate restructuring, and deregulation. The higher degree of competition draws attention to basic talent. Gender-blindness has been a hallmark of "high-tech" companies. The pressure to survive has encouraged opening the doors to both women and minorities. Deregulation also has facilitated new opportunities, particularly in banking, retailing, advertising, and accounting. For example, after the Wall Street financial community was deregulated, the proportion of women rapidly rose to one of four.[49] Since the October 1987 crash, of course, many of these newly hired women were among the 40,000-plus who were let go.

The greater relative openness of the peripheral firms to women in the 1980s is seen in the increase in the number of women partners in the 250 largest law firms. In 1987-88, 19% of the newly appointed partners were women. This increase still has not led to a strong position for women, however. In 1988 only 6% of all partners were women, up from 4.9% in 1984 and 2.8% in 1982.[50]

The powerful impact of patriarchal assumptions and sex-role stereotypes is evident in the legal field. U.S. Supreme Court Justice, Arizonan Sandra Day O'Connor, and the first female law professor at Columbia University and U.S. Appeals Court Judge, Ruth Bader Ginsburg, were both at the top of their law school classes, usually an indicator of a sure position in a major law firm. Upon graduation both were offered jobs as legal secretaries.

A 1985 report of a survey of women who had reached chief executive officer (CEO) rank in the U.S. firms[51] revealed that there are few women executives in the largest corporations, but that in selected industrial and entrepreneurial fields women were making inroads. Examples are Jane Evans of Genesco Inc.'s I. Miller shoe company; Sandra L. Kurtzig, founder and CEO of ASK Computer Systems; and Christie Heffner, head of Playboy Enterprises.

Unfortunately, many entrepreneurial women in the peripheral sector lose control of their small firms to the predation of large corporations in the core economy. For example, Theresa Myers is cofounder and president of Quarterdeck Office Systems, which developed Desqview, its only product. IBM, recognizing its potential, developed Topview, which threatened the existence of the smaller, more vulnerable firm.[52]

Regional variations exist in career opportunities for women.[53] The western and eastern parts of the United States have been much more receptive to women managers, professionals, and supervisors than either the Midwest or the South. The South paid considerably less to women vice presidents and other upper-level managers than any other region.[54]

The regional variations notwithstanding, *Working Woman* in 1988[55] stated that opportunities in the peripheral sector of the economy represented the "25 Hottest Careers" for women. The emphasis on the service economy was creating opportunities for women in real estate, personnel, and information systems. Corporate real estate management and service quality management for individuals with line management experience in product lines were jobs that were highlighted. The ten worst careers that were highlighted were generally those falling in Cells 5 and 6 of this peripheral part of the economy: telemarketers, word processing/data entry clerks, flight attendants, classical dancers, social workers, nurses, teachers, contractors, investment bankers, and—somewhat anomolously (from Cell 4 or possibly Cell 2)—major law firm attorney.

Cell 5 in the intermediate-peripheral sector encompasses occupations such as construction, crafts, retail trade, and clerical workers, as well as nurses, health workers, and finance. Women in the 1980s were employed in this general category, and many of the most heavily sex-segregated, female-dominated occupations fell here as well. For example, some of the occupations that occupy both intermediate and secondary segments of the peripheral economy include dental assistant (99% female), nurse (95% female), bank teller (91% female), billing clerk (90% female), nurse's aide (90% female), sales worker (74% female), and cashier (82% female).[56]

In the latter half of the 1980s, "9 to 5" and the National Association for Working Women charged that office automation was victimizing clerical workers and eliminating their jobs. Industry analysts tended to deny this assertion, countering with the belief that these clerical personnel were moving from administrative support and clerical jobs to executive, administrative, managerial, and sales jobs.[57]

Cell 6, the secondary category, is comparable to Cell 3 of the core economy in its high turnover, low pay, poor or no benefits, and unstable working conditions. Many of these workers are young and part-time workers. Examples of these jobs that were dominated by women in 1988 include food service workers (73% female), private household workers (85% female), and some retail sales clerks (74% female).[58]

The Self-Employed

The barriers to success in the core economy and at the middle and upper levels in the peripheral economy have contributed to a dramatic increase in the number of self-employed women. In the 1980s, about one-third of all new businesses were formed by women. Women-owned businesses were the fastest growing sector of the small business community. Between 1980 and 1990, the number of sole proprietorships owned by women grew 62.5%, while male-owned businesses grew only 33.4%.[59] Even so, although women-owned businesses accounted for 22% of all small businesses nationwide, they produced only 13% of the total small business sales.[60] Nevertheless, the director of the Office of Women's Business Ownership in the U.S. Small Business Administration predicts that women will own 50% of U.S. small businesses by the year 2000.[61]

The Public and Nonprofit Sectors

The public sector operates with an administered rather than a competitive labor market. Institutional and political processes rather than marginal productivity determine wages. The vast majority of government employees—more than four of every five—are employed by state and local government.[62]

An increasing number of women have attained high-level positions in the public sector indicated by Cell 7 in Figure 3.1. In the 1980s one of nine U.S. Supreme Court Justices was a woman (Sandra Day O'Connor from Arizona); two women in 1989-90 are U.S. senators; and about 5% of the U.S. House of Representatives are women. In the 1980s Elizabeth Dole was put in charge of a budget of more than $26 billion as U.S. secretary of transportation, and numerous other women attained high level federal and state administrative positions. At the federal level in 1987, 27% of all employees in GS9 or above were women, up from only 1% in 1960.[63]

Women had also made significant gains at the state level by 1990. Three women were governors (Rose Mofford in Arizona, Madeline Kunin in Vermont, and Kay Orr in Nebraska), and the number of women appointed to head state agencies doubled between 1981 and 1987. Reis[64] reported that 130 women held cabinet-level posts in 1987; only 70 held such positions in 1981. Following the sex-segregated patterns throughout the society, most of these positions were in social service agencies.

Arizona has offered more political opportunity to women than most states. In 1989 it had a female Democratic governor, a female Republican Speaker of the House, a female whip of the Democratic party, and 30% of its state legislators were female (37% in the Arizona House and 17% in the Senate). Under former Governor Bruce Babbitt, it ranked fourth in the nation in terms of the number of female cabinet officers. Revealing the importance of politics and ideology, under Babbitt's successor, Evan Mecham, Arizona's ranking dropped to 35th (of only 38 states counted).[65]

Women are becoming more visible and more powerful in state bureaucracies as well. In 1986, women filled 25% of the top state jobs in California, 18% in Texas, and 13% in Arizona and Utah.[66]

The nonprofit private sector employs a high percentage of women in child care, nursing homes, hospitals, schools, and other human welfare/service occupations. Salaries tend to be lower and the size of the employing institution smaller than in the for-profit sector.

In the nonprofit sector women have historically played a major administrative role. In the health care field, for example, traditionally church-sponsored, nonprofit hospitals have been run by church women and Catholic orders. Middle management for women in health care was usually restricted to being in charge of the nursing department, cleaning and laundry, linens store, the catering department, and private staff, clearly reflecting large-scale "household" management skills.

Although women's status in managerial positions has improved overall in health services, private as well as public, women have not kept pace with men in competition for top posts. The American College of Health Care Executive data for 1987 shows 490 women CEO affiliates, an increase of 172 since 1979. This number compares poorly with the 4,589 male CEOs in health care. Moreover, although women constituted 52.7% of the students in health care administration training programs, fewer than 10% are among top management.[67]

Relatively few of the women employed in the public sector, particularly in governmental positions, work in the more prestigious occupations found in Cell 7 of Figure 3.1. The vast majority are in the more vulnerable Cells 8 and 9, and are highly subject to being replaced by contract labor with the privatization movement, making their position in the society even more marginal and tenuous. In 1988, Gregory Lewis reported that:

> In the federal civil service, clerical work is the quintessential female occupation. In 1982, 49% of the government's female employees performed clerical work and 85% of its clerical workers were women. The number of clerical workers in the United States doubled between 1950 and 1974, with women accounting for 95% of the growth and increasing their share of clerical jobs from 61% to 77%.[68]

There is no question that, in the public as well as in the private sector, female-dominated jobs have lower entry levels, less mobility across grade levels, and lower top levels.[69]

The position of women in the nonprofit sector, the more vulnerable part of the economy, can be readily illustrated by the situation facing the classified staff in the Arizona Universities Personnel System (separate from the State of Arizona Personnel System) in June 1990. The universities' classified staff salaries were between 5.59 and 11.76% behind comparable State of Arizona employees, and from 8.66 to

15.26% behind the overall Arizona market, including both private and public employers.[70] At this point in time, 64% of these employees needed salary adjustments greater than 10% for them to even reach parity with other Arizonans employed in the same type of job by their very own state employer!

The Volunteer Sector

Volunteer work exists mostly in the public and nonprofit sector, but can exist elsewhere as well. These jobs either garnish no pay or relatively little pay compared with the training required to perform the job. To illustrate some patterns in this area, women's participation in religious leadership will be examined.

Although there are many ways to express leadership in religious movements and institutions, the most commonly recognized form of religious authority comes with being a member of the clergy. The Women's Movement in the 1960s and 1970s gave rise to the demand for women to enter these ranks. In 1989, the U.S. Bureau of Labor Statistics reported 9% of all employed clergy were women.[71]

Percentages of female clergy vary considerably from state to state. The highest rate in 1980 was in the District of Columbia, which had more than 20% of its clergy being women.

According to a Ford Foundation study of six mainstream denominations,[72] there were 37 ordained female ministers in Arizona in 1980. Only 19 of these were serving in churches; 7 were Presbyterian, 6 were Methodist, and 8 were pastors in the Assembly of God churches, most of whom serve Indian congregations.

The low numbers of women clergy are due to several factors. First, most religions are grounded in a patriarchal world view. In addition, most have a tradition of unquestioning voluntary service. Being aggressive about penetrating the ranks of the male-dominated clergy is not psychologically compatible with traditional views of women. As Auffret notes:

> Conservative dominations still believe that women have no business in the pulpit, their leaders sometimes quoting St. Paul's teaching that women should remain silent in church and look to their husbands for religious teaching. Southern Baptists Associations in Oklahoma City and Vallejo, California, recently refused to seat representatives from three of their congregations that ordained women admonishing them to stop their "non-Biblical practice."[73]

In the 1980s, the numbers of women in seminaries increased sharply. They were half of the Master of Divinity students in the United Church of Christ; about one-third in the United Methodist Church, the United Presbyterian Church (USA), and the Disciples of Christ Church; and about one-fourth in the American Baptist Church and the Lutheran Church of North America.[74] Yet, most of these seminarians shy away from seeking the position of pastor and from speaking from the pulpit. Many seek jobs as counselors, hospital or jail chaplains, choir directors, or education directors. Women who do become clergy or attain any type of paid position tend to suffer from the same problems found by women seeking positions of leadership and authority elsewhere. A study of 11 protestant denominations released by the National Council of Churches in 1984 revealed that whereas the average salary for male clergy was $20,790, for female clergy it was about $15,000.[75]

Conclusion

This brief overview of the segmented labor market in the United States clarifies the importance of examining such issues as career success, pay equity, and achieving leadership positions within each segment of the economy. If one ignores the economic segment in which people are employed, then there is a tendency to focus on individual explanations of wage discrimination, such as educational levels, work experience, and family responsibilities. Such explanations often blame the victim exclusively and encourage policymakers to overlook the structural nature of economic problems. Within the neoclassical economic perspective from which the individualistic arguments are typically drawn, debates about comparable pay for work of comparable worth have little meaning. Yet in the 1980s, it became clear that sex-segregation by industry and by economic sector are critical for assessing pay equity and advancement opportunities.[76] Variations in individual characteristics have seldom been able to explain more than 50% of gender-based pay inequities. By the late 1980s, women and men attained the same median education levels, but men's salaries far surpassed women's.[77] In 1987, executive women on the average earned 42% less than their male counterparts.[78]

Notes

1. U.S. Department of Labor, Bureau of Labor Statistics, *Handbook of Labor Statistics* (Washington, DC: Government Printing Office, 1989), Table 18, p. 90; cf. L. Baum, "Corporate Women: They're About to Break Through to the Top," *Business Week* 22 June 1987, 72-88.

2. Anonymous, "Women Are Changing the Work Force," *Credit Union Magazine,* 50(10) (1984): 54-57.

3. Derived from U.S. Department of Labor, *Handbook,* Table 18, 90. In 1988 there were 114,968,000 total employed workers in the United States. Of these 45.0% or 51,735,600 were women. Of the 14,216,000 total employed in the executive, administrative, and managerial category, 39.3% or 5,586,890 were women. These 5,586,890 women represent about 10.89% of the total 51,735,600 employed women.

4. The 8,629,110 men represent 13.6% of all the employed 63,232,400 men in 1988. Derived from U.S. Department of Labor, *Handbook,* 90.

5. U.S. Department of Labor, *Handbook,* 90.

6. J. B. Forbes and J. E. Piercy, "Rising to the Top: Executive Women in 1983 and Beyond," *Business Horizons* (September-October 1983): 38-47.

7. J. B. Forbes, J. E. Piercy, and T. L. Hayes, "Women Executives: Breaking Down Barriers?" *Business Horizons* 31(6) (November-December 1988): 6-9.

8. Juanita Cox-Burton, "Leadership in the Future—A Quality Issue," *S.A.M. Advanced Management Journal,* 53(4) (Autumn 1988): 41.

9. For a basic overview of economists' views of gender and labor markets, see Francine D. Blau and Marianne A. Ferber, *The Economics of Women, Men, and Work* (Englewood Cliffs, NJ: Prentice-Hall, 1986); and Barbara R. Bergmann, *The Economic Emergence of Women* (New York: Basic Books, 1986), 19. Discussions of segmented labor market theory as it pertains to occupational sex segregation can be found in Barbara F. Reskin, ed., *Sex Segregation in the Workplace: Trends, Explanations, Remedies,* Committee on Women's Employment and Related Social Issues, Commission on Behavioral and Social Sciences and Education, National Research Council (Washington, DC: National Academy Press, 1984).

10. Joan Scott, *Gender and the Politics of History* (New York: Columbia University Press, 1988), Ch. 2.

11. Scott, *Gender and the Politics of History,* Ch. 5.

12. Jane Bayes, "Occupational Sex Segregation and Comparable Worth," in *Comparable Worth, Pay Equity, and Public Policy,* eds. Rita Mae Kelly and Jane Bayes (Westport, CT: Greenwood, 1988), 15-47. All material cited from this book is reprinted by permission of Greenwood Publishing Group, Inc., Westport CT. Copyright © by Greenwood Press.

13. Bayes, "Occupational Sex Segregation," 32-45. The dual labor market theory is derived from P. B. Doeringer and M. H. Piore, *Internal Labor Markets and Manpower Analysis* (Lexington, MA: D.C. Heath, 1971).

14. The dependencia theory component stems in part from the work of R. E. Muller, *Revitalizing America: Politics for Prosperity* (New York: Simon & Schuster, 1980).

15. M. J. Piore, "Notes for a Theory of Labor Stratification," in *Conference on Labor Market Segmentation,* eds. R. C. Edwards, M. Reich, and D. M. Gordon (Lexington, MA: D.C. Heath, 1975), 125-150.

16. Piore, "Notes for a Theory." See also Bayes, "Occupational Sex Segregation," 35.

17. Bayes, "Occupational Sex Segregation," 36.

18. Faye C. Huerta and T. A. Lane, "Participation of Women in Centers of Power," *Social Science Journal* (April 1981): 71-86.

19. Thomas Dye and Julie Strickland, "Women at the Top: A Note on Institutional Leadership," *Social Science Quarterly* (June 1982): 333-341.

20. Lance de Haven-Smith, *Philosophical Critique of Policy Analysis* (Gainesville: University of Florida Press, 1988), 109.

21. Bayes, "Occupational Sex Segregation," 37.

22. Cynthia Fuchs Epstein, *Deceptive Distinctions: Sex, Gender and the Social Order* (New Haven: Yale University Press, 1988), 145.

23. Aaron Wildavsky, *The Politics of the Budgetary Process,* 3rd ed. (Boston: Little, Brown, 1979).

24. Bayes, "Occupational Sex Segregation," 39-43.

25. Irene Pane, "A Woman's Place Is at GE, Federal Express, P & G . . . ," *Business Week* (Industrial/Technology Edition) 23 June 1986, 75, 78.

26. Stella G. Guerra, "Women in America are Shooting for the Stars," *Vital Speeches* 52(23) (September 15, 1986): 726-729.

27. U.S. Department of Labor, *Handbook,* Table 18, 90-95.

28. H. R. Northrup, "Professional Women in R & D Laboratories," *Research and Technology Management* 31(4) (July/August 1988): 44-52.

29. Cindy Skrzycki, "Board Room Doors Open Wider for Women," *Washington Post* 3 December 1987, C1.

30. Skrzycki, *Washington Post.*

31. J. Kagan, "Cracks in the Glass Ceiling: How the Women Really Are Faring in Corporate America," *Working Women* 11(10) (October 1986): 107-109.

32. Kagan, "Cracks in the Glass Ceiling." See also, Mary Billard, "Women on the Verge of Being CEO," *Business Month Magazine* 23 April 1990, 26-47; and Anonymous, *Fortune Magazine* 23 April 1990, 337-96.

33. Forbes, Piercy, and Hayes, "Women Executives," 9.

34. G. Dawson, E. Ladenburg, and R. Moran, "Women in International Management," in *Businesswoman: Present and Future,* eds. David Clutterbuck and Marion Devine (London: MacMillan, 1987), 76-90.

35. U.S. Department of Labor, *Handbook,* Table 18, 90-95.

36. Bayes, "Occupational Sex Segregation," 41.

37. U.S. Department of Labor, *Handbook,* Table 18, 90-95.

38. Bayes, "Occupational Sex Segregation," 41; and F. D. Blau, *Equal Pay in the Office* (Lexington, MA: D.C. Heath, 1977).

39. Sharon Nelton and K. Berney, "The Second Wave," *Nation's Business* 75(5) (May 1987): 18-27.

40. Forbes, Piercy, and Hayes, "Women Executives," 7.

41. F. D. Blau and M. A. Ferber, "Occupations and Earnings of Women Workers," in *Working Women: Past, Present, Future,* eds. K. S. Koziara, M. H. Moskow, and L. D. Tanner (Washington, DC: BNA Books, 1987), 37-68.

42. Baum, "Corporate Women," 72-88.

43. Rita Mae Kelly and Jane Bayes, eds., *Comparable Worth, Pay Equity, and Public Policy* (Westport, CT: Greenwood, 1988); Mary M. Hale and Rita Mae Kelly, eds., *Gender, Bureaucracy, and Public Policy* (Westport, CT: Greenwood, 1989).

44. Bayes, "Occupational Sex Segregation," 42.

45. Bayes, "Occupational Sex Segregation," 42.

46. G. Broom and D. Dozier, "Advancement for Public Relations Role Models," *Public Relations Review* 12(1) (Spring 1986): 37-56; Lynda J. Stewart, "Women in Foundation and Corporate Public Relations," *Public Relations Review* 14(3) (1988): 20-23; and J. S. Hill, "Women Find Equality is Foreign," *Advertising Age* 58(24) (1987): 62-63.

47. Joanie Wexsler, "Are Women's Telecom Careers Measuring Up?" *Telecommunication Products and Technology* 6(2) (February 1988): 20-26.

48. C. Wilson and L. Lannon, "Women Confident, Comfortable in Powerful New Roles," *Telephony* 25 (June 20, 1988): 38-44.

49. Anne B. Fisher, "Where Women are Succeeding," *Fortune* 116, 3 August 1987, 78-86. See also Charlotte Sutton and Kris K. Moore, "Attitudes Toward Executive Women: Do They Differ Geographically?" *Personnel Administrator* 31(5) (May 1986): 75-88.

50. Epstein, *Deceptive Distinctions,* 164.

51. J. Braham, "Women at the Top," *Industry Week* 224(5) (March 4, 1985): 106-114.

52. M. Zientara, "A Lender, a Vendor, and a Micro Defender," *Computer World* 22(13) (March 28, 1988): 12-14.

53. Fisher, "Where Women Are Succeeding."

54. Fisher, "Where Women Are Succeeding." Cf. Laura L. Vertz, "Pay Inequalities Between Women and Men in State and Local Government: An Examination of the Political Context of the Comparable Worth Controversy," *Women & Politics* 7(2) (Summer 1987): 43-57.

55. Michelle Morris, Holloway McCandless, and Elizabeth A. Conlin, "25 Hottest Careers 1988: The 10 Worst Careers for Women," *Working Woman* 13(7) (July 1988): 55-66, 92-93.

56. The percentages are from U.S. Department of Labor, *Handbook,* Table 18, 90-95.

57. Mitch Betts, "Clerical Growth Slowing as Women Move Upscale, Study Says," *Computer World* 20.17, 28 April 1986, 13.

58. U.S. Department of Labor, *Handbook,* Table 18, 90-95.

59. Sharon Nelton, "The Age of the Woman Entrepreneur," *Nation's Business* (May 1989): 22-31.

60. N. Gerdes, "Sales at Women's Businesses Show They're Well Below Men's," *Arizona Republic* 18 June 1989, F3.

61. Nelton, "The Age of the Woman Entrepreneur," 23.

62. Bayes, "Occupational Sex Segregation," 43.

63. Mary Ellen Guy, *From Organizational Decline to Organizational Renewal* (New York: Quorum Books, 1989).

64. D. Reis, *The Appointment of Women: A Survey of Governor's Cabinets 1981-1988,* (Washington, DC: National Women's Political Caucus, 1988).

65. For details on women in Arizona politics, see Rita Mae Kelly, ed., *Women and the Arizona Political Process* (Lanham, MD: University Press of America, 1988).

66. Hale and Kelly, *Gender, Bureaucracy, and Democracy.*

67. Debra Caplan, "Women Health Care Managers: An Economic Update," *Health Care Management Review* 13(1) (1988): 71-79; and Laura Dempsey-Polan, "Women: Once and Future Leaders in Health Administration," *Hospital and Health Care Administration* 33(1) (Spring 1988): 89-98.

68. Gregory B. Lewis, "Clerical Work and Women's Earnings in the Federal Civil Service," in *Comparable Worth, Pay Equity, and Public Policy,* eds. Rita Mae Kelly and Jane Bayes (Westport, CT: Greenwood, 1988), 51.

69. Kelly and Bayes, *Comparable Worth,* 51; see also S. Peterson-Hardt and N. D. Perlman, *Sex-Segregated Career Ladders in New York State Government: A Structural Analysis of Inequality in Employment,* Working Paper No. 1 (Albany: Center for Women in Government, State University of New York, 1979).

70. Rita Mae Kelly, and Barbara Mawiney, "ASU Salaries" (paper presented to the Faculty Women's Association and selected Arizona legislators, October 1989). Available on request from Rita Mae Kelly, Director, School of Justice Studies, Arizona State University, Tempe, AZ 85287-0403.

71. U.S. Department of Labor, *Handbook,* Table 18, 90-95.

72. S. Auffret, "Equality in the Pulpit," *Arizona Republic, Arizona Magazine* 1 July 1984, 12. See also Roger W. Stump, "Women Clergy in the United States: A Geographical Analysis of Religious Change," *Social Science Quarterly* 67 (June 1986): 337-352.

73. Auffret, "Equality in the Pulpit," 14.

74. Auffret, "Equality in the Pulpit," 10-14.

75. J. L. Weidman, *Women Ministers: How Women Are Redefining Traditional Roles* (San Francisco: Harper & Row, 1985).

76. Kelly and Bayes, *Comparable Worth.*

77. M. A. Von Glinow, and A. K. Mercer, "Women in Corporate America: A Cast of Thousands," *New Management* 6(1) (Summer 1988): 36-42.

78. Baum, "Corporate Women," 72-88.

PART II

Sex, Gender, Stereotypes, and Success

For an individual the process of becoming a major business, political, or economic leader involves the interaction of socialization and human agency. *Socialization* refers to the process by which individuals learn to become part of particular social groups and society as a whole. It is also the process that teaches roles, values, and ways of thinking. *Human agency* refers to the control each person exercises over her or his personality and social roles.

In the last half of the 20th century, women who sought career success often found great tension between the childhood socialization they received to become women and the behavior required to become successful in a male-centered workplace. In Part II of this volume we explore the links among gender culture, socialization, and career success.

Women clearly meet more challenges and barriers in their efforts to reach higher level management and leadership positions than men.[1] The three major categories of barriers that women are more likely to confront are *internal barriers,*[2] such as gender role socialization, a passive self-concept, and role prejudice; *support availability barriers,*[3] such as limited financial resources, education and training, collegial networks, role models and mentors, and domestic restraints; and *structural barriers,*[4] such as employer biases, sex-segregated jobs, sexual harassment, and pay inequities.

Each of the broad categories of barriers is strongly related to sex-role ideologies, gender culture, socialization patterns, and adult sex-role biases. Part II of this volume describes the elements of these phenomena that are most directly related to the efforts of women to become successful as managers and leaders. Additionally, Part II assesses the aspects of the socialization processes that show promise for alleviating the barriers to career success and can be used as points of intervention for improving the odds of girls becoming top leaders or managers. Facilitators of career success often mirror the barriers. Having successful female role models as a child, being raised in a supportive environment that encourages female achievement and skill/ability development, having financial, educational, and training supports, and having a distinct career path with a history of full-time continuous employment, for example, facilitate success. Absence of these factors does not.

Chapter 4 examines the literature on childhood socialization and sex-role development. It assesses the extent to which gender differences in adult leadership and behavior in the economy are related to biological differences, sex-role identity, and moral development. Chapter 5 explores how sex-roles and sex-role stereotyping influence the opportunities available to women in the economy, building on our knowledge of the gendered-nature of the U.S. segmented labor market presented in Chapter 3. Chapter 6 analyzes available data on the relationship of gender to power, communication, stress, and the behavioral/leadership styles of managers. Chapter 7 articulates the way careers link individuals to organizations and to the broader social culture and the impact that gender has on careers.

Notes

1. B. A. Gutek and L. Larwood, eds. *Women's Career Development* (Newbury Park, CA: Sage, 1987).

2. K. M. Benedict, "When Women Succeed: Organizational Settings and the Structure of Careers," *Dissertation Abstracts International* 41 (1980), 799-A (University Microfilms No. 79-16471); E. P. Cook, "A Framework for Sex Role Counseling," *Journal of Counseling and Development* 64(4) (1985): 253-258; and D. W. Stewart, "Women in Top Jobs: An Opportunity for Federal Leadership," *Public Administration Review* 36(4) (1976): 357-364.

3. J. H. Bayes, "Women in Public Administration in the United States: Upward Mobility and Career Advancement" (paper presented at the XIIIth World Congress of the International Political Science Association, Paris, France, July 1985); K. M. Benedict,

"When Women Succeed"; W. H. Greene and A. O. Quester, "Divorce Risk and Wives' Labor Supply Behavior," *Social Science Quarterly* 63(1) (1982): 16-26; N. F. Russo, "After Consciousness-raising What? Women Learn From Women" (paper presented at the First Regional Conference on Women's Studies, New York, NY, February 1973); L. L. Vertz, "Women, Occupational Advancement, and Mentoring," *Public Administration Review* 45(3) (1985): 415-423; and G. L. Zellman, "The Role of Structural Factors in Limiting Women's Institutional Participation," *Journal of Social Issues* 32(3) (1976): 33-46.

4. Bayes, "Women in Public Administration" (paper); T. F. Brereton, "The Problems of Race and Sex in Public Agency Staffs," *Public Administration Review* 37(5) (1977): 604-607; C. C. Cherpas, "Dual-career Families: Terminology, Typologies, and Work and Family Issues," *Journal of Counseling and Development* 63(10) (1985): 616-620; J. M. Col, *Barriers to Women's Advancement in Administration and Management,* unpublished manuscript (Sangamon State University, Springfield, IL, 1985); B. A. Gutek, *Sex and the Workplace* (San Francisco: Jossey-Bass, 1985); N. R. Hooyman and J. S. Kaplan, "New Roles for Professional Women: Skills for Change," *Public Administration Review* 36(4) (1976): 374-378; A. H. Hopkins, "Perceptions of Employment Discrimination in the Public Sector," *Public Administration Review* 40(2) (1980): 131-137; C. A. MacKinnon, "Introduction," *Capital University Law Review* 10(3) (1979): i-viii; C. A. MacKinnon, *Sexual Harassment of Working Women: A Case of Sex Discrimination* (New Haven, CT: Yale University Press, 1979); L. C. Pogrebin, *Getting Yours* (New York: Avon, 1975); C. F. Ross and R. E. England, "State Government's Sexual Harassment Policy Initiative," *Public Administration Review* 47(3) (May/June 1987): 250-262; D. D. Van Fleet and J. G. Saurage, "Recent Research on Women in Management," *Akron Business and Economic Review* 15 (1984): 15-24; Vertz, "Women, Occupational Advancement"; and Zellman, "Role of Structural Factors."

4

Gender Culture and Socialization

Society, it is said, is like "'a gigantic Alcatraz,' a prison of already constructed definitions."[1] Humans enter into a world already shaped by gender, class, race, ethnicity, nationality, and existing sociopolitical economic systems. As Sondra Farganis notes:

> One's life is lived by learning from others—significant others, generalized others, agents of socialization—what one must do to make it through the terrain of lived experience. Who one is—that is, the already existent class and status into which one is born—determines how the terrain is traversed almost as predictably as will one's eye color, or ear length, or predisposition to a genetic problem such as Tay-Sachs or sickle cell anemia. One's socially ascribed status is pre-set, "there," a vise into which one's particular self is placed and away from which one can move with varying degrees of ease or difficulty.[2]

Gender culture is a generic term for the variety of ways in which persons are shaped by socialized sex-role expectations and ways in which sex differences are manifested. Clearly, the meaning of being a man or a woman, of being masculine or feminine, has altered considerably in the 20th century. Up to the 1970s and the Women's Movement, male and female were strongly associated with bipolar notions of masculinity and femininity. In the 1970s androgyny became popular, the notion that the ideal person, particularly the ideal professional, was a person who shared the instrumental masculine self with the more expressive feminine self.

In the 1980s androgyny retreated in popularity among socialization experts and a more multiplistic and pluralistic approach to gender appeared. Concern existed that androgyny produced a "hollow identity."[3] Ascribed roles were confused with and negated by attained roles. A female's feminine identity was subsumed or totally absorbed by her worker identity. Many did not appreciate the loss of the "viva la difference" notion between the sexes. Homogeneity was not necessarily what was desired or what constituted empirical reality. Nonetheless, the parallel between androgyny and liberal equality retains appeal to many scholars, particularly liberal feminists, as well as to activists.

Although the terms of the debate change over time, consensus exists that sex and gender differences remain. Important questions are, which parts of the gender culture are malleable, and which ones are likely to be found unchangeable, due to biology or consistency in socialization processes?

Analyses of sex roles have focused on three basically different orientations: social biology, social learning, and social cognition. Biological analyses rely heavily on the reproductive, physical, and hormonal differences between males and females. Social learning theories focus on how rewards and punishments shape sex-role behaviors. Social cognition theories identify cognitive "schemas" or "scripts" as the core of sex-role development. In recent years the latter two theories have blended together in some ways.[4] Both stress that children learn an ill-defined, fuzzy set of sex-role schemas associated with their culture, which they then apply in their behavior and identity development. More recently, scholars have stressed the interaction among the organism, the environment, and cognition.

Biological Differences

Sex differences are associated with biological differences. Historically, it was widely believed that men and women differed sharply in intellectual and physical abilities, in addition to differing in reproductive capacities. For example, until the 1980s the stereotypical, as well as the "scientific" view, was that males were superior in their mathematical abilities, were more aggressive, and had greater visual-spatial acuity, while females possessed superior verbal ability.[5] Indeed, to be male or to be female was, for most practical purposes, to be classified into mutually exclusive categories.

By the 1990s most of these views had changed dramatically. Amo. scientists some consensus still exists that males more readily deal with algebra than females, but recent studies reveal no meaningful differences with regard to arithmetic or geometry.[6] In addition, it is now recognized that girls tend to do as well as boys when they take math classes; the difference is that the girls opt out of taking such classes at much higher rates than boys. By the time adulthood is attained, the percentage differences as well as the actual math abilities between the sexes is considerable.[7]

Males are also still thought to be more adept at selected aspects of visual-spatial ability, but it is no longer concluded that they have across-the-board superiority. Differences in verbal ability are now considered less significant,[8] although females still perform better than males at all ages in perceptual speed, the ability "to perceive details quickly and accurately and to shift attention from one item to the next rapidly."[9] Some social development experts[10] still see an overall female advantage in verbal ability and a male advantage in mathematical and visual-spatial ability. As with beauty, sex differences and their importance for adult performance is often dependent on the eyes of the observer.

The gender difference found in visual-spatial ability has been projected to cognitive style[11] in a way negative to women. From a series of experiments with a rod and a frame tilted at various angles, it was discovered that men made fewer errors than women in adjusting the rod to the true vertical without the frame. From this finding Witkin and his colleagues concluded that men had an independent cognitive style, whereas women had a field dependent style.[12] As Hyde notes, it would be just as accurate, perhaps more accurate, and certainly less pejorative to women, if the authors had concluded that "women are context-sensitive and men are context-insensitive."[13]

Although, in 1990, it is now thought that both men and women can be equally aggressive, it appears that different stimuli trigger the aggression. Men are more likely to initiate aggression and to respond to physical challenges whereas women are more likely to get angry because of unfair treatment.[14] Girls also appear to be more likely to take steps to avoid quarrels and to self-select out of high conflict/dominance situations whereas boys are inclined to seek them out.[15] Reviews of multiple studies of sex differences in nurturance and aggressiveness[16] reveal that females tend to be more nurturing as adults as well as during childhood, and that in a variety of cultures males are consistently found to be more aggressive, more physical, and more dominance-oriented.

Other studies have found a link between nonverbal expressions of dominance and sexual attractiveness. "Dominant males were seen as more sexually attractive in three studies; no such relationship was found for females."[17]

In previous eras these differences—and many others—were thought to be biologically determined and unchangeable. In 1990 more confidence exists that education and socialization can provide individuals with sufficient levels of skill, whether in mathematics, verbal, or analytical ability, to compete with members of either sex. As the debate over Scholastic Aptitude Test (SAT) scores makes clear, many achievement-related sex differences were created by the wording of tests, not by biological differences.[18] Moreover, it is now recognized that at least half of the top 1% of people with the highest IQs are female. The lack of public achievements by women are not in native ability and must be sought elsewhere.

In 1990, most sex differences are viewed as variations in degrees rather than dualistic opposites. Figure 4.1 illustrates the switch in thinking. The bell-shaped curves depicting male and female abilities overlap considerably, indicating that on average, even when differences exist between the sexes, the differences do not signify mutually exclusive abilities or skills.

Even when one sex is thought to have an advantage (such as males are thought to have in algebra and coordination of most body movements) large numbers and percentages of women will still be superior to large numbers and percentages of men. Society is clearly better off using female talents than not using them and relying on less able males. In addition, the variation in ability among males, even mathematical and visual-spatial ability, is substantially greater than the ability differences between males and females. Among females, less sharp extremes in ability and performance occur.[19] Group variations within each sex are sufficient to permit large numbers of women to compete on equal footing with large numbers of men. With regard to major workplace issues, at any point of the bell-shaped curve (Figure 4.1), differences between men and women are less significant than differences among women themselves and among men themselves.

As new technologies enable individuals to perform tasks previously accomplished by manual labor, the traditionally male occupations that require physical strength, like the military, will increasingly rely on people trained to operate sophisticated machinery.[20] Although women are demonstrating competence in meeting these changing needs,[21] not

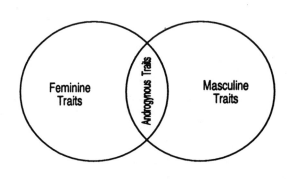

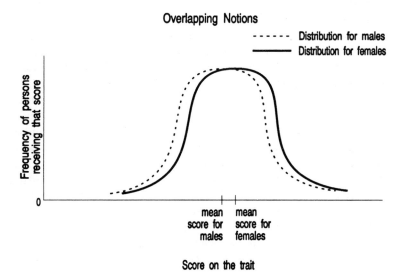

Figure 4.1. Notions of Sex Differences

SOURCE: The bottom figure depicting Overlapping Notions is adapted from *Half the Human Experience: The Psychology of Women,* 3d ed. (p. 140), ed. J. S. Hyde (Lexington, MA: D.C. Heath, 1985). Reprinted by permission.

all women are suited to all such physically demanding jobs. The gradual movement of women into such positions has, however, helped to break down myths suggesting that women are physically inferior.

Women's migration into the military and law enforcement has accompanied an increasing support of women's participation in sports. Women were barred from entering the original Olympic Games in 1896; they now compete in most events. Five women now serve on the International Olympic Committee.[22] Additionally, small but growing numbers of women "serve at every level of international sport."[23] This international competition has set a precedent for expanded participation in sports by women at all levels of the U.S. society. Title IX has also opened opportunities on school athletic teams for women. Before the passage of this law, which limits discrimination against students, faculty, and staff in federally assisted education programs, women accounted for only 7% of interscholastic athletes, and no colleges offered women's athletic scholarships.[24] By 1982, women accounted for 35% of the interscholastic athletes, and by 1984, more than 10,000 athletic scholarships were offered to women.[25] Sociologist Susan Greendorfer has argued that, by playing in high school and college sports, men gain "an incredible advantage, because most workplaces are structured on a competitive model."[26] *Health* magazine editor Gordon Bakoulis Bloch comments, "Sports have always been part of the glue that has kept the old-boy network alive and kicking; now women can reap the same benefits from the contacts they make through sports."[27] American businesswomen not only have demonstrated an interest in playing and following professional sports, they have also found that sports talk can open doors with new clients.[28] This change in understanding of the nature of sex differences has opened important new workplace opportunities for women.

In the 1980s, even the assumption that only women can carry and nurse a child was being challenged, as efforts were made to enable men to have fetuses implanted in their abdomens and devices were developed to facilitate a baby sucking from the father. Test tube babies and genetic engineering in general have opened new doors for cross-sex behavior that once would have been considered absolutely impossible. Advances in reproductive technology, especially in birth control and abortion, have also reduced the ease with which reproductive differences can be used to establish dichotomous, mutually exclusive differences between the sexes. Only the most naive or the most rigid believers in sex differences can still argue that biology is destiny and that, because of physiological differences, males belong in one sphere of life and females in another.

Environmental Factors

Simone de Beauvoir once wrote that, "one is not born a woman, but rather becomes a woman."[29] We learn, we imitate, we identify. We are socialized by our parental family, school, religion, friends/peers, the mass media, and the organizations and people with whom we work. Gender differences in socialization that have relevance for career choices and success abound. These differences are thought to be particularly meaningful in terms of shaping ambition, skill development, moral development, attitudes toward power, and behavioral/leadership styles.

The Family

Imitation of same-sex models, particularly parents, is recognized as central to the socialization process. Boys will tend to imitate their fathers or a favored older male, whereas girls will tend to imitate their mothers or a favored older female. If these parents act out and believe in the traditional sex-role stereotypes, they are likely to reward boys for being leaders, encouraging competitiveness, autonomy, aggressiveness, and independence, and to discourage girls from similar behavior. Seeing that they are rewarded for being gentle, caring, nurturing, and supportive of others, girls respond increasingly in these ways until such behavior becomes habitual. To break out of this pattern is difficult.

In the 1980s, increasing numbers of parents chose a more egalitarian approach to child rearing, expecting girls as well as boys to be competitive in sports, to excel in math and science, to be independent, and to be leaders. In addition, as more and more mothers worked outside the home, it became increasingly likely that daughters would have as their mothers female role models who themselves had successful careers. Imitation of professional and managerial mothers facilitates similar career success in daughters, just as imitation of professional and managerial fathers facilitates similar career success in sons.[30]

Ambition typically precedes achievement. Parents who hold egalitarian views about sex-roles tend to expect their daughters to perform well in school and to have high career aspirations. Yet, they also expect their daughters to use the family as a referent more than their sons. Beginning early in childhood, girl's play is focused on mimicking family life and responsibilities. In 1966 and in 1975, less than 6% of high school and college women did not intend to marry.[31] Moreover, even in the 1980s, a majority of girls still gave "mother" or "wife" as their primary occupational goal; young boys seldom mentioned "father" or "husband" as their career aspiration.[32]

Males also use the family as a referent. The outcome is different, however, because their experience in an intact family is different. Men are assumed to need and/or deserve more leisure time and greater freedom from housework and other caretaking functions. Women are assumed to accept these family and nurturing responsibilities as central to their womanhood. As will be pointed out in Chapter 5, these differences in orientation toward the family and the adult responsibility that women and men are expected to have within the family and in their roles as wife/husband, mother/father, daughter/son, and initiator or receiver of sexual interest strongly influence career opportunities in the workplace.

One consequence of the differential emphasis on family responsibilities is that, even in egalitarian family environments, girls more often than boys tend to opt for occupations more compatible with child care responsibilities, such as being an elementary rather than a university teacher, or being a nurse instead of a doctor, or being a science technician rather than a scientist or engineer. Societal patterns become norms to be followed rather than simply choices that other generations have made.[33]

To achieve one needs to be ambitious; to be ambitious means one must be motivated. Studies consistently show that "adult sex differences in cognitive abilities are motivational, and that motivational differences lead to different learning experiences."[34] This motivational difference is found to be related to the "reliably more persistent and single-minded pursuit of high levels of occupational achievement among males, but only small differences in abilities".[35] It is also found to have significant influence on girls' decisions to take or avoid mathematics in high school and college. Given that mathematics is the "critical filter"[36] for jobs in the core economy and high-prestige professions, such as engineering, medicine, computer science, the physical sciences, and business, it is vital to reverse the decision of girls not to take math. Gender equity and parity in career success will not occur if skills to compete are not obtained.

Studies of factors affecting career choices of females in the labor force indicate that entrepreneurs and managers both "scored higher than did secretaries in achieving motivation, locus of control, internality, and sex role 'masculinity.' . . . Women owners had more parental models, both mothers and fathers, who had engaged in occupational ownership than did either the managers or secretaries. This suggests that very early experience may be significant in determining important career behaviors that are seen later in life."[37]

Two studies in 1985 show that "the motivation influences of aspiration, mastery, and career commitment are significantly related to the background, personal, and environmental dimensions."[38] H. S. Farmer finds that the environmental changes are having a significant effect on girls' career and achievement motivations, reflecting again the impact of the Women's Movement and the demand for female labor. Farmer also found a change in boys; they are now anticipating playing a shared role in parenting as well as having a career.[39] In the same study, girls were found to have higher career aspirations than boys.

The critical role of parents in sex-role development can hardly be overstated. Studies consistently show that both mothers and fathers impact their child's sex-role identity and that fathers are much more likely to be traditional in the roles and behaviors they encourage. "The process of [sex-role] differentiation is attributed to the powerful socialization pressures of the family and society through differential reinforcement and the process of identification with the same sex parent."[40] The power of parental sex-role expectations on themselves and their children can be seen in several findings: a baby dressed in pink and labeled a girl will be given dolls, labeled cuddly, weaker, smaller, softer, and more finely featured than a baby dressed in blue and labeled a boy; and girls will be smiled at and parents will do things for them—rewarding them for dependent behavior. Boys, on the other hand, will be taught how to do a task and praised for their independence and ability. Fathers, in particular, are found to stress competence, task performance, achievement, careers, and occupational success for their sons, but to reinforce dependency behavior on parts of daughters.[41] It is almost self-evident that parents who do not encourage achievement and career ambition for their daughters will be less likely to provide them with the financial, emotional, and other intellectual supports required to obtain the educational and other human capital training needed to succeed. The professional mother becomes important here, not only as a role model, but also as the source that can ensure availability of such resources.[42]

According to Nancy Chodorow, early childhood socialization accounts for much of the difference in adult masculine and feminine characteristics.[43] The difference stems from the way gender identity is formed for males and females. Females achieve gender identity in the ongoing relationship with their mother. They are taught relational and empathetic skills and their identity is forged within the family relationship. In contrast, males are encouraged to develop independence and organizational skills. They must separate from their mothers in order to achieve a masculine identity, thus their individuation and self-concept are forged in relation to the larger world.

These differences in psychological development are thought to affect not only the way an individual perceives him or herself but also society's view of the individual. When societal expectations or role demands meet self-concept, the result is often individual confusion. This confusion is thought to be greater for females on the average than for males simply because their orientation to the larger world has been more limited.[44] By the same token, their self-image lacks individuation, as they view themselves functioning only in relationship to the whole. Female ethical concerns highlight relationship and understanding; as a result relationship often takes precedence over achievement. Socialization literature stresses that females are more cooperative, more empathetic, and emphasize interpersonal relationships much more than males—from childhood through advanced age.[45] A consequence of this gender difference is that, when individual achievement is highlighted, women often experience a higher degree of success anxiety when that achievement is perceived to be at the expense of another. As we will see in Chapter 6, numerous observers argue that these differences in socialization lead to substantial differences in managerial and decision-making styles as adults.

From 1960 to 1988, the number of female-headed households (single or divorced) raising children alone more than tripled. More than one of five children live with only one parent.[46] Usually it is the father who is absent, raising the question, "Does a father's absence make a difference in a girl's sex-role development?" Studies show that no effect is found on preadolescent girls, but that effects do appear during adolescence. Girls without fathers showed more anxiety and discomfort around males, and tended to be more sexually precocious and "inappropriately aggressive" toward males.[47] Girls from divorced families tend to marry earlier, be pregnant when they marry, and be less satisfied with their partner, ultimately leading to more divorces.

Birth Order and Social Class

Birth order and social class have also been found to be important mediators of sex-role socialization and career success.[48] Birth order studies show that high achievers are more likely to be first born, only children, or last born. For both sexes, family size, the number and gender of siblings, relationship to parents, and social class interact with birth order to impact career success. In general, birth order is important because, as the first or only child (or the last), the child is more likely to receive financial resources and more attention, both of which are essential for success. Many female achievers have not only been first born, they also have had no brothers, suggesting that having no competition for such resources from males was critical.[49] In the 1980s, as the average number of children declined to less than 2.0, such birth order concerns undoubtedly have less impact.

Studies of successful women in the 1970s debated whether achieving women were deviants or the products of an enriched environment.[50] Research supported the enrichment perspective. For example, all female presidents and vice presidents of U.S. businesses in a 1977 study of managerial women were first-born children who felt special as children, had parents with high educational levels, and a mother with a strong employment record with positive feelings toward her work.[51] Similar patterns were found among the very highest female political leaders.[52]

Adolescence, Peers, and the Opposite Sex

Adolescence has been a critical point in the development of achievement and ambition for girls. Until reaching puberty, girls are encouraged to excel as much as boys. Then, in preparation for adulthood, which historically meant wifehood and motherhood, the stress switched to the adoption of feminine attitudes and behaviors. Academic excellence, achievement, and femininity have historically *not* been viewed as being compatible.[53] The impact on self-concept has been considerable. For example, although gender differences are small in elementary school, by the eleventh and twelfth grades girls were found to be significantly more concerned with being liked and were more selfconscious, whereas boys were more concerned with achievement and competence.[54]

Numerous studies have found that sex roles mediate intellectual accomplishments and achievement aspirations.[55] Children, and adolescents in particular, strive to be consistent with their self-defined gender categorization. "Simply labeling a task as appropriate for either boys or girls has had the effect of increasing expectancy for success, appeal of the game, task persistence, quality of performance, and achievement level attained . . . when the task was sex-appropriate."[56] Girls and women are consistently found to have higher success expectations and higher performance standards when the area of achievement was considered appropriate for females.[57] In addition, the females showing the greatest fear of achievement were those with the strongest traditional sex-role expectations.[58] The fear of success syndrome appears to be a fear of inappropriate sex-role behavior.[59]

If women are to be achievement oriented and successful in careers, the female sex role needs to be perceived as more compatible with achievement-oriented behaviors, and males need to become accepting of that behavior. These data draw attention to the importance of role models of the same sex, and highlight again why having a successful mother in a positive relationship with an adult male (spouse or significant other) is so critical to the self-esteem and achievement aspirations of the daughter.

Another difficulty in developing female achievers concerns the dating game. Because girls mature at a faster rate than boys, they tend to seek and date older males who, because of their age, are more knowledgeable and more experienced. This differential establishes a pattern of deference and an assumption that men are more likely to be knowledgeable about the world than women.[60] Historically, girls did not have the option of taking the initiative in the dating game. Rather, they had to use their appearance and "feminine wiles" to attract males. One longitudinal study of fifth- and sixth-grade girls, begun in the 1930s,[61] found that the more attractive girls had, as women, married the most well-to-do, successful men. This demonstrated that, as late as the 1960s, "a woman's status [was] determined by her appearance, a man's by his achievements."[62]

In the 1980s, dating patterns changed, enabling girls to take the initiative. Relationships came to be more emphasized than marriage. In 1970, 35.8% of all U.S. women age 20 to 24 had never married; by 1987, that percentage had risen to 60.8%.[63] The reduced interest in early marriage reflected the pursuit of more education for young women and an effort to resist the constraints associated with the wife/mother role.

Television

Children in the United States watch an average of 20 hours or more of television each week, and television plays a major role in most children's lives before they learn to read and write.[64] The content of television shows can shape viewers' conception of gender roles,[65] and television can have considerable impact on children's perceptions of gender. The influence of TV on the development of children's gender identities raised concern in the 1970s.[66] One 1974 study of shows popular at the time found only 34 significant female characters, "and those were presented in very traditional female roles characterized by dependence and over-emotionalism. There was not a single instance in which a married woman worked outside the home."[67]

Fortunately television shows have changed substantially over the last 15 years. Women in such shows as *Murphy Brown, The Cosby Show,* and even *Star Trek—The Next Generation* express nontraditional attitudes and pursue careers. Nevertheless, while the number of female main characters has significantly increased over the 1980s, women are still underrepresented. A 1989 study found that nearly 71% of prime time characters are men, while only 29% are women.[68] This study also revealed that women were more likely than men to be identified by their marital status (59% of women compared to 32% of men), more likely to be engaged in housework (20% of women compared to 3% of men), more likely to be pursuing a romantic relationship, and more likely to be victimized.[69] Although some women characters do have successful careers, "less than a third of the married women and half of the single and formerly married women are portrayed as working outside the home." Three-fourths of male characters are identified by an occupation outside the home.[70] Even commercials create false gender expectations by portraying successful women as primarily young and beautiful.[71] If children's acceptance of women's advancement is to improve, the media portrayal of women must also continue to improve.

Printed Matter

Children's literature has historically been very male-centered. A 1971 study of the Caldecott Award winning books discovered that most stories were about boys, men, male animals, or male adventures.[72] A follow-up 1972 study found that males appeared in pictures 11 times more frequently than females and that "most of the women in picture books have status by virtue of their relationships to specific men—they are the wives of the kings, judges, adventurers, and explorers, but they themselves are not the rulers, judges, adventurers, and explorers."[73]

Like television programming, children's literature has also improved its portrayal of gender roles. Follow-up studies on the Caldecott Award winners in the 1980s found that, by 1985, the ratio of male to female characters had risen from a low of 78% males to 22% females in the period from 1971 to 1975 to 57% males to 43% females in the period from 1981 to 1985.[74] The ratio of illustrations of men and women also improved from 75% males to 17% females in the period from 1976 to 1980 to 63% males to 37% females in the period from 1981 to 1985.[75] Again, these statistics demonstrate that male bias continues to permeate the media socializing American children; however, this improvement can allow future business leaders to better appreciate women's contributions. Gayle Kimball, a professor of women's studies at California State University, Chico, notes that parents can help shape their children's attitudes by screening books their children read.[76]

The Schools

Schools have been notorious for perpetuating the traditional sex-role stereotypes. Teachers consistently pay more attention to boys than girls. They also tend to reward males for independence and task performance and reward females for passivity and dependence behavior. By giving different feedback to each sex, they can instill a learned helplessness in girls.[77] In the classroom setting, girls "receive less teacher attention than boys, unless girls stay physically close to the teacher and lose needed opportunities for inventive and independent experiences." Greenburg continues, "boys receive attention whether they stay near to or far from the teacher."[78]

Schools often have sex-typed tracking systems as well, with higher proportions of girls going into English, history, and the social sciences at the college preparatory track, and more males going into the physical sciences and math. In vocational areas, girls are channeled into home economics, typing, and bookkeeping, whereas boys are channeled more into mechanical and technical courses.

Textbooks and tests also perpetuate traditional sex-roles. Even in 1990, women are rarely pictured as political leaders, scientists, and public achievers. An analysis of 24 best-selling teacher education texts reveals that, as educators, teachers are not being made aware of the problem of sexism in the classroom. Of the 24 texts reviewed, 23 gave less than 1% of their space to the issue of sexism; one-third did not mention sexism at all; not a single text provided future teachers with curricular resources or strategies to counteract sexism in the classroom.[79] The content of textbooks for students gives the basic message that females are less important and less visible than males. In addition, educational achievement tests contain more male than female pronouns and references. Item content analysis of social science texts also revealed that the majority of the professors, doctors, presidents of companies, and members of professional teams, as well as famous persons in history, were male. Moreover, most biographies were about men. When women or girls did appear, they were more often portrayed in passive roles and/or stereotyped occupations.[80]

Conclusion

The fact that changes in many of the historically more negative patterns of socialization for girls have occurred cannot be disputed. Yet remnants of the impact of these patterns on female aspirations and achievement potential remain. The women trying to move up the career ladder in the 1990s, who are now in their mid-thirties and forties, were socialized during a more traditional period. Studies of the female identity patterns of this age group during adolescence revealed three different approaches: being traditional, anticipating no career and being a wife/mother; being achievement- and success-oriented for oneself with no intention of marrying or having children; and finally being bimodal and committed to both family and career, the "superwoman" of the 1980s.[81] As Hyde points out, none of these approaches really resolves the identity conflict between femininity and achievement.[82] The first two each reject the other; the third attempts to be all things to all people. The women in 1990 who are in their fifties and sixties, who should be at the top of their careers, were raised during an even more traditional period. Sex-role ideology and traditional sex-role development patterns hang heavy on the lives of both males and females playing the 1990s' competitive game of "success." We might need to await the 21st century to witness the development of more viable options.

Notes

1. Sondra Farganis, *The Social Reconstruction of the Feminine Character* (Totowa, NJ: Rowman & Littlefield, 1986), 48; and Peter L. Berger and Thomas Luckman, *Social Construction of Reality: A Treatise in the Sociology of Knowledge* (Garden City, NY: Doubleday, 1966), 62.

2. Farganis, *The Social Reconstruction*, 48.

3. T. R. Sarbin and K. E. Scheibe, "A Model of Social Identity," in *Studies in Social Identity*, eds. T. R. Sarbin and K. E. Scheibe (New York: Praeger, 1983); J. G. Morawski, "The Troubled Quest for Masculinity, Femininity, and Androgyny," in *Sex and Gender*, eds. Phillip Shaver and Clyde Hendrick (Newbury Park, CA: Sage, 1987), 54; and Martha T. Mednick, "On the Politics of Psychological Constructs," *American Psychologist* 44(8) (August 1988): 1118-1123.

4. Douglas T. Kendrick, "Gender, Genes, and the Social Environment: A Biosocial Interactionist Perspective," in *Sex and Gender*, eds. Phillip Shaver and Clyde Hendrick (Newbury Park, CA: Sage, 1987), 32-34.

5. E. E. Maccoby and C. N. Jacklin, *The Psychology of Sex Differences* (Stanford, CA: Stanford University Press, 1974). See also, Joan E. Grusec and Hugh Lytton, *Social Development: History, Theory, and Research* (New York: Springer-Verlag, 1988), 363-410.

6. G. N. Powell, *Women & Men in Management* (Newbury Park, CA: Sage, 1988), 47.

7. A. Anastasi, "Reciprocal Relations Between Cognitive and Affective Development with Implications for Sex Differences," in *Nebraska Symposium on Motivation, 1984: Psychology and Gender*, ed. T. B. Sonderegger (Lincoln: University of Nebraska Press, 1985), 1-36.

8. Powell, *Women & Men in Management;* Grusec and Lytton, *Social Development*, 363-410.

9. Janet Shibley Hyde, *Half the Human Experience: The Psychology of Women* 3rd ed. (Lexington, MA: D.C. Heath, 1985), 189.

10. For example, see Grusec and Lytton, *Social Development*.

11. H. A. Witkin, "Origins of Cognitive Style," in *Cognition: Theory, Research, Promise*, ed. C. Sheerer (New York: Harper & Row, 1964).

12. Witkin, *Cognition*.

13. Hyde, *Half the Human Experience*, 196.

14. Powell, *Women & Men in Management*, 48-49.

15. Carol Gilligan, *In a Different Voice: Psychological Theory and Women's Development* (Cambridge, MA: Harvard University Press, 1982).

16. Summarized by Grusec and Lytton, *Social Development*, 378-379.

17. Kendrick, "Gender, Genes, and the Social Environment," 35.

18. Jean Evangelauf, "SAT Called a 'Defective Product' that Is Biased Against Women," *Chronicle of Higher Education* 35(34), 3 May 1989, A3; "National Merit Scholarship Program Unfair to Girls, Test Group Charges," *Education Week* 8(34), 17 May 1989, 3; Tom Waters, "SAT Bashing," *Discover* 10(8) (August 1989): 28.

19. Grusec and Lytton, *Social Development,* 370-372.

20. Ralph P. Witherspoon, "Female Soldiers in Combat: A Policy Adrift," *Minerva* (Spring 1988): 1-27.

21. Witherspoon, "Female Soldiers in Combat"; and Amy Laboda, "Women with Navy Wings: They Fly Everywhere but into Battle, and on that Point They've Just Begun to Fight," *Flying* (January 1990): 39-51.

22. Anita L. DeFrantz, "Women and Leadership in Sport," *Journal of Physical Education, Recreation and Dance* 59 (March 1988): 46-48.

23. DeFrantz, "Women and Leadership," 47.

24. Mary Bohlig, "Women Coaches/Administration: An Endangered Species," *Scholastic Coach* 57 (February 1988): 89.

25. Bohlig, "Women Coaches."

26. Gordon Bakoulis Bloch, "Sports and Your Career," *Working Woman* 14(6) (June 1989): 138.

27. Bloch, "Sports and Your Career," 138.

28. Sam Friedman, "Sports Helps Women Be 'One of the Boys,' " *National Underwriter: Property & Casualty/Risk Benefits Management Edition* 93(30) (24 July 1989).

29. Simone de Beauvoir, *The Second Sex,* trans. H. M. Paushley, New York Modern Library (New York: Vintage Books, 1952), 301.

30. Rita Mae Kelly and Mary Boutilier, *The Making of Political Women: A Study of Socialization and Role Conflict* (Chicago, IL: Nelson-Hall, 1988); Grusec and Lytton, *Social Development,* 393.

31. Elaine Donelson, "Becoming a Single Woman," in *Women: A Psychological Perspective,* eds. E. Donelson and J. Gullahorn (New York: John Wiley, 1977).

32. Esther R. Greenglass and Reva Devins, "Factors Related to Marriage and Career Plans in Unmarried Women," *Sex Roles* 8 (1982): 57-72.

33. Kendrick, "Gender, Genes, and Social Environment," 31-32.

34. Kendrick, "Gender, Genes, and Social Environment," 24; see, e.g., Anastasi, "Reciprocal Relations"; and J. Eccles, "Sex Differences in Achievement Patterns," in *Nebraska Symposium on Motivation, 1984: Psychology and Gender,* ed. T. B. Sonderegger (Lincoln: University of Nebraska Press, 1985), 97-132.

35. Kendrick, "Gender, Genes, and Social Development," 24; cf Eccles, "Sex Differences in Achievement Patterns."

36. Julia A. Sherman, "Mathematics, the Critical Filter: A Look at Some Residues," *Psychology of Women Quarterly* 6 (1982): 428-444.

37. S. H. Osipow, "Counseling Psychology: Theory, Research and Practice in Career Counseling," *Annual Review of Psychology* 38 (1987): 274.

38. Osipow, "Counseling Psychology," 273.

39. H. S. Farmer, "Model of Career and Achievement Motivation for Women and Men," *Journal of Counseling Psychology* 32 (1985): 363-390; and Ruth E. Fassinger, "A Causal Model of College Women's Career Choice," *Journal of Vocational Behavior* 27(1) (August 1985): 123-153; H. S. Farmer, "Career and Homemaking Plans for High School Youth," *Journal of Counseling Psychology* 30 (1983): 40-45.

40. Dee L. Shepherd-Look, "Sex Differentiation and the Development of Sex Roles," in *Handbook of Developmental Psychology,* ed. Benjamin B. Wolman (Englewood Cliffs, NJ: Prentice-Hall, 1982), 412.

41. Shepherd-Look, "Sex Differentiation," 419.

42. Kelly and Boutilier, *The Making of Political Women;* and Mary M. Hale and Rita Mae Kelly, *Gender, Bureaucracy, and Democracy* (Westport, CT: Greenwood, 1989).

43. Nancy Chodorow, *The Reproduction of Mothering: Psychoanalysis and the Sociology of Gender* (Berkeley: University of California Press, 1978).

44. Grusec and Lytton, *Social Development,* 374-378; Chodorow, *Reproduction of Mothering.*

45. Grusec and Lytton, *Social Development,* 377.

46. U.S. Bureau of the Census, *Statistical Abstract of the United States, 1989* (Washington, DC: Department of Commerce, 1989), 40-50. See also, J. Glick, "Cognition and Social Cognition: An Introduction," in *The Development of Social Understanding,* eds. J. Glick and A. K. Clarke-Stewart (New York: Gardner, 1978); Shepherd-Look, "Sex Differentiation," especially 423-424; and Margaret Anderson, *Thinking About Women: Sociological Perspectives on Sex and Gender* (New York: Macmillan, 1988), 76-77.

47. Shepherd-Look, "Sex Differentiation," 424.

48. S. A. Basow, *Sex Role Stereotypes: Traditions and Alternatives* (Monterey, CA: Brooks/Cole, 1980); B. H. Hess and M. B. Sussman, *Women and the Family: Two Decades of Change* (New York: Haworth, 1984); Kelly and Boutilier, *The Making of Political Women;* and L. J. Weitzman, *Sex Roles* (New York: Oxford University Press, 1975).

49. J. S. Crawford, *Women in Middle Management* (Ridgewood, NJ: Forkner, 1977); Kelly and Boutilier, *The Making of Political Women;* M. T. S. Mednick, S. S. Tangri, and L. W. Hoffman, *Women and Achievement* (New York: John Wiley, 1975); A. J. Lott, "Social Psychology," in *Handbook of General Psychology,* ed. Benjamin Wolman (Englewood Cliffs, NJ: Prentice-Hall, 1973); and Basow, *Sex Role Stereotypes.*

50. E. M. Almquist and S. S. Angrist, "Role Model Influences on College Women's Career Aspirations," *Merrill-Palmer Quarterly* 17(3) (1971): 263-279.

51. Margaret Hennig and Anne Jardim, "Women Executives in the Old Boy Network," *Psychology Today* 10 (January 1977): 76-81.

52. Kelly and Boutilier, *The Making of Political Women.*

53. Hyde, *Half the Human Experience,* 160.

54. Florence R. Rosenberg and R. G. Simmons, "Sex Differences in the Self-Concept in Adolescence," *Sex Roles* 1 (1975), 147-159; and Patricia Y. Miller and William Simon, "Adolescent Sexual Behavior: Context and Change," *Social Problems* 22(1) (October 1974): 58-76.

55. For a brief summary see Shepherd-Look, "Sex Differentiation," 425.

56. Shepherd-Look, "Sex Differentiation," 425.

57. A. H. Stein and M. M. Bailey, "The Socialization of Achievement Oriented Females," *Psychological Bulletin* 5(51) (1973): 345-366; Matina S. Horner, "Fail: Bright Women," *Psychology Today* 3(6) (1969): 36; and Anderson, *Thinking About Women,* 85-88.

58. Shepherd-Look, "Sex Differentiation," 425.

59. Kay Deaux, *The Behavior of Women and Men* (Monterey, CA: Brooks/Cole, 1976).

60. Hyde, "Half the Human Experience," 163.

61. Glenn H. Elder, "Appearance and Education in Marriage Mobility," *American Sociological Review* 34 (1969): 519-533.

62. Hyde, *Half the Human Experience,* 163.

63. U.S. Bureau of the Census, *Statistical Abstract of the United States, 1989* (Washington, DC: Department of Commerce, 1989): 43.

64. Michael Morgan and Nancy Signorielli, "Cultivation Analysis: Conceptualization and Methodology," in *Cultivation Analysis: New Directions in Media Effects Research,* eds. Nancy Signorielli and Michael Morgan (Newbury Park, CA: Sage, 1990), 13.

65. Kevin Durkin, *Television, Sex Roles and Children: A Developmental Social Psychological Account* (Philadelphia, PA: Milton Keynes Open University Press, 1985).

66. Faye H. Dambrot, Diana C. Reep, and Daniel Bell, "Television Sex Roles in the 1980s: Do Viewers' Sex and Sex Role Orientation Change the Picture?" *Sex Roles* 19(56) (1988): 387-401.

67. Shepherd-Look, "Sex Differentiation," 426.

68. Nancy Signorielli, "Television and Conceptions About Sex Roles: Maintaining Conventionality and the Status Quo," *Sex Roles* 21(516) (1989): 341-361.

69. Signorielli, "Television and Conceptions About Sex Roles," 350-352.

70. Signorielli, "Television and Conceptions About Sex Roles," 350-351.

71. Gayle Kimball, *50-50 Parenting* (Lexington, MA: D. C. Heath, 1988), 67-68.

72. A. P. Nilsen, "Women in Children's Literature," *College English* 29 (1971): 918-926.

73. Shepherd-Look, "Sex Differentiation," 426; see also L. J. Weiztman, D. Eifler, E. Hokada, and C. Ross, "Sex Role Socialization in Picture Books for Pre-school Children," *American Journal of Sociology* 77 (1982): 1125-1150.

74. Wilma Holden Dougherty and Rosalind E. Engel, "An 80s Look for Sex Equality in Caldecott Winners and Honor Books," *The Reading Teacher* 40(4) (January 1987): 395.

75. Dougherty and Engel, "An 80s Look for Sex Equality," 396.

76. Kimball, *50-50 Parenting,* 76.

77. C. S. Dweck and F. E. Goetz, "Attributions and Learned Helplessness," in *New Directions in Attribution Research* Vol. 2, eds. J. H. Harvey, W. Ickles, and R. F. Kidd (Hillsdale, NJ: Lawrence Erlbaum, 1977); and Selma Greenberg, "Educational Equity in Early Education Environments," in *Handbook for Achieving Sex Equity Through Education,* ed. S. S. Klein (Baltimore, MD: Johns Hopkins University Press, 1988), 457-469.

78. Greenberg, "Educational Equity," 462.

79. David Sadker and Myra Sadker, "The Treatment of Sex Equity in Teacher Education," in *Handbook for Achieving Sex Equity Through Education,* ed. S. S. Klein (Baltimore, MD: Johns Hopkins University Press, 1988), 147-148.

80. Carole L. Hahn and Jane Bernard-Powers, with Lisa Hunter, Susan Groves, Molly MacGregor, and Kathryn P. Scott, "Sex Equity in Social Science," in *Handbook for Achieving Sex Equity Through Education,* ed. S. S. Klein (Baltimore, MD: Johns Hopkins University Press, 1988), 280.

81. M. Dellas and E. L. Gaier, "The Self and Adolescent Identity in Women: Options and Implications," *Adolescence* 10 (1975): 399-407.

82. Hyde, "Sex Differentiation," 165.

5

Sex-Role Spillover: Personal, Familial, and Organizational Roles

Americans have traditionally equated the role of "worker" with the roles of breadwinner, father, and husband. As women enter the work force, they have been expected to meet this male-centered standard. At the same time, women also have been expected to follow their traditional roles of wife or girlfriend, mother, daughter, and sex partner/object. The intertwining of women's expanding economic power and less rapidly evolving sex roles has produced the gendered dimension of the U.S. segmented labor market.

In 1986 more than 80% of women in the work force were of childbearing age.[1] A large proportion of employed women experienced significant conflicts between their roles as workers, wives, mothers, daughters, and family caretakers, all of which they were expected to play simultaneously.[2] These concurrent demands caused many women to suffer from two conditions: role overload, which results when a person is expected to fulfill more roles than she or he can handle; and role strain, which results from conflict between two or more roles. Table 5.1 contrasts the traditional family and organizational roles of men and women.

AUTHOR'S NOTE: This chapter was researched and written with Phoebe Morgan Stambaugh.

TABLE 5.1 Comparison of Traditional Family and Organizational Roles

Wife	Husband	Employee	Manager
• homemaking	• provider of living wage	• subordinate follows policy	• makes and administers policy
• consumer-family goods	• initiating sex partner	• must be pleasant and receptive to clients and management	• is staff's link to organization
• attractive, receptive sex partner	• key decision maker		
• supportive— "little woman behind big man"	• family's link to political/economic system		

Mother	Father	Employee	Management
• childbirth	• provides means for rearing (education, etc)	• complete loyalty to organizational needs— continuous, uninterrupted, productive work	• controls staff's movement through merit system
• childrearing	• nurturer for whole family		• complete loyalty to company policy/ goals
• always available for children's needs	• key discipliner		

Daughter	Son	Employee	Management
• respect and honor of mother	• heir apparent	• complete trust in superiors	• finds talented staff and grooms for management
• adoration of father	• "chip off the old block"	• loyalty to superiors and organization	• carries on "legacy" through protege
• "daddy's little girl"			
• attractive—good "catch" for promising son-in-law			

Girlfriend/ Sex Partner/Object	Boyfriend/ Male Sex-Actor	Employee	Management
• attractive: potential wife/mother	• successful: potential provider	Woman	Woman
		• attractive, pleasant, supportive	• attractive, interpersonal, managerial
• passive: waits to be asked out	• assertive: makes the date	Man	Man
		• aggressive, jocular, dominant	• successful, assertive, commanding

Working Women and the Home

The Wife Role (Housekeeper/Homemaker/Hostess)

In the 1950s and 1960s wives employed outside the home to augment their husbands' income gradually gained acceptance in the role of supplemental workers. By the 1980s, middle-class women had become more than just guardians of their family status and lifestyle; many had also launched careers. At the same time, many couples found that both spouses needed to work to maintain a middle-class standard of living.[3] Wives were not the only women entering the paid labor force; 45% of all employed women were single, separated, or divorced.[4] Further, 23% of all households consisted of nonmarried, single women.[5] The median weekly earnings in 1989 for a male-supported household without an employed wife were $486. For families with both spouses working, the median earnings were $668; yet, for a female-supported household, median weekly earnings totaled only $334.[6] These statistics indicate that increasing numbers of women have fallen into or have barely escaped poverty.

Regardless of income or marital status, female workers must deal with home and hearth in ways that male workers do not. In *The Second Stage,* Betty Friedan recognized that, while women were pulled into the public realm, men were not enticed into the private domain.[7] The resulting lopsided division of familial responsibilities led to a condition Friedan termed the "superwoman" syndrome. While women attempted to excel at both the traditional female sex roles and the male role of paid laborer, men avoided the women's traditional role of housekeeper/homemaker/hostess. Consequently, women entering the paid labor force encountered a Herculean task that only a mythical "superwoman" could have completely fulfilled.

Empirical studies demonstrate the burden this condition places on women. Arlie Hochschild's study of couples and housework shows that this imbalance of roles requires women to put in a "second shift" as housekeeper, consumer, and caregiver.[8] Skow reports that working wives spend 15 fewer hours at leisure each week than their husbands, and when faced with scheduling conflicts, women tend to reduce leisure time before reducing time spent on child care.[9] A study reported in *The American Woman* compared married men and women who spend equal hours in the paid work force. This study found that women put in an additional 18 hours per week doing home labor.[10] Fathers average only 12 minutes per day in primary child care.[11] Even women who claim to have egalitarian arrangements at home still put in more energy, time, and labor during this second shift than do their spouses.[12]

Although custom has decreed that women be more available for family care, this role expectation has not been viewed positively in the workplace. Ten executive men were asked by *Executive Female* magazine to participate in a roundtable discussion about the strengths and weaknesses of female peers. One executive claimed:

> People have to have families—you can't argue that—but within the business environment, it's a negative. A woman always wants to go home at 5:00 to be with her family. Men have families too, but they don't leave. . . .[13]

Men make sacrifices in order to make money and to gain power. These executives suggested that women may be hitting the glass ceiling because they are not ready to make the same sacrifices for their careers.

This perception shifts the blame for women's difficulties in the workplace to women, rather than on recognizing socially institutionalized and individually internalized stereotypes. In addition, reports indicate that this type of perception about women is becoming increasingly inaccurate. A roundtable discussion of ten successful female executives by *Nation's Business* indicates women are not only "ready to make the sacrifice" but also are making the personal concessions necessary for career advancement.[14] One IBM executive found that her 10 to 12 hour workdays made it impossible to keep a commitment to a family evening meal. "I took a close look at that ritual and decided it had to go."[15] Letting go of time-honored practices is one of the many sacrifices women, especially those in the primary labor market, have to make.

To be most competitive, especially in the primary job sector, requires not being a "wife," but actually having an effective substitute. Many careers command complete loyalty and submission to organizational goals with total submersion into corporate culture. Most management and executive careers are project-driven. Deadlines are not flexed to accommodate family or personal schedules. High-powered careers blur the lines between the personal and private realms. Work often takes place with a client over dinner, with the boss at a show, with co-workers on the golf course, and frequently out of town. It is assumed a babysitter is available, that the children are always well, or that there are no children at all.

Companies frequently expect employees will not be burdened with responsibility for cleaning the home, purchasing consumer goods, and caring for children. In addition, the higher level professional is expected to have a partner who serves as hostess to the boss and clients, stands in line to buy the theater tickets, makes reservations for the restaurant, packs the luggage for out-of-town meetings, and drives the higher status spouse (usually the man) to the airport in mid-workday. Without the help of "wives," married career women and career women with children suffer a real disadvantage competing for important contracts, key line positions or out-of-town jobs.

The Mother Role (Childbearing and Child Rearing)

In 1990 more than 70% of women age 25 to 34 were in the labor force. In 1950, there were only 35%. Lenhoff reports that 80% of all women in the workplace are of childbearing age, and 93% of them will become pregnant while working.[16] Overall, approximately three-fourths of women in the work force will be affected by pregnancy and motherhood. Given that about 50 million women are in the labor force, that means about 37.2 million women will be directly affected by pregnancy and child-care policies. This estimate does not include the millions of children, elderly relatives, and spouses that are indirectly impacted.

The number of working mothers has increased sharply since the 1950s, when only 12% of women with children under the age of six worked. In 1988, approximately six of every ten mothers with a child under age six were employed. Half of all married mothers with infants younger than one year were in the labor force. In 1990, fewer than 5% of families had a father who worked and a mother who stayed home caring for the children. By 1995 it is estimated that two-thirds of all preschool children will have mothers in the work force, and that four of five school-age children will have employed mothers.[17]

Neither U.S. employers nor the government have been quick to respond to these radical changes. In 1987 the Bureau of Labor Statistics estimated that only 2% of businesses with 10 or more workers sponsored child-care centers; an additional 3% provided financial assistance for day-care services; and only 6% offered help in the form of information, referral, or counseling services.[18] AT&T reported in 1989 that families juggle up to four different kinds of child-care arrangements each week.[19] Although the number of day-care centers built in or near the workplace increased from 110 in 1979 to 4,000 in 1989,[20] most workers have to rely on other family members, neighbors, religious institutions, or personally devised arrangements. In 1989, churches provided one-third of the child-care services.[21] In 1989, only 14% of U.S. corporations offered child-care benefits to their employees, arguing that the bottom line costs outweighed benefits.

The options for integrating the roles of mother and career woman have not been great. Women have been expected to fit into the male model of work, which forces them to either avoid being a mother, adopt a "father's" approach to child care, or seek alternative work hours and work forms. Table 5.2 presents a summary of some of the employment alternatives developed to date with a brief assessment of the advantages and disadvantages of each.

A common solution to the motherhood conflict for ambitious career women has been avoidance. Whereas 90% of male executives age 40 and under are fathers, only 35% of their female counterparts are mothers.[22] As the biological clock ticked close to menopause, more and more career women of the 1980s sought alternative approaches to the work force. Women who put off having children until the last possible moment were not rewarded for their sacrifice. Instead, their choices regarding pregnancy and maternity leave became a test of organizational loyalty.[23] The more seniority and/or responsibility a woman has, the more childbirth is likely to be viewed as an organizational disruption. Employers often want reassurance that the motherhood role will not supersede the employee role.

Large numbers of women, especially those with well-paying jobs, addressed the stress of role overload and role strain due to motherhood as single working fathers have previously done. They hire other women to assist in mothering and family chores. This "fatherly" approach to child care, house care, and family consumption is a major factor in the rise of the service economy and self-employment of women in the peripheral sector of the labor market.[24]

Although the need for child care has led to more jobs for women and greater flexibility for women owners and managers of such services, the resulting businesses and jobs have also contributed to pay inequities and employment of women in jobs that lack career growth potential. Although nearly one-half of all day-care teachers have bachelor degrees or at least some college training, the average salary of these professionals—mostly women—was only $5.35 per hour in 1988, a salary that amounts to about $9,363 a year. This sum is less than the

TABLE 5.2 Advantages and Disadvantages to Alternative Work Styles

Alternative	Advantages	Disadvantages
Flextime		
Flexible arrival/exit time: can arrive at work anytime during a 2-3-hour grace period.	The most stressful time of day is the "rush hour" getting to and from the workplace—flexibility reduces this stress.	Studies indicate single women are the users, not parents. Flextime is not considered appropriate for supervisors and managers of personnel.
Compressed work week: most common ones are 40 hours in 4 days or 32 hours over a weekend.	Allows parents one or more full days of access to businesses, schools, and medical facilities. Weekend shifts popular among nurses.	High fatigue among workers. Adds the need for special child care arrangements for the extended working days.
Part-time work		
Part-time professionals: works less than 32 hours per week yet receives pro-rated amount of benefits afforded to full-time employees.	A parent spends more time on child care without losing "professional status."	May not have access to the more important projects and tasks given to those who are available through the entire work day.
Part-time partnership tracks: accomplished based on total number of billable hours, total amount of income, or total number of hours worked.	Allows professionals like doctors and lawyers to keep on a partnership track during child-rearing years.	May take twice as long to gain partnership as a traditional track. Many professions are project-oriented so may often work more hours than contracted.
Job sharing: two or more people share one job either simultaneously or alternatively.	Well received by helping professionals like teachers and counselors—avoids burn-out and helps maintain creativity. Affords the most flexibility in time spent at work.	Must be done on a voluntary basis. With professionals, employer will get more than "half" of their energy and talents—employee gets half the pay.
Extended leave		
Maternity leave: extended leave for mothers of newly born or adopted children.	Helps women make the adjustment to motherhood while still guaranteeing her job at work.	Does not offer men the opportunity to learn and practice primary child-care responsibilities.
Paternity leave: same as maternity leave but for fathers.	Promotes bonding of father to child at birth and fosters new role development for fathers.	Although the job is guaranteed, maternity or paternity leave may result in loss of positioning for key promotions.

(continued)

TABLE 5.2 Continued

Alternative	Advantages	Disadvantages
Parental leave: same as maternal and paternal.	If each spouse could take turns, the time period for which a full-time parent is available is doubled.	This system can work only if both have access to leave—an unlikelihood today.
Homework Telecommuting	Allows women to combine homecare, childcare, and work for pay in the home. Saves time and cuts the cost of commuting and day-care tuition. Also allows flexibility of scheduling.	The isolation of home-based work keeps women from networking and prevents positioning for key opportunities. Also, without physical boundaries, can result in even more role strain and overload.

$9,431 federally defined poverty level for a family of three.[25] As the need for day care increased in the 1980s, the average salary of day-care teachers declined by 27% from 1977 to 1988.[26]

The low salaries reflect a dilemma facing U.S. women. Day care services bear large price tags. In 1986, the estimated cost of purchasing in-home care was $8,000 per year, $5,000 for day care per year, and $2,500 for a year of full-time preschool tuition—costs comparable to college tuition.[27] Women who must hire other women to watch their children typically do not earn salaries high enough to pay day-care providers higher wages.

Working women still earn only 74 cents to every working man's dollar.[28] Even the highest level executive women suffer dramatic pay gaps. According to the U.S. Chamber of Commerce in May 1987, "corporate women at the vice-presidential level and above earn 42 percent less than their male peers."[29]

In addition to the burden of affordability, a shortage of licensed day-care centers makes it unlikely that a good center will be conveniently located. Many centers cater to those who work a regular day shift. Women who work odd shifts, who are going to school, or who often have after-hour meetings find themselves struggling to find additional home care and solutions to the restrictive drop-off and pick-up hours at the day-care center. And those few centers that can accommodate parents after 6:00 p.m. often charge an additional fee for these "off hours."

Many licensed day-care centers have age restrictions preventing enrollment of young babies. Often maternity or pregnancy leaves are not long enough to meet the age requirements for enrollment. In addition, care for physically challenged or sick children is rare and very expensive. In 1987, approximately 67% of all child care still took place in a home.[30] (See Figure 5.1 for the location of child care in the three largest cities of Arizona.)

School-age children pose additional problems. While public schools dismiss students in early afternoon, the average workday ends at 5:00 p.m. Lack of transportation to a care center or prohibitive costs of two to three hours of care per child often results in children caring for themselves after school. According to the Arizona Latchkey Task Force, in Maricopa County alone, 35,000 children need after-school care but do not receive it.[31] One in nine latchkey children is from a middle-income family, and one in three is from a lower-income level. More than half of the care of school-age children in Tucson, Arizona, is organized through public school programs like "Play and Learn."[32]

Family work alternatives, like those in Table 5.2, put women—especially mothers—on a separate "Mommy Track." This Mommy Track reinforces the superiority of the present male career model, preventing married women and mothers from developing a more appropriate female work model. These alternatives relieve the conflict between work and home but typically become formidable barriers to long-term career success.

At the Workplace: Workers as Surrogate Daughters, Wives, Girlfriends, and Sex Partners/Objects

Career women suffer role stress in two directions. Not only does the public role of worker create overload and conflict within the home, but the spillover of traditional sex-role expectations into the workplace is a critical career barrier to women.[33] Unlike their male peers, women are often perceived in the limited roles of surrogate daughters, wives, or mothers rather than as workers. Working women may find that they are judged by their presence, attractiveness, and attitudes rather than their talents and skills as professionals. One reason for this spillover may be that institutions adhere to a family model. In fact, with divorce so prevalent, the corporation may be a more stable institution than marriage.[34]

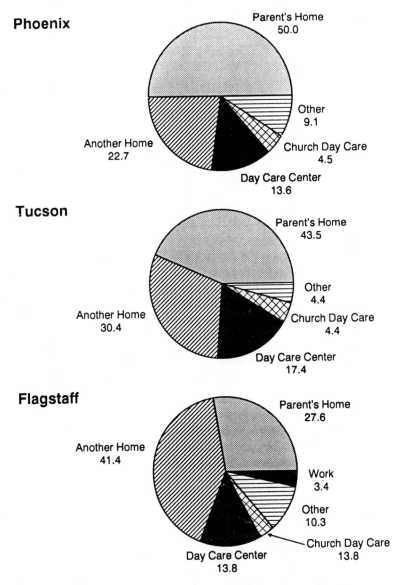

Figure 5.1. Child Care Used Most in Arizona's Major Metropolitan Areas

SOURCE: From P. MacCorquodale, "The Economics of Home and Family," in *Women and the Arizona Economy: The First Arizona Woman's Town Hall,* eds. Janice Monk and Alice Schlegel (Tucson: University of Arizona, Southwest Institute for Research on Women, 1986), p. 110. Reprinted by permission.

For a man, the apprenticeship role may be the first of many stages in his career. For a woman, however, the novice role may be the "end of the line." As "daddy's little girl" female proteges are granted the privileged inequality of the little girl, a privilege their male peers don't have—to fail and to lean on someone. However, "as long as her need for approval is stronger than her need for self-expression, a woman may always be trapped in this subordinate daughter role,"[35] also called the "office daughter syndrome." A study of 18 California families owning businesses found that none of the fathers of daughters had planned on their daughters succeeding them.[36] Unexpected events led to the daughters entering the business. Once in the business, 44% felt obliged to be nurturing of their fathers as well as of the business. The daughters reported feeling it necessary to kiss their dad and to continue being "daddy's little girl." Most daughters helped their fathers remain at the head of the company longer, rather than pushing him out as soon as possible, as sons often do. So few fathers assume their daughters will take over that almost no studies have been done on the topic. In one study reported in 1990, 78% of the fathers interviewed "had difficulty handling their daughters' dual family and business roles—as did 89% of the daughters. Unlike sons, daughters find themselves competing at work in their fathers' eyes with male managers from outside the family."[37] One woman interviewed shared that her father would not listen to her evidence regarding the behavior of the hired male manager.

The difficulties daughters have with their own fathers often carry over to male mentors. With less than 10% of top executive positions being held by women, it is rare that an aspiring woman finds a female mentor. Therefore, a woman's mentor will more likely be a man. Executive men who adhere to using a family model for relating to their co-workers may hesitate to invest in females as proteges because "daughters" have a tendency to grow up, go away, get married, and have babies. The organizational "sons" are viewed as a better bet to become the "heir apparent."

In addition to the daughter role, significant numbers of women also must cope with the girlfriend role. In 1980, Mary Ann Cunningham made the headlines of all the major newspapers, not because she was a graduate of Harvard and the executive vice president of a Fortune 500 corporation, but rather because she was perceived by her male co-workers to be "sleeping her way to the top." Interestingly enough, she never denied having sex with the president but rather insisted they were "truly in love."[38]

The occasional headlines about office romances reflect a change that occurred in the 1980s. The office became a place for professionals and career-oriented individuals to "meet, date, and relate." Workplaces, not unlike the sex-segregated dormitories of the 1960s, had become "co-ed."

Being a successful professional often means working long hours under tight deadlines, being available on an on-call basis, and working long stints out of town. The same institutions that afford little time for house and child care make it equally difficult for singles to develop and nurture romantic relationships. According to Lisa A. Mainiero's latest report on office romance, the sexual revolution that exploded on college and university campuses in the 1960s and 1970s had moved to the workplace in the 1980s.[39] Although Mainiero finds romance at work a positive influence on worker morale and productivity, Barbara Gutek finds that sex in the workplace actually reduces productivity and is generally detrimental to women workers.

Perhaps the most central traditional role for women is that of sex partner (or sex object) and procreator. When this role supersedes appropriate worker roles, the work environment becomes "eroticized."[40] *Playboy* pin-ups in the workplace, off-color graffiti, teasing and flirting behaviors, and physical touching are all manifestations of the spillover of inappropriate sex-role expectations into the workplace.

Women in such workplaces may be accused of capitalizing on their abilities as sex partners/objects rather than as creative employees. Like Mary Ann Cunningham, they may be charged with sleeping their way to the top. Gutek suggests that one may use her "feminine wiles" to get a better typewriter, a free out-of-town excursion, a car phone, or an office with a window, but Cunningham's notoriety stands testament to the fact that sex will not necessarily take you to the top.

The spillover of sex roles into the business environment can become the career woman's nightmare—sexual harassment. Survey research (see Table 5.3) has indicated that from 45% to 90% of all working women experience sexual harassment. This wide margin in estimating the prevalence of sexual harassment is due to an inability of the scientific, business, and legal communities to reach a consensus on a precise definition of this problem. Table 5.3 highlights the survey research efforts to date. Although it is true that harassers can be of either sex, reports of female harassment of males is rare. According to a recent study of Arizona upper-level government employees (grades 23-30), only 7% of the males surveyed had experienced requests for sexual

TABLE 5.3 Summary of Survey Research on Sexual Harassment

Study	Description	Results
1976: Safran, *Redbook*	Questionnaire printed in Redbook. 9,000 responses.	90% of respondents reported being sexually harassed in their lifetime.
1980: Reily, U.S. Navy	Replicated *Redbook* questionnaire with women in Navy.	90% of respondents reported sexual harassment.
1981: Collins & Blodgett, *Harvard Business Review*	Questionnaire printed in HBR yielded a 25% response rate.	Results reveal a gender difference in definition of problem, severity of problem, and prevalence.
1981: U.S. Merit Systems Review Board, Federal Government	Randomly sampled all federal governmental employees.	42% of women had been sexually harassed while 15% of men reported sexual harassment.
1985: Gutek, *Sex in the Workplace*	Random telephone poll of the general population of Los Angeles residents.	21% of the women and 9% of men had been sexually harassed based on respondent's definition of sexual harassment.
1986: Powell, *Business Horizons Magazine*	Questioned students (business undergraduates and MBAs) about ethics and appropriateness of sexual intimacy at work.	Women and MBAs more likely to view intimacy at work negatively than undergraduates.
1987: Feldman, *Personnel Magazine*	Questionnaires to 300 human resource managers and subscribers. 20% response rate.	44% of respondents had received a complaint of sexual harassment.
1988: Ford & McLaughlin, *Business Horizons Magazine*	Poll resulted in 247 responses from human resource managers.	50% had received complaint within last year. 50% of women polled believed they had been sexually harassed.

(continued)

favors—contrasted with 21% of the women.[41] Women at lower levels experience higher rates of harassment. Probably the most famous sexual harassment case of the 1980s has been the Jim Bakker-Jessica Hahn affair. In this case, both Bakker and Hahn claimed to be victims of harassment.

TABLE 5.3 Continued

1988: Sandroff, *Working Woman* *Magazine*	Questionnaire to every director of personnel, human resource manager, and EEOC officer for the Fortune 500 companies.	90% of the Fortune 500 companies have complaints of sexual harassment.
1989: Hale & Kelly, *Gender,* *Bureaucracy and* *Democracy*	Survey of the top eight grades of employees in the Arizona state government.	10% of women had reported unwelcome sexual advances.

SOURCES: From Phoebe Stambaugh's "Sexual Harassment: The Politics of Discourse," unpublished paper, School of Justice Studies, Arizona State University, Tempe, Arizona, 1989. Research studies include: C. Safran, "What Men Do to Women on the Job." *Redbook* (1980), 149, 217-223; P. J. Reilly, *Sexual Harassment in the Navy. (Monterey, CA: U.S. Naval Postgraduate School, 1980); G. C. Collins and T. B. Blodgett (Eds.), When the Executive Is a Woman* (Cambridge, MD: Harvard University Press, 1981), 46-64; U.S. Merit Systems Protection Board, *Sexual Harassment in the Federal Workplace: Is It a Problem?* (Washington, DC: Government Printing Office, 1981); Barbara A. Gutek, *Sex and the Workplace.* (San Francisco, Jossey-Bass, 1985); Gary N. Powell, "What Do Tomorrow's Managers Think About Sexual Intimacy in the Workplace?" *Business Horizons,* 29(4) (July/Aug. 1986), 30-35; C. Feldman, "Sexual Harassment Policies." *Personnel Magazine (1987); Robert C. Ford and Frank S. McLauglin, "Sexual Harassment at Work." Business Horizons* 31(6) (Nov./Dec. 1988), 14-19; Ronni Sandroff, "Sexual Harassment on the Fortune 500." *Working Woman* 31(12) (December 1988), 69-73; Mary M. Hale and Rita Mae Kelly (Eds.), *Gender, Bureaucracy, and Democracy: Careers and Equal Opportunity in the Public Sector* (New York: Greenwood Press, 1989).

Fifteen years of case law indicates three conditions that must be proved before sexual harassment is charged: (1) the behavior must be *unwelcomed,* (2) it must be *repetitive,* and (3) it must be considered *offensive* by the subject of the action.[42]

Typically, male victims assert that they are targets of a much younger, provocatively dressed, attractive "girl."[43] In these cases, the young women refuse to take a "hint"; the "victims" of sexual harassment typically see to it that the young women are transferred or dismissed. The most prevalent sexual harassment cases, however, involve male superiors who press female subordinates for sexual favors.

A more subtle form of harassment stems not from any one person's behavior but from a *hostile environment.* Hostile behaviors often develop at office parties, picnics, and other "fun" activities where drinking and unprofessional behavior are encouraged. Workplaces where flirting and sexual touching is accepted are highly "eroticized"[44] and are more likely to harbor sexual harassers than environments free of sexual expectations.

Such sexual harassment of women in traditional male careers by co-workers may be the result of the defensive posture of the men.

Sexual harassment is used to remind the invading women that their primary role is that of a sex object, not of a professional.

There is evidence that sexual harassment occurs across all industries, including the Fortune 500 companies.[45] Employees in all occupations are harassed—supervisors have been harassed by their staff[46] and teachers often endure harassment by their students.[47] It is prevalent in the military,[48] in the government,[49] and in academic institutions.[50] The scope of the problem is difficult to assess because most cases go unreported.[51] This fact may reflect a fear held by victims that nothing will be done to address the problem adequately. One case that has become an important exception to this rule occurred in Arizona. Leta Ford, a manager for Revlon, brought suit against her employer.[52] The courts ruled in Ford's favor because she was able to produce a "paper trail" of complaints and grievances over a 13-month period and to demonstrate that Revlon had not taken action to stop the harassment.

The 1986 Supreme Court opinion in the case of *Meritor Savings Bank v. Vinson* has been widely used by organizations to formulate their sexual harassment policy.[53] In the *Vinson* decision, victims of sexual harassment won the battle but lost the war. In the first year after *Vinson,* the courts ruled against the plaintiff and in favor of employers in 20 of 31 federal district court cases.[54] The majority of appeals court decisions have also favored the employer.[55] Therefore, it appears that the judicial opinions on sexual harassment have served to create effective sexual harassment policies that *avoid liability.* However, it is not clear to what degree these policies actually prevent sexual harassment.

In October of 1989, the House Ethics Committee found representative Jim Bates (D-Calif.) guilty of sexually harassing two members of his staff.[56] The women claimed his behavior created a hostile environment. Bates apologized to the two women but stated: "Times are changing. Members of Congress are going to be scrutinized for their personal and professional behavior . . . sexual harassment is very serious and not to be taken lightly. *I did not know what sexual harassment meant until this came up.*"[57]

It is clear from Rep. Bates's last remark that, even though sexual harassment has been a long-standing problem for women and a political issue for more than ten years, many still are not aware of the basic dimensions of the problem: (1) of what sexual harassment is, (2) that it is harmful, and (3) that the consequences can be harsh. Increased media attention would do much to increase the public's awareness of the problem.

Conclusion

Establishing a successful career in the 1990s requires integrating one's private and public lives. The task is much more than an individual or even an organizational matter. It involves a reconceptualization of sex-role ideology; the acceptance of this new ideology by both men and women; and the adoption of this way of thinking by the nation's political, economic, and judicial institutions.

Notes

1. Sarah Hardesty and Nehama Jacobs, *Success and Betrayal: The Crisis of Women in Corporate America* (New York: Franklin Watts, 1986).

2. Susan N. C. Lewis and C. L. Cooper, "Stress in Dual-Earner Families," in *Women and Work, an Annual Review* Vol. 3, eds. Barbara Gutek, Ann H. Stromberg, and Laurie Larwood (Newbury Park, CA: Sage, 1988), 146-151.

3. Joseph H. Pleck, *Working Wives, Working Husbands* (Beverly Hills, CA: Sage, 1985).

4. U.S. Bureau of the Census, Current Population Survey Report (Washington, DC: Government Printing Office, 1988), 60.

5. Rebecca M. Blank, "Women's Paid Work, Household Income and Household Well-Being," in *The American Woman: 1988-89,* ed. Sara E. Rix (New York: W.W. Norton, 1988), 123-161.

6. U.S. Bureau of Labor, *Handbook of Labor Statistics* (Washington, DC: Government Printing Office, 1989), 200.

7. Betty Friedan, *The Second Stage* (New York: Summit, 1981).

8. Arlie Hochschild, *The Second Shift* (New York: Viking, 1989); and "House Approves $22 Billion for Child Care: GOP Proposals Lose—Senate OK Still Needed," *Arizona Republic,* 6 October 1989, C4.

9. John Skow, "The Myth of Male Housework," *Time* August 1989, 62.

10. Blank, "Women's Paid Work, Household Income," 151-160.

11. Blank, "Women's Paid Work, Household Income."

12. Hochschild, *The Second Shift;* and "House Approves $22 Billion for Child Care," *Arizona Republic.* See also P. MacCorquodale, "The Economics of Home and Family," in *Women and the Arizona Economy,* eds. Janice Monk and Alice Schelgle (Tucson: University of Arizona Press, 1986), 99-133; and Linda Heller, "The Last of the Angry Men," *Executive Female* (September/October 1983): 33-38.

13. Heller, "Last of the Angry Men," 38. For additional information see MacCorquodale, "The Economics of Home and Family," 102.

14. Sharon Nelton and Karen Berney, "Women: The Second Wave," *Nation's Business* (May 1987): 18-22.

15. Nelton and Berney, "Women: The Second Wave," 18.

16. Donna Lenhoff, "Family Medical Leave Act," in *The Women's Economic Justice Agenda: Ideas for the States,* eds. L. Tarr-Whelan and L. C. Isensee (Washington, DC: National Center for Policy Alternatives, 1987), 99-103.

17. U.S. Department of Labor, *Child Care: A Work Force Issue* (Washington, DC: Government Printing Office, 1988), Table B-21; and Milo Geyelin, "States Try to Balance Job, Family," *Wall Street Journal* 4 May 1990, B1.

18. Roger Thompson, "Caring for the Children," *Nation's Business* 76 (May 1988): 20.

19. Robert E. Allen, "It Pays to Invest in Tomorrow's Work Force," *Wall Street Journal* 6 November 1989, A16.

20. Rachelle Garbarine, "Building Workplace Centers to Reduce Turnover," *New York Times* 15 October 1989, 32.

21. Hochschild, *The Second Shift;* "House Approves $22 Billion for Child Care," *Arizona Republic,* 4C.

22. Claudia Wallis, Scott Brown, Melissa Ludtke, and Martha Smiligis, "Onward Women!" *Time* 4 December 1989, 80-89.

23. Hardesty and Jacobs, *Success and Betrayal.*

24. L. Elisabeth Beattie, "Battling Another Bias in Business Lending," *Business Week* 31 October 1984, 14-16.

25. Tamar Lewin, "Study Finds High Turnover in Child Care Workers," *New York Times* 18 October 1989, A10.

26. Lewin, "Study Finds High Turnover in Child Care Workers."

27. Elizabeth Ehrlich, "Child Care, the Private Sector Cannot Do it Alone," *Business Week* October 1986, 52-53.

28. Blank, "Women's Paid Work, Household Income."

29. Wallis, "Onward Women!" p. 85.

30. Blank, "Women's Paid Work, Household Income."

31. Arizona Latchkey Task Force, "Ten Facts About Latchkey Children," Fact Sheet, 1987. (Single-page handout.)

32. MacCorquodale, "The Economics of Home and Family."

33. Barbara A. Gutek, *Sex and the Workplace* (San Francisco: Jossey-Bass, 1985).

34. Paula Bernstein, "Family Ties, Corporate Bonds," *Working Woman* 10(5) (May 1985): 85-87; 138-139.

35. Psychologist Susan Locke, as cited in Bernstein, "Family Ties," 139.

36. "A Daughter Heir Apparent Isn't Heir," *Wall Street Journal* 9 February 1990, B12.

37. "A Daughter Heir Apparent," *Wall Street Journal,* B12.

38. Mary Ann Cunningham, *Power Play* (New York: Simon & Schuster, 1984).

39. Lisa A. Mainiero, *Office Romance: Love, Power, and Sex in the Workplace* (New York: Rawson of McMillan, 1989).

40. Gutek, *Sex and the Workplace.*

41. Mary M. Hale and Rita Mae Kelly, *Gender, Bureaucracy and Democracy* (Westport, CT: Greenwood, 1989), 58.

42. Cynthia Fryer Cohen, "Implications of Meritor Savings Bank, FSB v. Vinson et al.," *Labor Law Journal* 38 (April 1987): 243-247.

43. Constance Backhouse and Leah Cohen, *Sexual Harassment on the Job* (Toronto: Prentice-Hall, 1981).

44. Gutek, *Sex and the Workplace.*

45. Ronni Sandroff, "Sexual Harassment in the Fortune 500," *Working Woman* December 1988, 69-73.

46. Lillian Wilson Clarke, "Women Supervisors Experience Sexual Harassment, Too," *Supervisory Management* 31(4) (April 1986): 35-36.

47. Claire Herbert, *Talking of Silence: The Sexual Harassment of School Girls* (New York: Palmer, 1989).

48. P. J. Reily, "Sexual Harassment in the Navy." Unpublished master's thesis. U.S. Navy Post Graduate School, Monterey, California, 1980.

49. U.S. Merit Systems Protection Board, *Sexual Harassment in the Federal Workplace: Is it a Problem?* (Washington, DC: Government Printing Office, 1987).

50. Billie Wright Dziech and Linda Weiner, *The Lecherous Professor* (Boston: Beacon, 1984).

51. Patricia V. Markunas and Jean M. Joyce-Brady, "Underutilization of Sexual Harassment Grievance Procedures," *Journal of the National Association for Women Deans* 50 (Spring 1987): 27-32.

52. *Ford v. Revlon,* Arizona State Supreme Court (1987).

53. Cohen, "Implications of Meritor Savings Bank."

54. Bureau of National Affairs, Inc., "Sexual Harassment," in *Corporate Affairs, Nepotism, Office Romance and Sexual Harassment* (Washington, DC: Bureau of National Affairs, 1988), 59-108.

55. Bureau of National Affairs, "Sexual Harassment."

56. Associated Press, "Lawmaker Harassed 2 Women on Staff, Is Rebuked by Panel," *Arizona Republic* 19 October 1989, A13.

57. Associated Press, "Lawmaker Harasses 2 Women on Staff." Emphasis added.

6

Gender, Success, and Behavioral/Leadership Styles

Gender is a social construct of physiological sex and, as such, is a changeable reflection of each individual. Women are not biologically or sociologically different from men in the sense that men are the comparative norm. Rather, each of us is *unique* in our own right. As noted in Chapters 4 and 5, a number of contributing factors determine the characteristics and traits with which an individual chooses to construct her or his work force behavior.

In this chapter we examine the extent to which gender differences exist in orientation to power, language and communication, response to stress, professional image, moral development, and being a team player. We then assess how these differences influence managerial behavioral styles. In the process we explore the extent to which existing data suggest women must become androgynous or follow a male managerial style to be successful.

Sex-role differences in private life, socialization, and work experiences, along with the masculine role expectations of bureaucracies, suggest that women might not be as successful as men in the workplace. By 1990 an ongoing debate had developed over whether women want the same type of success as men, whether they are able to demonstrate the behavior and leadership required for modern organizations to compete at high levels, and whether successful female managers need to adopt male behavioral styles in order to lead and compete.

AUTHOR'S NOTE: This chapter was researched and written with Marcia Cech-Soucy.

Early research on the subject of women in management blamed women's difficulties in attaining higher level positions exclusively on either personal attributes derived from early childhood socialization patterns or the positions women tend to hold within the organization which promote certain behavioral characteristics. Either way, the ensuing stereotypes of women executives left an impression of their being less capable, not only physically and emotionally, but tactically as well. Some traits that were thought to have inhibited women from advancing were low self-esteem,[1] fear of success,[2] lower organizing and decision-making capabilities,[3] lower motivation and skills,[4] need for dominance,[5] poor understanding of organizational power,[6] and inadequate socialization to organizational norms.[7]

Rosabeth Kanter[8] argues instead that structural factors in the organizations themselves have prevented women from performing successfully.[9] This chapter will cover a number of these areas of concern. It examines how and why men and women function in particular ways as executives.

The Male Nature of Bureaucracies and Definitions of Success

Bureaucracies were developed by men, primarily by white men. Max Weber's ideal type of bureaucracy stressed the need for expertise, hierarchical structure, interchangeability of personnel, records, job security, and organizational rationality. It should be no surprise that feminists have asserted that bureaucracies have a male orientation and a male bias.[10] This bias requires, it is argued,[11] that women who become managers and who have successful careers must become like men, not only in their training but also in their behavior. In the 1970s, it also seemed as though women needed to look like men, wearing pin-striped, dark suits, pants, and masculine accessories. Scholars, like Rosabeth Kanter, pointed out that successful women managers were highly likely to behave like men because they had to be trained like men to have the necessary expertise, they had to have traversed the same or similar career paths, and they typically had only male role models or mentors to guide them.[12] In the 1980s, the larger number of female executives and the changing nature of organizational structures led to questioning the assumption that a traditional male understanding of success needed to be followed. Nonetheless, success of some sort remains a concern.

Success connotes movement along a continuum. A successful person typically is high in some hierarchy, with the most successful being at the very top. He or she tends to receive a larger salary, have more respect, recognition, status, and greater freedom in selecting job assignments, hours, and commitments, as well as more responsibility for other workers and the organization. Those at the very top tend to have all these items. Because positions at the very top are limited and salary is linked to position, salary and position both have come to be particular denotations of success. Upward mobility within a hierarchy, "reaching the top," "moving up," breaking through the "glass ceiling," all convey the idea that achieving a top position within an organizational structure is success. At lower levels, being on a "fast track" of assignments and positions that demonstrate progress toward advanced line authority are indicators of a good career path. Receiving positive performance evaluations and increasing organizational responsibility—and higher salaries—provide evidence of the successful career.

Historically, the high achievers in society were men who had wives performing supportive hostess/social secretary/homemaker/ wife/mother/general backup roles. Even single women found it hard to match this "two person, single career" competition.[13] Large numbers of married women and women with children, whether single or married, either dropped out, took "Mommy Tracks," or traded some symbols of success, such as greater freedom and discretionary assignments, for a high position and/or a high salary.

In the 1980s some men, as well as women, opted for changing the meaning of success to have a greater balance between home and work. As many as 56% of the men surveyed by the recruiting firm Robert Half International indicated that they "would give up as much as a quarter of their salary to have more family or personal time. About 45% said they would probably refuse a promotion that involved sacrificing hours with their family."[14] With men doing increasing amounts of housework (about 30% of it in the mid-1980s compared to 20% in the 1960s)[15] and more and more fathers becoming the primary child-care provider while their wives are working (about 18% of dual-parent workers),[16] male, as well as female, concerns about career success are altering.

This questioning of the meaning and value of different parts of life will undoubtedly continue in the 1990s and the 21st century, changing career aspirations and paths for men as well as women. Nonetheless, these definitional and aspirational changes will not alter the basic realities that women who do choose to compete with men for high-level positions will still have to face. These realities include the physiological and socialization differences of males and females, the fact that organizations and society vitally need competent and effective leaders and managers, and that a concern exists among employers and employees alike as to whether female differences in behavioral and leadership styles represent alternate means to achieve similar ends or a less effective manager and leader.

Power

According to social psychologist David McClelland, the power motive and the uses of power are integral to the practice of management and to understanding organizational behavior.[17] The best leaders and executives tend to score high on the power motive and be effective in the use of power. Yet women have been chastised for their fear of power,[18] and gender is recognized as having a power differential with females being of lower status than males.[19] The concept of "The personal is political"[20] is to make us aware of the numerous ways in which simple interactions between men and women are really acts of power, acts of dominance of men over women, whether it be a pat on a secretary's bottom, sexual harassment, or men feeling more free to touch women regardless of place or position.

The fact that men dominate in the power positions of society is evident. The reasons for the dominance are less clear. One line of reasoning sees a physiological basis for the difference. D. E. Berlyne, for example, found that the exercise of power produces a positive effect on the nervous system.[21] An increase in catecholamines (adrenaline, epinephrine, norepinephrine, endorphins, and dopamine) occurs by the activation of the sympathetic nervous system. Anger, aggression, and pleasure are produced by these catecholamines. McClelland reports that men experience this positive effect more than women.[22] On the basis of this research it is argued that "the need for power is a socially learned set of associations between the arousal or exercise of power and the experience of positive affect."[23]

In spite of the noted sex differences in catecholamine response to emotional stimuli, specific studies of females and power-arousing stimuli have not found significant gender differences. "Several studies have shown that the behavior of high power motivated males and females are similar to each other and yet different from their low power counterparts."[24] Both choose occupations that will permit them to influence and have power over others. In the one study that reported women high in power were "less overtly assertive and competitive than men,"[25] it was suggested that stereotypic sex-role expectations for women caused the variation.[26]

Combining a high power motivation with a high leadership motivation is strongly related to career success for managers, engineers, scientists, and executives.[27] Performance ratings and promotion were found to be highly associated as well. David McClelland links low affiliation, high power, and high activity inhibition as key factors in effective leadership.[28] Given the previous findings that females typically score higher on affiliation and lower than males in both power and achievement motivation, one might conclude that females are disadvantaged as a group. Nonetheless, McClelland[29] in a study on subjects who expressed "high inhibited power and need for power greater than the need for affiliation" reported that their behavior "appeared to reflect respect for institutional authority, discipline, and self-control, caring for others, altruism, and concern for a just world."[30] Perhaps, the message is that fewer women will have the power, achievement, and leadership motives given current sex-role socialization and sex-role ideologies, but that those who do have these motives will behave similarly to men. After more than 25 years and several hundred studies, it appears that both power and leadership motivation are important for managerial success, especially when social influence is more vital to success than the technical expertise of the manager. It also appears that "organizations can be designed either to facilitate or to inhibit the arousal and exercise of power."[31] Further research on the implications of this conclusion for women and managerial career success are clearly needed.

Various studies of gender differences in power orientations have found no significant differences in power salience, power drive, power anxiety, power enjoyment, and power style.[32] Gender differences do exist in ambivalence toward holding and exercising power. Only among women is there a relationship between education and power anxiety: the higher a female's education, the lower the anxiety. Higher educated men score higher on power enjoyment.[33] A difference also exists in how power is defined. Women tend to view power as a means to promote change, whereas men tend to view power as a means of having influence over other people—"power to" versus "power over."[34] For managers and leaders, concern must exist for both legitimate position power, the power that comes with the role of manager, and personal power, the power that comes as the result of who and what the individual is. Historically, males were socialized more directly for position power, whereas women were socialized to deal more with personal power. Decisiveness, assertiveness, accountability, taking the initiative, and taking charge of planning the work and directing subordinates are vital skills for successful management. As already noted in Chapters 4 and 5, these abilities and behaviors have often led to females being chastised for being unfeminine, being "bitchy," bossy, pushy. The line between appropriate managerial assertiveness and the appearance of angry aggressiveness in women is fine, particularly if the beholder of the behavior has a traditional feminine sex-role mind-set. Practice, training, and self-reflection on feedback and reactions can help master an appropriate style to cope with this.

In most settings where managerial or leadership behavior occurs, male competition is highly valued and expected. Females are not socialized to be as competitive as males, nor are adolescent females encouraged to compete with males.[35] As adults, however, women must deal with both competitive males and a competitive male environment. This environment typically consists of sharp banter, repartee, "zingers" of others, and often sexist comments and jokes. In addition, although men are allowed to show anger in the workplace, women are looked down on if, in their frustration, they cry. As Alice Sargent notes, "When most of the daily interchange of an organization is conducted in a competitive mode, women often feel ignored, invisible, and excluded. . . . As they become frustrated and angry, they may explode in tears or show some other form of frustration-releasing behavior. Men are often incredulous at this situation. 'No one was preventing this woman from participating, so why on earth is she blowing up like this?' "[36]

Personal power is related to an individual's capacities, the ability to establish such characteristics as trust, mutual respect, credibility for good judgment, and reliability. Influence goes to those with insight, problem-solving abilities, creative capacities, and the ability to perceive others' needs. Many women "behind the throne" had this type of personal power.

Charisma is another type of personal power. It is more often associated with men, such as John F. Kennedy and Ronald Reagan, than with women. In men personal attractiveness combines with likability, style, intellect, and leadership to produce the charismatic man. "Charisma in men is often associated with highly controlling, assertive behavior, as well as strength, humor, energy, warmth, and articulateness."[37] Female charisma is less commonplace. Sargent suggests "that for a woman to be responded to as charismatic, she must combine personal attractiveness, strength, and energy; sensitivity, warmth, and humor; being 'together' and self-aware in a way which is perceived as feminine—in other words, she does not defy the female sex-role stereotype."[38]

Personal power also comes from being an idea-person, making the right suggestion at the right time. Unfortunately, studies indicate that women are often not listened to in meetings and that their ideas are legitimated only when men repeat or adopt them.[39]

The acquisition of power calls for control over tangible resources and information, together with the establishment of favorable relationships with co-workers. The current work force requires such leadership skills as cooperation, development of positive relationships and team building, and the adoption of win-win approaches to dispute resolution. These are skills women can develop to high levels.[40]

Identification of one's power strengths and weaknesses, the power-points in the organization, and the requirements for career advancement is needed for women to succeed no matter how technically or socially skilled they are. The pursuit of power need not be for self-aggrandizement. It can be a useful tool for empowering and benefiting others.[41]

Women can meet the challenges of executive positions by first accepting the ownership of power. Power is important to meeting the goals of the corporation for effectiveness, efficiency, and productivity.[42] Power is influence; by virtue of position the manager has power. It is important for the nontraditional manager (e.g., the female manager) to open communication between herself and her subordinates to insure the recognition of legitimate power. Power also consists of using rewards and punishments, the coercive power of discipline. Nontraditional managers need to pay special attention to the manner in which they reward and discipline members of their own group (e.g., other women or employees of the same race).[43] Power also rests on expertise, on one's own and those the manager/leader supervises.

A 1988 study of 273 male and female supervisors found no significant difference in the power bases used by men and women to influence subordinates.[44] Both male and female supervisors indicated they use the same three power bases, employed in the following order: (1) use of expertise; (2) use of the position itself as legitimate power; and (3) reward-power depending on what is available through the company for employees.[45]

After comparing the use of reward-power by male and female managers, G. H. Dobbins suggests that males and females distribute rewards based on different norms.[46] Male leaders tend to distribute rewards based on equity (each member's reward is directly related to his or her input), whereas female leaders tend to distribute rewards on the basis of equality (all group members receive the same reward, regardless of input). He also notes that females respond less harshly toward females performing poorly than toward males performing poorly. Male leaders respond equally toward male and female subordinates. This conclusion is disputed by W. R. Todd-Mancillas and A. Rossi.[47]

Todd-Mancillas and Rossi have done a comparative review of three studies analyzing the gender differences in managerial styles with regard to personnel disputes among members of the intermediate labor market of the core economy (see Chapter 3).[48] They began the review with two basic assumptions: First, that men and women's styles of management do, in fact, differ significantly. Second, that women must assimilate into the male culture, adopting the "take-charge" style of men in order to succeed. They found that women may be more communicative in their management styles than men. A significant and positive correlation exists between employee job satisfaction and the extent to which they perceive supervisors as supportive and openly communicative.

In the Todd-Mancillas and Rossi study, male managers had a much greater preference for using power for disciplining female than male employees.[49] Female managers, on the other hand, exhibited no such tendency to treat female employees differently from male employees. When a situation arose that challenged the manager's competence, male managers were much more likely to respond using power. Female managers were prone to use communication or communication coupled with power.

Language and Communication

Communication is one of the areas of women's strength. Research into whether written communication styles differ between men and women, and whether combinations of style variables are specific to either gender, revealed in 1988 no difference between males and females in the number of words—positive or negative—or the number of clichés they used.[50] In fact, there were no noticeable differences at all.

The female advantage appears to stem more from interpersonal interaction, style, and a greater disposition to use communication than other sources of power.

Psychologists have consistently found gender differences in language use. Women are thought to swear less, to use words like "lovely," "nice," "pretty," and more precise terms for colors, such as "lavender," than are men. Men's speech tends to be harsher with more exclamations.[51] Studies show females to be more correct in their speech, following the cultural norms on language more closely than males. Women also tend to add a short phrase to declarative sentences that turns a statement into a question, making them seem less certain of their statements and weaker when speaking. Although such questions might be used to facilitate communication, men often interpret them as a means of avoiding conflict, as an indicator that the speaker is unsure of herself or does not know an answer. Women also generally use more supportive language and words, such as "mm hmm" than men, who, in turn, tend to use more hostile verbs.[52]

Gender differences exist in intonation as well. Women tend to use "intonation patterns of surprise, unexpectedness, cheerfulness, and politeness." Women also have four levels of pitch they can use in speech (whereas men have only three), with the fourth being the highest one. Obviously, this additional tone expands women's ability to express themselves; the ability has also been interpreted as contributing to female speech being seen as "overly emotional and high-pitched."[53]

Interruption patterns are also gender-linked. Although within each sex grouping, interruptions are about the same for both males and females, in cross-sex groupings women are interrupted quite often by men. Women seldom interrupt men.[54] Since the interruption gives men control during an interpersonal exchange, such speech patterns have been interpreted as forms of male dominance and power. Studies also show that empirically the total time spent talking is greater for men than women.[55]

Nonverbal communication is important for managerial success. Communication with body language often conveys more than with words alone. The politics of touching at the workplace has been noted frequently, particularly in the negative context of sexual harassment. Touching is a form of dominance. Usually males touch females, older people touch younger people, and individuals of higher status touch individuals of lower status.[56] The implications of these findings are that women should be aware of the role of touching in power relationships.

If a woman wants to enhance her own power, she would do well to increase touching of others (in sexually neutral ways) and reduce the touching she receives.

The tendency toward greater familiarity with women extends to expecting a smaller interpersonal distance from women than men. With men, closeness is often viewed as invasion of personal space. Women also smile more than men. Although some allude to this smiling as an act of submission, few empirical studies have been done on its impact on women's power or ability to manage.[57]

Generally, the way women are referred to in the English language tends to devalue them. The word "girl" is often the counterpoint to "man," and the male pronoun "he" is used in school and other texts using the rationale that "he" subsumes "she" just as "man" is supposed to subsume "woman."

A 1985 study of pronoun usage and its effect on children indicated that sexist pronoun usage "can affect the concepts children form of occupations, and . . . there is reason for concern about its effect on broader issues such as girls' self-confidence."[58]

Response to Stress

In addition to the general concern that a female might become pregnant, concern exists that stress-related factors might keep women from being high achievers in the business world. Many high achievers feel chronically overwhelmed at work, and women are among them. In order to understand the problem, it is necessary to look at both the demands of the job and personalities in the workplace.[59] One male commentator, G. S. Bullivant, asserted in 1984 that a woman's response to stress is chemically different from that of a man, whose heart rate, blood pressure, and production of adrenalin reach much higher levels. Referring to conditions of socialization during early childhood development, Bullivant comes to the conclusion that "each sex responds better to the opposite sex." And he leaps to the conclusion that "a female staff can be better managed by a male, since he can stand slightly apart and remain an authority figure."[60] Although Bullivant notes that, because of her sympathetic and approachable stance, a female manager can be highly effective, he does not go on to conclude that women might manage men better than another man would.

Other researchers studying stress among women, have identified the "Type E" woman, a person who needs to be "everything to everybody."[61] Men apparently do not have this fixation because, aside from having fewer family responsibilities, they learn to delegate responsibility. Men also tend to be Type A persons, individuals who are intense workaholics, highly subject to heart attacks. Stress may be related to management style and the performance expectations of the organization, and can be reduced by hiring strategically and including staff in day-to-day decisions regarding routine.[62] On the basis of surveys conducted in 1983 and 1986 of both male and female managers of the 50 largest companies in the United Kingdom, it was concluded that higher stress levels among female managers stemmed from insufficient role models, isolation at the workplace, male prejudices, and role strain and role conflict between home and work.[63]

Understanding female response to stress is important for managers because behavior changes during stressful times. "Specifically the theory and supporting evidence demonstrate that when under stress, due to problematic relationships with their superiors or group members, leaders rely on prior experience and do not make effective use of their intelligence."[64] This regressive behavior might work, but gender differences in socialization suggest that this response to stress might be more damaging for women than for men. In addition, control of stress should promote not only better leaders, but also more rational decision making and behavior in the organization.

Professional Image and Stress

The physical differences between men and women raise questions regarding appropriate professional images. Even among men, physical differences, such as height and good looks, are correlated with more power and money. Women, frequently shorter than men, often feel less confident and less powerful because of their height. *Working Woman* gives the following suggestions for coping with being shorter: (1) talk in a lower voice, (2) stand away from a taller person so the contrast will not be noticed, (3) try to arrange meetings so that everyone is seated, (4) use appropriate clothing to look taller, (5) take up more space by spreading papers to create the illusion of a larger person, and (6) be the one who initiates business encounters.[65]

Women's concern for appearance created the demand for Liz Claiborne, Inc. The demand for professional apparel has been so great that it put this company on the Fortune 500 list in 1986.[66] A survey done by *Working Woman* regarding the importance of a woman's professional image indicated that 75% of the respondents had made a concerted effort to develop one.[67] Almost every woman reported that she was careful to act and dress in ways that are appropriate to her career, although not necessarily suited to her individual style. The most damaging behaviors to be avoided in promoting a woman's professional image include: (1) crying in the office (78%), (2) wearing miniskirts (76%), (3) flirting (72%), and (4) losing one's temper (78%). According to an article in *Executive Female,*[68] crying in the office is upsetting to women, not because they think it is wrong or bad, but because it sets up a conflict between their desires to be genuine and expressive and their desire to live up to the masculine ideal of being objective and in control.

Conflict and stress are unavoidable in the workplace. Tension and frustration build up to intolerable levels, and when this happens, it is our natural instinct to seek release, usually by yelling or crying. Men tend to yell; women tend to cry. Although tears are less destructive than anger, removing anger from the workplace is discussed less than removing crying. Both expressions of frustration need to be addressed.[69]

Gender and the Successful Manager/Leader

Research suggests that no significant gender differences exist in managerial aptitude;[70] however, women and men managers are often perceived as having quite different behavioral styles.[71] Men supposedly are more focused on competition, winning, and domination, are said to take more risks, to be better team players, and to be more independent, assertive, opportunistic, and impersonal than women in their work relations.[72] Women administrators are viewed as being better than men at giving information, strengthening interpersonal relations, being receptive to ideas, and encouraging effort and subordinate development,[73] and at assuming supportive roles.[74]

Behavioral styles are difficult to explore. The examination of specific, individual behavioral traits can be misleading, particularly when assessing the impact that sex can have on managerial style and success. We know that behaviors such as aggressiveness, competitiveness, and dominance receive different reactions depending on the sex of the actor. Behavior that is perceived as "bitchiness" in women is often perceived as gruffness or acceptable aggressiveness in men.

Although some of the variation in perception is undoubtedly due to traditional sex-role bias and sexist social structures and patterns, it is also possible that men and women combine different behaviors in different ways so as to produce alternate impacts. The remainder of this chapter explores this possibility and assesses the relationship such variations in behavioral style patterns have for successful careers.

Scholars have examined gender differences in behavioral traits in all sectors of the economy. Here we will highlight the findings of the Center for Creative Leadership, which examined such differences for major corporations, a study sponsored by the Leadership Foundation of the International Women's Forum, and the findings from studies of public high-level administrators in the states of Arizona and Wisconsin.

Personality Traits and Leadership Ability in the Private Sector

The Center for Creative Leadership has identified a number of personality traits considered synonymous with strong leadership ability and collected from various data banks the managers and executives who participated in management development programs from 1978 to 1986. Scores of high-level male and female executives from large companies with more than five thousand employees were selected for study. The tests measured personality dimensions, behavior in problem-solving groups, and overall management skill. Out of all these measurements, only a few statistically different sex differences emerged.[75]

Overall results of the comparison of personality traits revealed the men and women to be essentially similar in terms of dominance, capacity for status, sociability, social presence, self-acceptance, responsibility, self-control, tolerance, good impression, achievement via independence, intellectual efficiency, and flexibility. The women scored lower than their male counterparts on only a few items: overall sense of well-being or comfort level experienced in the corporate setting, socialization, communality, achievement via conformity, and having sufficient time and energy to meet all the demands facing them.[76] Women also tend to score significantly higher than men in taking an assertive lead during the cooperative group exercises. The results indicate that women are less comfortable, less prepared through socialization, and less familiar with the male environment of the corporate setting. Given that substantial numbers of the female participants of this study, which began in 1978, are essentially pioneers in the corporate environment, these findings are not surprising.

In *Breaking the Glass Ceiling,* Ann M. Morrison, Randall P. White, and Ellen Van Velson reported the results of their interviews of 76 executive women and 22 higher-level executives (16 men and 6 women) working in large corporate settings; that is, in companies with earnings at the Fortune 100 level. The project was a more intensive examination of the Center for Creative Leadership's previous studies seeking facilitators and barriers to entering and being successful in the highest echelons of corporate America, the top 1% of jobs in the work force. They found six major facilitators of female executive success: support from above, a strong achievement record, an ambition to succeed, managerial ability, a propensity to take career risks, and the capacity to be "tough, decisive, and demanding."[77] Three "deadly flaws" leading to derailment for women were "1. The inability to adapt, 2. wanting too much (for oneself or for other women), 3. performance problems."[78] Women who derailed from achieving the higher executive positions consistently lacked three things the successful women had: "the ability to manage subordinates," "taking career risks," and "having help from above."[79] Compared to successful men, successful women were cited more frequently as "having had help from above," "being easy to be with," "being able to adapt," "taking career risks," "being tough," "having the desire to succeed," and "having an impressive presence."[80] The authors conclude, "it appears that in order to approach the highest levels, women are expected to have more strengths and fewer faults than their male counterparts."[81]

Although the authors of *Breaking the Glass Ceiling* conclude that few differences exist in specific personality traits and behaviors, they assert that the way women combine the traits and behaviors is critical. This is because the band of acceptable behaviors is narrower for women. "The narrow band of acceptability, then, means that women must be better than men and also better than the stereotyped view of women. It is not enough for an executive woman to ace the success factors . . . , she must accomplish these feats in precisely the right way, and that means combining seemingly contradictory behaviors."[82]

In 1989, the Leadership Foundation of the International Women's Forum funded a study of men and women leaders in its membership organizations, medium-sized, less traditional, fast-growing, rapidly changing organizations.[83] The results indicated that men and women

the female elements of "process-oriented" and "do things by the book" certainly are not exclusively female styles within bureaucracies. Driven by concern for equity and accountability, all public bureaucracies include these elements. . . . As Kanter (1977) aptly demonstrated, those in positions of limited power tend to rely heavily on rules regardless of gender. Because professional women tended to be clustered in powerless positions, this characteristic became associated with them; however, the position, not gender explains this stereotype. . . . This exercise demonstrates that bureaucratic stereotypes are ambiguous and gender stereotypes require a context.[91]

In addition to comparing gender and bureaucratic stereotypes, Duerst-Lahti and Johnson[92] also asked the Wisconsin upper-level civil servants which traits characterized their behavior. They found that both sexes perceived themselves as behaving within gender-appropriate stereotypes.

Men's behavior includes significantly more of the traits creative and opportunistic. In fact, being opportunistic is the only characteristic that is significantly different across all pay ranges as well. Men see being opportunistic as part of their style in a way women do not. Women see their style as complying significantly more with two feminine characteristics, being attractive and being affectionate.[93]

Men were also reported adopting the feminine characteristic of trusting. Women adopted many more male stereotypical traits than the men adopted female stereotypical traits—by a ratio of four to one—in part because the bureaucratic traits included more male than female traits. "Women cross gender stereotypes on the characteristics task oriented, managerial, assertive, and straightforward and frank."[94] All these are characteristics important for managerial success.[95]

In the Arizona study it was hypothesized that men would be more likely to describe themselves as competitive, dominant, risk-taking, and team oriented, and as more independent, assertive, and opportunistic than women; and that women would view themselves, more than do the men, as skilled in interpersonal transactions, creative, process-oriented, loyal, acting "by the book," and less willing to use intimidation.

Statistical tests (the t-test) of the behavioral items did not reveal marked variations between the Arizona males and females for either upper-level (grades 23-30) or middle-level (grades 18-22) state administrators. For the upper-level sample, the males indicated they were more *trusting,* whereas the females rated themselves higher on *independent, assertive, and attractive.*

Among the middle-level public administrators a few significant differences also appeared on the specific items. The males rated themselves as being more *competitive,* more *intimidating,* and more *managerial.* The females rated themselves as being more *process-oriented,* more *independent,* and more *attractive.*

The value placed on particular gender traits by current managers is perhaps more important than the historical stereotypes. Duerst-Lahti and Johnson[96] addressed this question. They found in Wisconsin at least,

> that gender neutral traits are valued most in the consequential categories of important and most important. Contrary to expectations, masculine traits do not dominate and feminine traits are clearly valued. Five of ten masculine traits and six of nine feminine traits rate as consequential. Feminine traits do slightly better on traits registering as consequential, . . . If bureaucratic natives ever did prefer predominantly masculine traits, they no longer do by this measure.[97]

The lack of substantial and consistent variations among men and women on individual traits suggests that, even if gender differences in behavior do influence career advancement or managerial or leadership ability, their impact is limited primarily to a clustering of characteristics into behavioral patterns.

Gender-Related Styles

Recent research suggests that viable, gender-based behavioral styles, distinct from either assimilationist or androgynous styles, are developing. Leaders who display sex-role behavior, regardless of whether they are male, female, or an androgynous combination, have been found to be more effective managers by their subordinates.[98] Men and women may approach their jobs differently, using somewhat different styles to accomplish their ends, but this difference in approach may enhance a woman's job performance.[99] These collective findings suggest that the exploration of specific, behavioral characteristics can be misleading; it is the gender-specific overall behavioral style that clusters traits in particular ways that matters.

Two separate studies recently have been completed that provide empirical examinations of the profile of the male versus female styles. One by Carolyn Desjardins[100] is based on Carol Gilligan's work in the area of moral psychology. The other by Rita Mae Kelly, Mary M. Hale, and Jayne Burgess[101] used factor analysis, an analytical clustering technique, of 22 specific behavioral traits to develop their profiles.

The Desjardins Study

Gilligan was a colleague of the late Lawrence Kohlberg,[102] who developed a theory of moral development in juvenile males that defines morality as justice or fairness reasoning and emphasizes the movement toward objectivity and universality as ideal. This moral mode sees relationships in terms of inequality and equality and emphasizes autonomy and reciprocity. It is referred to as the "justice/rights" mode. In attempting to apply this definition to the study of a group of women facing real-life dilemmas concerning the morality of abortion, Gilligan uncovered a different moral orientation used by women, one that comes from relationship and caring.

According to this recent research, the identity and moral development each of us experience as we mature is quite different for males and females; these experiences are further differentiated by social and economic class.[103] These differences help to create a distinct ethical framework for men as compared to women. The approach to managerial style, including decision making, power relationships, peer interaction, delegation style, and stress management are all thought to be influenced by each individual's self-concept, and by each individual's ethical framework.

According to Gilligan,[104] in early childhood development in a patriarchal society built on the nuclear family, females achieve gender identity in the ongoing relationship with their mothers. For females, intimacy precedes identity, and separation from the whole, especially abandonment, is threatening. Succeeding at the "games" they play is always secondary to the relationship with those playing. In contrast, males are encouraged to develop independence and organizational skills. For males, identity precedes intimacy, and intimacy is threatening. Males learn to compete with friends and "play" or interact with enemies with the objective of gaining power over, rather than relationship with, them. Although variance in development occurs through social and economic class for males and females alike, and the end results are unique in many aspects of the whole, they are nevertheless calculable by gender.

In comparison with the male, Gilligan and others[105] assert that female morality emphasizes responsibility and care. Morality is conceived in interpersonal terms, and goodness is equated with helping and pleasing others. A woman approaches decision making, for example, with consideration of others and often feels guilty if she puts her own considerations first. Responsibility means being responsive to others. Her dilemma appears when, in the world at large, that approach is no longer feasible without sacrificing personal success. For the mature male, morality consists of the protection of individual rights, and "goodness" is equated with not violating the rights of others.[106] A man comes from a point of responsibility to himself, a responsibility he takes for granted and without guilt. His dilemma is how to achieve his goals without infringing on the rights of others, but he remains in full, competitive knowledge that the goal is autonomous power over others without limitation or restriction. These differences in socialization interact with basic physiological differences, enhancing the expectation, if not the reality, that men and women are different in leadership and management positions. Figure 6.1 illustrates the gender-based worldview proposed by Desjardins.

Although it is probably impossible to elaborate a male model that all would agree is a national or international norm, certain characteristics of masculine managerial/leadership behavior have been identified that fit the model developed by Desjardins and are distinctive from a common female approach to similar situations.[107] Among these is a difference in motivation for seeking leadership positions. Women tend not to be as goal-oriented as men. Service to the profession or to others tends to be their motivation, taking precedence over loyalty to a chief executive officer (CEO). Male supervisors often interpret this difference as meaning women are not as ambitious as men.

Studies also have found that women prefer a participative leadership style, rather than the authoritative or consultative styles preferred by most men. The authoritative and consultative styles are defended as being cleaner, easier, more efficient, taking less time, and diluting position power less. An old Chinese saying illustrates the difference: A man's charm is in his strength. A woman's strength is in her charm. A masculine style would emphasize leading from position power, relying

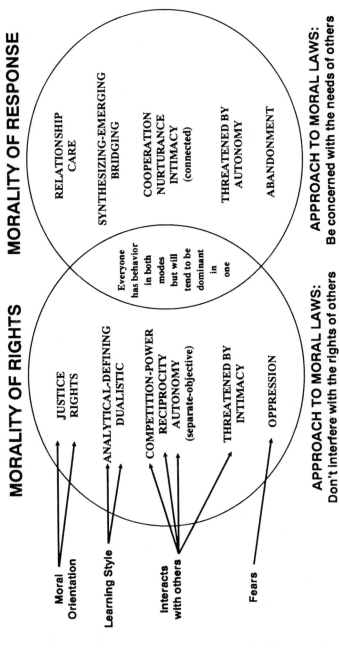

MORALITY OF RIGHTS   **MORALITY OF RESPONSE**

JUSTICE
RIGHTS

ANALYTICAL-DEFINING
DUALISTIC

COMPETITION-POWER
RECIPROCITY
AUTONOMY
(separate-objective)

THREATENED BY
INTIMACY

OPPRESSION

RELATIONSHIP
CARE

SYNTHESIZING-EMERGING
BRIDGING

COOPERATION
NURTURANCE
INTIMACY
(connected)

THREATENED BY
AUTONOMY

ABANDONMENT

Everyone
has behavior
in both
modes
but will
tend to be
dominant
in
one

Moral
Orientation

Learning Style

Interacts
with others

Fears

APPROACH TO MORAL LAWS:
Don't interfere with the rights of others

APPROACH TO MORAL LAWS:
Be concerned with the needs of others

Figure 6.1. Morality of Rights/Morality of Response
SOURCE: Reprinted from National Institute for Leadership Development (unpublished handout material) with permission from Carolyn Desjardins.

116

on control of resources and the authority of the organization. A feminine style pays more attention to personal abilities, charisma, interpersonal relationships, and personal commitment by and to others.

Men in leadership roles often emphasize avoiding conflict and open confrontation. Research[108] indicates that men avoid conflict by reverting (1) to authority—"I am right," or "I have the right to make the decision" or (2) to passive resistance—efforts to avoid losing. They avoid conflict by not acknowledging it and by sabotaging efforts to implement agreements. In contrast to men, an alternative collaborative win-win strategy tends to be more appealing to women. Women executives, in contrast to men, are characterized as being comfortable working in team settings, preferring win-win approaches to conflict management, and placing a high priority on managing relationships.[109] Rather than avoid the conflict, this approach would require accommodation and asking: "What do we each want? Can we accomplish individual and collective objectives and still maintain good relationships?"

Some important, but beneficial differences in the way women act as legislators compared to men have been identified.[110] Women tend to be more sympathetic to and to champion issues pertaining to women's rights, children, and human rights. They also tend to understand more clearly the impact that reductions in human-resource programs can have on the people affected. Women continue to bring a new perspective to issues important to women, having noticeably different policy priorities than men. Women tend to think in the gray area of compromise, win-win, as opposed to the black and white area of win-lose.[111] Ethics are also high on their agendas, and women tend to pay more attention to detail while men focus on the larger picture.[112]

To test the reality of the hypothesized gender difference in moral orientation as it pertains to managers and leaders, Desjardins studied 72 community college CEO's, half of whom were male and half of whom were female. (This group of managers would fall into the intermediate category of the labor market in the public sector of the economy described in Chapter 3.)

Although the majority of interviewees exhibited behaviors in both the justice/rights mode (male) and the connecting/care mode (female), a clear and substantial gender difference existed in the ways the behaviors clustered. Sixty-six percent of the women had a majority of behaviors, motivations, and ideas in the connecting/care mode; 17% fit the justice/rights mode; and another 17% had an equal number in each mode. Of the men studied, 28% fit the connecting/care mode; 50% were into the justice/rights mode; and 22% had an equal number in both modes. The overlap between the justice/rights and connecting/care modes is significant, and the ability of either gender to adopt a point of view other than their own gender-linked mode is apparent. Nonetheless, the difference between men and women with regard to these two moral orientations is quite striking.

The Kelly, Hale, and Burgess Study

In their study of gender and the behavioral styles of Arizona state-level administrators, Kelly, Hale, and Burgess[113] also provide evidence supporting this concept of gender-related managerial styles. In their study, they asked:

- Are there meaningful patterns of relationships among the 22 behavioral items enumerated in Table 6.1 that vary by sex?
- If so, do these patterns reflect particular gender-linked traits which support the view that males and females have distinctive managerial/leadership styles?

To answer these questions a factor analysis was performed separately on the 42 female and the 208 male Arizona high-level public administrators. The results of this empirical analysis produced six separate factors for both groups. For the males (see Table 6.2), these six factors accounted for 59% of the variance in the data. For the females (see Table 6.3), the six factors accounted for 70% of the variance. Although both analyses produced the same number of factors, the content was quite different.

For the male administrators, the first factor reflected behavioral characteristics of *The Boss,* an independent, assertive, dominant, competitive, ambitious, and creative risk-taker. The second factor reflected a *Manipulative Opportunist,* characterized by the traits of attractive, affectionate, and opportunistic. The third factor depicts a *Loyalist,* someone who is trusting, loyal, and frank. The fourth factor suggests *The Coach,* a person who is interpersonal, team-oriented, and managerial. The fifth factor, *The Bureaucrat* fits the stereotype, consisting of process-oriented, task-oriented, predictable, and by-the-book. The sixth male factor reflects an *Intimidator* and contains only one trait: intimidation.

TABLE 6.2. Factor Analytic Behavioral Patterns Identified in Upper-Level Male Administrators (Arizona Grades 23-30)

	The Boss Factor 1	Manipulative Opportunist Factor 2	The Loyalist Factor 3	The Coach Factor 4	The Bureaucrat Factor 5	The Intimidator Factor 6	h^2
Rotated Factor Matrix							
Independent	.73651						.58
Assertive	.70018						.60
Creative	.62772						.53
Risk-Taking	.58046						.53
Dominant	.56540						.58
Competitive	.49088						.47
Ambitious	.44170						.97
Attractive		.82761					.72
Affectionate		.81620					.73
Opportunistic		.60394					.59
Trusting			.73221				.65
Loyal			.64937				.57
Frank			.48790				.39
Interpersonal				.76054			.70
Team-Oriented				.66717			.66
Managerial				.56143			.59
Process-Oriented					.66824		.72
Task-Oriented					.65807		.61
Predictable					.63071		.51
By-the-Book					.60660		.63
Intimidation						.74659	.63

(continued)

TABLE 6.2 Continued

	The Boss Factor 1	Manipulative Opportunist Factor 2	The Loyalist Factor 3	The Coach Factor 4	The Bureaucrat Factor 5	The Intimidator Factor 6	h^2
Initial Statistics for Unrotated Factors							
Eigenvalue	4.99	2.07	1.61	1.56	1.20	1.03	
% of Total Variance	23.8	9.9	7.7	7.4	5.7	4.9	
% of Cumulative Variance	23.8	33.7	41.3	48.8	54.5	59.4	

SOURCE: Reprinted with permission from Rita Mae Kelly, Mary M. Hale, and Jayne Burgess, "Gender and Managerial Leadership Styles: A Comparison of Arizona Public Administrators," *Women & Politics* 11(2) (1991), Table 3. Copyright held by Haworth Press Inc.

TABLE 6.3. Factor Analytic Behavioral Patterns Identified in Upper-Level Female Administrators (Arizona Grades 23-30)

	Attractive Manager Factor 1	The Entrepreneur Factor 2	The Gentle One Factor 3	Individualistic Opportunist Factor 4	The Processor Factor 5	The Task Master Factor 6	h^2
Rotated Factor Matrix							
Managerial	.82814						.75
Competitive	.76881						.76
Ambitious	.73900						.81
Assertive	.62494						.79
Independent	.61987						.47
Frank	.61906						.76
Attractive	.61898						.53
Interpersonal	.48437						.73
By-the-Book		−.79100					.72
Risk-Taking		.74624					.72
Creative		.69456					.62
Predictable		−.67595					.61
Loyal			.82831				.74
Trusting			.78333				.64
Intimidation			−.57442				.69
Affectionate			.55013				.82
Team-Oriented				−.76624			.65
Opportunistic				.65963			.70
Process-Oriented					.81685		.79
Dominant					−.58281		.77
Task-Oriented						.82007	.80

(continued)

TABLE 6.3 Continued

	Attractive Manager Factor 1	The Entrepreneur Factor 2	The Gentle One Factor 3	Individualistic Opportunist Factor 4	The Processor Factor 5	The Task Master Factor 6	h^2
Initial Statistics for Unrotated Factors							
Eigenvalue	5.03	2.99	2.76	1.73	1.21	1.12	
% of Total Variance	24.0	14.2	13.1	8.2	5.8	5.4	
% of Cumulative Variance	24.0	38.2	51.4	59.6	65.4	70.8	

SOURCE: Reprinted with permission from Rita Mae Kelly, Mary M. Hale, and Jayne Burgess, "Gender and Managerial Leadership Styles: A Comparison of Arizona Public Administrators," *Women & Politics* 11(2) (1991), Table 4. Copyright held by Haworth Press Inc.

Among the 42 high-level female Arizona administrators, the first factor reflects *The Attractive Manager,* a person with the following traits: managerial, competitiveness, ambitious, assertive, independent, frank, attractive, interpersonal. The second factor suggests *The Entrepreneur,* a person who does not go by-the-book, who is not predictable, and who is risk-taking and creative. The third factor reflects *The Gentle One,* someone who is loyal, trusting, avoids using intimidation, and is affectionate. The fourth factor highlights an *Individualistic Opportunist,* containing a negative loading on team-oriented and being quite positive on opportunistic. The fifth factor connotes *A Processor,* being process-oriented and negative on dominant. The sixth factor, containing only task-oriented, suggests *A Task Master.*

The factor structures for the men and women Arizona high-level administrators are indeed quite different. The behavioral traits of dominance, intimidation, attractiveness, and affection do interact with the other behavioral characteristics differently for men and women as predicted.

The various and complex interactions of these factors reiterate the findings of the Desjardins and Wisconsin studies in that they indicate notable differences in male and female behavioral styles. None of the studies to date, however, has clarified the extent to which these differences are likely to be unchangeable. The entrance of women into higher levels of management and leadership is a relatively new phenomenon. The data reported here show only that substantial current variations exist, not that such variations will exist forever.

The findings do suggest, nonetheless, that men and women are likely to vary, currently and in the near future, in how they will deal with power, handle subordinates, and interrelate. The findings also suggest that, to the extent that women at higher levels are still expected to adopt a male model of behavior or to assimilate into the male mold, they will have difficulty. Full assimilation seems unlikely, and accommodation might well require thought and planning.

Alternative Guidelines for Accommodating to Male Structures

Several guidelines exist indicating ways women can accommodate themselves to structures demanding assimilation to a male-dominated form[114]:

1. Develop neutral topics to get acquainted with male workers and peers.
2. Take charge quickly, be direct.
3. Be assertive rather than aggressive.
4. Correct a male worker's mistakes by referring to specific events and approach the correction in private.
5. Stop the perception that women have less power than men by setting high goals and making and announcing clear decisions.
6. Combat the patronizing older male by keeping the conversation focused on business.
7. Avoid overfamiliarity with younger men.
8. Retain concern for the individual.

Other recommendations for effective management where accommodating to a prevailing male style is still necessary include the following[115]:

1. Learn to diagnose problems from an anthropological standpoint.
2. Understand the political power games played against women.
3. Take long-term approaches to organizational problems.
4. Use consensual, collaborative, participative leadership style.
5. Develop an action-oriented style of management.

Nancy Arnott in *Executive Female*[116] offers a slightly different guide for successful managers that in her judgment combines the best elements of male and female approaches yet will work in a setting demanding assimilation:

1. Listen for the hard facts and the emotional undertones, but guide the discussion to keep people's thoughts on track.
2. Gather information from all sources (balance qualitative with quantitative), weigh all sides, then make firm decisions.
3. Stay flexible. Be democratic enough to get the best from your people, but authoritative enough to give orders when necessary.
4. Accept that most gains require risk. Learn to manage risk, rather than avoid it.
5. Look for mentors of both sexes, and incorporate their strength into your style.
6. Don't get bogged down in picayune details; focus on the big picture.
7. Don't be afraid to show your feelings, but keep your emotions under control in crises and back up your arguments with facts, not feelings.

8. Put aside personal differences with colleagues and collaborate on common goals.

Conclusion

The question in 1991 is no longer whether men and women possess the same individual traits identified as necessary for effective leadership qualities. Rather, it is a question of how each individual in possession of these attributes chooses to cluster and apply her or his skills and abilities. Gilligan,[117] Statham,[118] and Desjardins,[119] among others, identify typical, gender-related approaches based on moral orientations. Kelly, Hale, and Burgess,[120] in their study of 250 top executives in Arizona state government, reveal alternative gender-linked patterns of clustering individual characteristics that produce leadership styles that currently are unique to each gender. These gender styles not only appear to utilize the personal strengths of the individual, but also are adaptive to positions within various organizations and the U.S. segmented labor market.

By masking their "noncorporate" feminine values, women may be paying a painfully high psychological and professional price, impeding their own progress by not developing their natural talents. Since the late 1970s feminists have promoted a managerial style that values women's experience, traditional values, and ways of behaving, feeling, and thinking, rather than one that encourages assimilation. Although stereotypical "femininity" per se is still not considered desirable in a manager, several of the androgynous combinations women employ rate as equally as desirable as masculine behaviors. A need exists in the business world for the development of the "female," for both men and women, to provide a long-needed balance against over dominance of male principles.[121]

Notes

1. Kay Deaux, *The Behavior of Men and Women* (Monterey, CA: Brooks/Cole, 1976).

2. Marion M. Wood and Susan T. Greenfield, "Women Managers and Fear of Success: A Study in the Field," *Sex Roles* 2 (December 1976): 375-387.

3. Joseph L. Moses and Virginia R. Boehm, "Relationship of Assessment-Center Performance to Management Progress of Women," *Journal of Applied Psychology* 60 (August 1975): 527-529.

4. B. Rosen and T. Jerdee, "Perceived Sex Differences in Managerially Relevant Characteristics," *Sex Roles* 5 (1978): 837-843.

5. Kathryn M. Bartol, "Male Versus Female Leaders: The Effect of Leader Need for Dominance on Follower Satisfaction," *Academy of Management Journal* 17 (July 1974): 225-233.

6. Rosen and Jerdee, "Perceived Sex Differences," 837-843; and James Tergorg, "Women in Management: A Research Review," *Journal of Applied Psychology* 62 (December 1977): 647-664.

7. Tergorg, "Women in Management."

8. R. M. Kanter, *Men and Women of the Corporation* (New York: Basic Books, 1977).

9. Stephanie Riger and Pat Gilligan, "Women in Management: An Exploration of Competing Paradigms," *American Psychologist* 35 (October 1980): 902-910.

10. Rosabeth Kanter, *Men and Women of the Corporation* (New York: Basic Books, 1977); and Kathy Ferguson, *The Feminist Case Against Bureaucracy* (Philadelphia: Temple University Press, 1988).

11. See, e.g., Georgia Duerst-Lahti and Cathy Johnson, "Gender Style and Bureaucracy: Must Women Go Native to Succeed?" Paper presented at the Annual Meeting of the American Political Science Association, Atlanta, Georgia (September 1989), Figure 1.

12. Kanter, *Men and Women.*

13. H. Papanek, "Men, Women and Work: Reflections on the Two-Person Career," *American Journal of Sociology* 78(4) (January 1973): 852-872.

14. Claudia Wallis, "Women in the 90s," *Time* January 1990, 89.

15. Joseph Pleck, *Working Wives/Working Husbands* (Beverly Hills, CA: Sage, 1985); and cf. Joseph Pleck, "The Work-Family System," *Social Problems* 24 (1977): 417-427.

16. Wallis, "Women in the 90s," 89.

17. D. C. McClelland, *Human Motivation* (Glenview, IL: Scott Foresman, 1985).

18. Jo Freeman, *The Politics of Women's Liberation* (New York: McKay, 1975).

19. Janet Shibley Hyde, *Half the Human Experience: The Psychology of Women* (Lexington, MA: D.C. Heath, 1985).

20. Catherine A. MacKinnon, "Feminism, Marxism, Method, and the State: An Agenda for Theory," in *Feminist Theory,* eds. N. O. Keohane et al. (Chicago: University of Chicago Press, 1982).

21. D. E. Berlyne, "Arousal and Reinforcement," in *Nebraska Symposium on Motivation,* ed. D. Levine. (Lincoln: University of Nebraska Press, 1967).

22. McClelland, *Human Motivation,* 151.

23. Robert J. House and Jitendra V. Singh, "Organizational Behavior: Some New Directions for I/O Psychology," *Annual Review of Psychology* 38 (1987), 673.

24. House and Singh, "Organizational Behavior," 674.

25. House and Singh, "Organizational Behavior."

26. See also, D. G. Winter and A. J. Stewart, "Power Motivation," in *Dimensions of Personality,* eds. H. London and J. Exner (New York: John Wiley, 1978); and D. C. McClelland, *Power: The Inner Experience* (New York: Irvington, 1975).

27. House and Singh, "Organizational Behavior," 675.

28. McClelland, *Power: The Inner Experience.*

29. McClelland, *Power: The Inner Experience.*

30. House and Singh, "Organizational Behavior," 676.

31. House and Singh, "Organizational Behavior," 678.

32. I. E. Deutchman, "Socialization to Power: Questions about Women and Politics," *Women & Politics* 5(4) (1986): 79-89; and D. C. Jones, "Power Structures and Perceptions of Powerholders in Same Sex Groups of Young Children," *Women & Politics* 3(2/3) (Summer/Fall 1983): 147-164.

33. D. C. Jones, "Power Structures"; see also R. Jones, "Keeping Up: The Jones Principle," *Leadership and Organizational Development* 4 (1983): 26-31.

34. R. Jones, "Keeping Up"; and Mary M. Hale and Rita Mae Kelly, *Gender, Bureaucracy, and Democracy* (Westport, CT: Greenwood, 1989), 24.

35. Alice G. Sargent, *Beyond Sex Roles* 2nd ed. (St. Paul, MN: West, 1977).

36. Sargent, *Beyond Sex Roles,* 467.

37. Sargent, *Beyond Sex Roles,* 469.

38. Sargent, *Beyond Sex Roles,* 469.

39. Sargent, *Beyond Sex Roles.*

40. Carolyn Desjardins, "Gender Issues in Community College Leadership," *American Association of Women in Community and Junior College Journal* (June 1989).

41. M. D. Lamkin, "Power: How to Get It, Keep It and Use It Wisely," *Vital Speeches* 53(5) (December 1986): 151-154.

42. D. P. Ashton, *Non-traditional Authority Figures: New Leadership Styles for Women and Minorities* (Oakland: California School of Professional Psychology, n.d.).

43. Ashton, *Non-traditional Authority Figures.*

44. T. Vilkinas, "Do Women Use Different Influences?" *Women in Management Review* 3(3) (1988): 155-160.

45. Vilkinas, "Do Women Use Different Influences?"

46. G. H. Dobbins, "Equity vs. Equality: Sex Differences in Leadership," *Sex Roles* 15(9/10) (1986): 513-525.

47. W. R. Todd-Mancillas and A. Rossi, "Gender Differences in the Management of Personnel Disputes," *Women's Studies Communications* 8 (Spring 1985): 25-33.

48. Todd-Mancillas and Rossi, "Gender Differences."

49. Todd-Mancillas and Rossi, "Gender Differences."

50. Todd-Mancillas and Rossi, "Gender Differences."

51. Hyde, *Half the Human Experience,* 212.

52. Hyde, *Half the Human Experience,* 215.

53. Hyde, *Half the Human Experience,* 214.

54. Hyde, *Half the Human Experience.*

55. M. Swacker, "The Sex of the Speaker as a Sociolinguistic Variable," in *Language and Sex: Difference and Dominance,* eds. B. Thorne and N. Henley (Rowely, MA: Newbury House, 1975). See also, Hyde, *Half the Human Experience,* 215.

56. Nancy Henley, "Status and Sex: Some Touching Observations," *Bulletin of the Psychonomic Society* 2 (1973): 92-93; and Diana L. Summerhayes and R. W. Suchner, "Power Implications of Touch in Male-Female Relationships," *Sex Roles* 4 (1978): 103-110.

57. Hyde, *Half the Human Experience,* 219.

58. Hyde, *Half the Human Experience,* 223-225.

59. Leah Rosch, "The Professional Image Report," *Working Woman* 13(10) (1988): 91-96.

60. G. S. Bullivant, "Deadlier Than the Male?" *Credit Management* (November 1984): 28.

61. Waino W. Suojanen, et al., "The Emergence of the Type 'E' Woman," *Business* 37(1) (1987): 6.

62. K. Stechert, H. B. Braiker, J. Calano, and J. Salzman, "Stress Workshop: Balancing Your Career and Your Life," *Working Woman* 13(8) (August 1988): 59-68.

63. Richard Scase, R. Goffee, and A. Mann, "Women Managers: 1. Room at the Top, 2. Destroying the Myths," *Management Today* March 1987, 64-67.

64. House and Singh, "Organizational Behavior," 682.

65. Pamela Redmond Satran, "Short Power," *Working Woman* 12(6) (1987): 98-100.

66. Michelle Morris, "The Wizard of the Working Woman's Wardrobe," *Working Woman* 13(6) (1988): 74-80.

67. Rosch, "The Professional Image Report."

68. Mindy Schanback, "Big Girls Don't Cry," *Executive Female* (May/June 1988): 50-53.

69. Schanback, "Big Girls Don't Cry."

70. Jeane Marie Col, *Barriers to Women's Advancement in Administration,* unpublished manuscript (Springfield, IL: Sangamon State University, 1985); and Kanter, *Men and Women.*

71. Kathryn M. Bartol, "The Effect of Male Versus Female Leaders on Follower Satisfaction and Performance," *Journal of Business Research* 3 (January 1975): 81; Stephen M. Brown, "Male Versus Female Leaders: A Comparison of Empirical Studies," *Sex Roles: A Journal of Research* 5 (October 1979): 595-661; N. Carr-Ruffino, *The Promotable Woman* (Belmont, CA: Wadsworth, 1985); J. Melia and P. Lyttle, *Why Jenny Can't Lead: Understanding the Male Dominant System* (Saguache, CO: Operational Politics, 1986); Rosen and Jerdee, "Perceived Sex Differences"; and J. R. Stanley, *Gender Differences in Career Advancement: Collegial Relationships,* paper presented at the Second Annual Symposium of Texas Women Scholars, Austin, TX, 1987.

72. Margaret Hennig and Anne Jardim, *The Managerial Woman* (Garden City, NY: Anchor Press/Doubleday, 1977); J. Lipman-Blumen, *Gender Roles and Power* (Englewood Cliffs, NJ: Prentice-Hall, 1982); Melia and Lyttle, *Why Jennie Can't Lead;* Anne Statham, "The Gender Model Revisited: Differences in the Management Styles of Men and Women," *Sex Roles* 16(7/8) (1987): 409-429; and Stanley, *Gender Differences.*

73. John E. Baird, Jr. and Patricia Hayes Bradley, "Styles of Management and Communication: A Comparative Study of Men and Women," *Communication Monographs* 46 (June 1979), 101-111; and Statham, "The Gender Model Revisited."

74. A. Baron, "How We're Viewed by the Men We Boss," *Savvy* (July 1982): 15-18; N. Carr-Ruffino, *The Promotable Woman* (Belmont, CA: Wadsworth, 1985), 157-158; P. Dubro, "Perceptions of Men and Women Managers" (mimeo) (New York: New York School of Business Management, 1984); Rosen and Jerdee, "Perceived Sex Differences"; and Stanley, *Gender Differences.*

75. Ann M. Morrison, Randall P. White, and Ellen Van Velson, *Breaking the Glass Ceiling* (Reading, MA: Addison-Wesley, 1987), 49-54.

76. Morrison, White, and Van Velson, *Breaking the Glass Ceiling,* 49-54 and the appendix. See also, Catalyst, *Female Management Style: Myth and Reality* (New York: Catalyst, April 1986); and *Korn/Ferry International's Profile of Women Senior Executives* (New York: Korn/Ferry International, 1982).

77. Morrison, White, and Van Velson, *Breaking the Glass Ceiling,* 24.

78. Morrison, White, and Van Velson, *Breaking the Glass Ceiling,* 36.

79. Morrison, White, and Van Velson, *Breaking the Glass Ceiling,* 36.

80. Morrison, White, and Van Velson, *Breaking the Glass Ceiling,* 44.

81. Morrison, White, and Van Velson, *Breaking the Glass Ceiling,* 44.

82. Morrison, White, and Van Velson, *Breaking the Glass Ceiling,* 56.

83. Judy B. Rosener, "Ways Women Lead," *Harvard Business Review* (November-December 1990): 119-125.

84. Rosener, "Ways Women Lead," 120.

85. Rosener, "Ways Women Lead," 120.

86. Rosener, "Ways Women Lead," 120.

87. Natasha Josefowitz, "Management Men and Women: Closed vs. Open Doors," *Harvard Business Review* 58 (September-October 1980): 56-62.

88. Rosener, "Ways Women Lead," 120.

89. Rita Mae Kelly, Mary M. Hale, and Jayne Burgess, "Gender and Managerial/Leadership Styles: A Comparison of Arizona Public Administrators," *Women & Politics* 11(2) (1991), forthcoming.

90. Duerst-Lahti and Johnson, "Gender, Style."

91. Duerst-Lahti and Johnson, "Gender, Style," 11.

92. Duerst-Lahti and Johnson, "Gender, Style."

93. Duerst-Lahti and Johnson, "Gender, Style," 11.

94. Duerst-Lahti and Johnson, "Gender, Style," 11.

95. Duerst-Lahti and Johnson, "Gender, Style," 12.

96. Duerst-Lahti and Johnson, "Gender, Style," 13.

97. Duerst-Lahti and Johnson, "Gender, Style," 13.

98. Stephen C. Bushardt, Aubrey Fowler, and Regina Caveny, "Sex Role Behavior and Leadership: An Empirical Investigation," *Leadership and Organizational Journal* 8(5) (1987): 13-16.

99. Anne Statham, "Women Managers: Leadership Style, Development, and Misunderstandings," in *Women and Work: Selected Papers,* eds. W. Knezek, M. Barrett, and S. Collins, 17-36 (Arlington: University of Texas, Arlington, 1985).

100. Desjardins, "Gender Issues."

101. Kelly, Hale, and Burgess, "Gender and Managerial/Leadership Styles."

102. Lawrence Kohlberg, *The Philosophy of Moral Development: Moral Stages and the Idea of Justice* (San Francisco: Harper & Row, 1981).

103. Kohlberg, *The Philosophy of Moral Development;* and Carol Gilligan, *In a Different Voice: Psychological Theory and Women's Development* (Cambridge, MA: Harvard University Press, 1982).

104. Gilligan, *In a Different Voice.*

105. Gilligan, *In a Different Voice;* Desjardins, "Gender Issues"; and Statham, "Women Managers." See also Eva Feder Kittay and Diana T. Meyers, eds. *Women and Moral Theory* (New York: Rowman & Littlefield, 1987).

106. Gilligan, *In a Different Voice;* and Robin West, "Jurisprudence and Gender," *University of Chicago Law Review* 55(1) (Winter 1988): 1-72.

107. See Marilyn Loden Bilensky, *Feminine Leadership: Or How to Succeed in Business Without Being One of the Boys* (New York: Times Books, 1985); Natasha Josefowitz, *Paths to Power: A Woman's Guide from First Job to Top Executive* (Reading, MA: Addison-Wesley, 1980); and Kanter, *Managerial Women.*

108. Gwen Rubenstein, "Women on the Way Up," *Association Management* 38(10) (October 1986): 26-30.

109. Rubenstein, "Women on the Way Up."

110. Vera Katz, "Women Chart New Legislative Course," *Journal of State Government* 60(5) (September/October 1987): 213-215.

111. H. Gluck, "The Difference," *Journal of State Government* 60(5) (September/October 1987): 223-226.

112. For an overview of recent research on the difference women have made as legislators, see Rita Mae Kelly, Michelle St. Germain, and Jody Horn, "Female Public Officials: A Different Voice," *Annals of the American Academy of Political and Social Science* (May 1991): 77-87.

113. Kelly, Hale, and Burgess, "Gender and Managerial/Leadership Styles."

114. M. A. Allison and E. Allison, "Managing Men," *Working Woman* 10(10) (October 1985): 37-40.

115. Stephen J. Rexford and Lisa Molniero, "The 'Right Stuff' of Management: Challenges Confronting Women," *Advanced Management Journal* 51(2) (Spring 1986): 38-39.

116. Nancy Arnott, "Off Balance," *Executive Female* May/June 1988, 26-28.

117. Gilligan, *In a Different Voice.*

118. Statham, "Women Managers."

119. Desjardins, "Gender Issues."

120. Kelly, Hale, and Burgess, "Gender and Managerial/Leadership Styles."

121. Daniel Simmons and Rosemary Simmons, "The 'Good Manager': Sex-typed, Androgynous, or Likeable?" *Sex Roles* 12(11/12) (1985): 1187-1198.

7

Careers: Linking Individuals
to Organizations

Careers link individuals and organizations. Theory and research on this linkage over the past fifty years[1] reveal two major concerns: (1) how individuals shape their own careers and (2) how society, organizations, and careers shape individuals. This chapter explores these two themes. First, a model of career dynamics revolving around the concept of the internal and the external career is presented. Second, each type of career is examined in some detail. The *internal career* is concerned with the individual, her or his development, education, training, experience, motivation, career anchors, and orientations. To explore how the internal career unfolds for women, typical career stages are described, revealing that the different stages require different psychological and personal orientations. The importance of a person's career anchor is highlighted. Specific gender differences in how life phases interact with career stages and influence women's career anchors are explored, and broad strategies for advancing a career are reviewed. Then, the concept of the *external career* is examined. This concept draws attention to the organizational and societal roles in structuring careers. Focusing on the external career draws attention to career paths within occupations, career stages within organizations, and career types within society. A model of the external career that builds on the segmented labor market material presented in Chapter 3 is outlined.

Figure 7.1 depicts a model of career dynamics, illustrating how the internal and external career concepts are related and how they are linked to national and organizational cultures. The model grounds career dynamics on the basic assumptions undergirding the U.S. national heritage. As noted throughout this book, the traditional patriarchal sex-role ideology about women, family, and careers has strongly shaped our collective definition of how women relate to the economy. National sex-role ideologies influence the values, norms, and artifacts of particular organizational cultures, further defining the ways individuals approach work. Each person's ideas about career options develop from early interactions in families and schools, the agencies that do the most to reproduce our shared understandings of the career options open to us. These shared values, norms, and practices become part of the organizational culture which, in turn, creates the institutional context or design of work and the individual's perception of the external career.[2]

The Internal Career

Career Stages

Careers are often conceived in terms of stages and the life cycle. Although variations exist among individuals and across occupations, people who work consistently throughout their lives tend to pass through nine basic stages.[3]

In Stage 1 (Growth, Fantasy, Exploration), career has little meaning; people have vague ideas about occupations, work, and their personal implications. Becoming aware of alternatives is important.

In Stage 2 (Education and Training), investments are made in personal human capital. Some careers require extensive education and training, others little, but the choices that are made will impact one's entire work life.

In Stage 3 (Entry into the World of Work), regardless of quality of preparation, entry usually represents a "reality shock" and major personal adjustments. Occupational self-concepts begin to develop.

During Stage 4 (Basic Training, Socialization), organizational demands are placed on individuals, and significant personal learning about one's self, work, and careers occurs.

During Stage 5 (Gaining Membership), the trainee stage ends and full membership in an occupation or organization begins. Understanding of one's own talents, strengths, and weaknesses develops as reflection on motives and values and work experience unfolds.

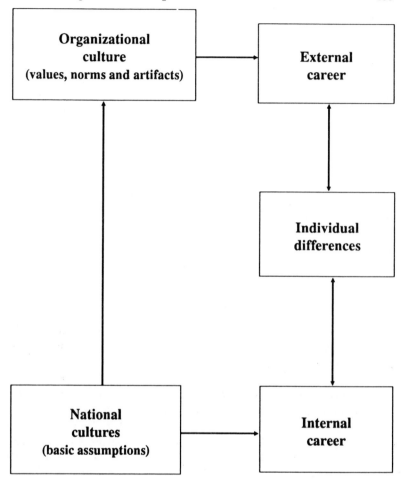

Figure 7.1. A Model of Career Dynamics

SOURCE: From C. B. Derr and A. Laurent, "The Internal and External Career: A Theoretical Cross-Cultural Perspective," in *Handbook of Career Theory*, eds. Michael B. Arthur, Douglas T. Hall, and Barbara S. Lawrence (New York: Cambridge University Press, 1989), p. 466. Copyright 1989 by University of Cambridge Press. Reprinted by permission.

Stage 6 (Gaining Tenure) usually occurs between 5 to 10 years on the job. At this stage, permanent membership or some sense of permanency in the occupation or position is given by the employing organization—with the understanding that tenure lasts only as long as the job exists.

During Stage 7 (Mid-Career Crisis, Reassessment), individuals either retain momentum, regain it, or level off. Most individuals enter a period in their mid-careers where they ask themselves a series of questions: "Have I entered the right career?" "Have I accomplished all I hoped to?" "What have I accomplished and was it worth the sacrifice?" "Should I continue or make a change?" and "What do I want to do with the rest of my life, and how does my work fit into it?" This reassessment can lead to crisis and change.

In Stage 8 (Disengagement), individuals slow down, become less involved, and prepare for retirement. Some deny this necessity and avoid planning for the next stage of life.

In Stage 9 (Retirement), the organization or occupation no longer provides a meaningful role for the individual. This loss of role can be devastating to some. Others choose to start a second career; still others opt for a more relaxed, nonworking life style.

Passage through these stages involves participation in the workplace. Whether or not an individual has participated successfully depends on other matters, not least of which are one's level of aspiration and one's reference group for comparison.

Career Anchors

Each of us has a preference about how we as individuals ought to fit into the life of work. The concept of a "career anchor" is used to describe the core element, the self-image that "both guides and constrains career decisions."[4] A *career anchor* "is that element in our self-concept that we will not give up, even if forced to make a difficult choice."[5] It is linked to our "life anchor," the decisions we each make about "how to integrate work, family, and personal priorities."[6] To have a career anchor, one must place enough emphasis on work that its importance requires thinking about work life in a relatively long-term and systematic way.

Success is related to one's career anchor. According to Edgar H. Schein, eight distinctive career anchors exist, with each revolving around how much an individual values the following: security, autonomy, technical/functional preferences, managerial work, entrepreneurship, service, challenges, and overall lifestyle.[7] Each career anchor reflects a different integration of talents, abilities, skills, and human needs. Table 7.1 summarizes the basic core of these career anchors in terms of the identity they give to a person along with the type of work,

TABLE 7.1 Career Anchors and Their Characteristics

Anchors	Description	Type of Work	Pay and Benefits	Promotion	Type of Recognition
			Type of Career Characteristics Desired		
Security/Stability	Identifies personal goals with that of the organization	Stable, predictable regulated work; often prefers one geographic location; work context important	Reliable, consistent based on length of service, pre-insurance and retirement benefits	Formal system like grade, rank or tenure	Loyalty, steady, performance recognized
Autonomy/ Independence	Willing to sacrifice security for freedom	Contract or project driven; delineated time-bound projects with clear	Merit pay, bonuses, portable benefits & cafeteria-style goals	More autonomy	Portable awards, medals, testimonials, prizes or awards, own "shop"
Technical/Functional Competence	Career defined by constant refinement of skills and abilities	Task-oriented, specializations, challenging, work content important	Pay based on education, and demonstrated expertise; external equity important; portable benefits	Professional promotional ladder parallel to executive ladder	Recognition from professional peers; self-development opportunities
Managerial Competence	Cmbination of motives, talents, and skills; "Jack of All Trades," managing the inter-personal and group competence	Ever-increasing responsibility showing analytical, decision-making process	Pay based on degree of responsibility; success, good company retirement benefits	Results-oriented or performance-based evaluations	Timely promotion to higher responsibility; titles, high incomes, bonuses, stock options, larger budget, status symbols

(continued)

TABLE 7.1 Continued

Anchors	Description	Type of Work	Type of Career Characteristics Desired			
			Pay and Benefits	Promotion	Type of Recognition	
Entrepreneur	Overwhelming drive to create	Invention of products, service, or new organization	Controlling percentage of company stock; ownership, patents; benefits not meaningful	Power and freedom to be creative; to be and do what person can	Name on the product or company; building a fortune on large enterprise	
Service	Dedication to a cause that is compelling	"Helping Professions" like nursing, teaching, or the ministry	"Fair Pay," portable benefits, money not central	Movement to position of more influence and freedom to serve cause	Recognition of contributions; support from peers and superiors	
Pure Challenge	Defines all work situations as self-tests	"Warriors" like strategists, sales-persons and athletes; competitive skills need exercising	Awards and stipends based on excellence, "winning"	Promotion to greater challenge	"Winning" and demonstrating skill is everything	
Life Style	Integration of family and personal life with work	Flexible with respect for family	Extensive, progressive, family-oriented benefits	Rewarded with more vacation or sabbatical	Respect given for worker's commitment to family	

SOURCE: Developed from E. H. Schein's "Individuals and Careers," in *Organizational Behaviors at Various Systems Levels*, ed. J. W. Lorsch, 155-171 (Englewood Cliffs, NJ: Prentice-Hall, 1987).

pay and benefits, promotion system, and type of recognition persons with these anchors tend to prefer.

Although women have as wide a variety of career anchors as men, the life-style anchor was first found among women.[8] Schein's description of this anchor is interesting, as it reflects some of the major difficulties women face in both career development and in breaking through the "glass ceiling." Schein states, "At first glance this concept seems like a contradiction in terms. People who organize their existence around 'life-style' are, in effect, saying that their career is less important to them and therefore that they do not have a career anchor."[9] He included it in his discussion, however, "because a growing number of graduates who are highly motivated toward meaningful careers are insisting that the careers be meshed with total life-style. It is not enough to *balance* personal and professional life; it is more a matter of finding a way to *integrate* the needs of the individual, the family, and the career."[10]

The person with a life-style career anchor desires flexibility the most. In contrast to the autonomy-oriented person, however, this individual will work for an organization that provides the appropriate options. Among these are being able to travel or move if family needs require or permit it, "part-time work if life concerns require it, sabbaticals, paternity and maternity leaves, day-care options (which are becoming especially relevant for the growing population of single parents), flexible work hours, and so on."[11] As Schein notes, individuals with the life-style anchor seek a proper "organizational attitude" rather than specific programs.[12]

The existence of these career patterns has several implications for both employing organizations and individuals who seek viable careers. *For individuals,* some soul-searching and reflection on the nature of one's career anchors is in order. By analyzing these anchors and understanding their implications for our career choices, patterns, and trade-offs to attain success, individuals will be better able to manage and plan their own careers—and to supervise subordinates in the attainment of success in theirs. *For organizations,* attention to "more flexible career paths, incentive systems, and reward systems to meet a wider range of individual needs, even within a particular job category"[13] is in order. In addition, greater clarity of what the organization actually needs from an individual and the basis for performance appraisal will facilitate an improved relationship between the organization and the individual.

Women's Life Phases and Career Stages

Although the notion of career anchors and the internal career are relevant to women as well as to men, women clearly neither follow the same developmental paths as men nor do their careers typically reflect the same patterns, paths, and anchors as those of men. Until the 1980s, most career theories and studies were grounded on male models of both success and work. As has been stressed throughout this book, such models are seldom fully applicable to women.

Numerous scholars have noted that sex-role ideology merges with sex-role socialization processes to ensure that females will relate to work life differently from males. Women derive their identity, maturity, and strength from attachment to significant others. And, as Gallos notes, "Women's career gains and professional accomplishments are complements, not substitutes, for strong interdependent relationships,"[14] and "Both . . . [phase and stage] . . . theories emphasize the centrality of relationships, attachments, and caring for women, affecting how women view the world around them and how they choose to live their lives."[15] (Note: Phase theories focus on expectations revolving around one's age. Stage theories focus on typical experiences one goes through regardless of age.)

Perhaps the most important message that research on women and careers gives is that the traditional sex-role remains central to women's identity. Hence, the psychological stance toward work for the average woman is different from that for the average man. "Work is something important to do [for women] rather than something to be [for men]."[16] Numerous studies have found that interpersonal commitments and self-definition dominate women's career aspirations, pathways, and patterns.[17] Others report that the age expectations for women do not match with career age expectations as well as they match for men.[18]

Bardwick[19] and Gallos[20] assert that the phases and pace of career development differ considerably for women compared to men. The need to deal with the importance of relationships constantly affects women's career decisions. For example, during the *early adult transition phase* (ages 17 to 28) women must face what to do about marriage and/or commitments to significant others. Although men also must address this relationship issue, the decision made has substantially less impact on their careers and other life choices. These other relationship commitments often lead women to prioritize career and family options differently than men. Women remain more fluid in their early adult years, particularly about career choices and geographical location.

This psychological fluidity can appear to be a less strong commitment to one's own career and imply uncertainty about one's own goals. Uncertainty often becomes confused with "weak ego boundaries"[21] with the consequence that young women are often taken less seriously than their male counterparts as they enter the work world. Even in a dual-career work environment, it is the woman's career that often suffers during this phase.

The next phase, the *settling down period* (ages 30 to 40), also typically has different meaning for men and women. As Gallos[22] notes, "Becoming one's own woman requires more than achieving professional success." For those who haven't had children, the biological clock calls. For those who have children, the difficulties of juggling home and work loom large, making many question whether a balance or proper integration of personal life and work is actually feasible. Even women who have foregone marriage and children face a challenge— whether their sacrifice was worth it. Although large numbers of women with children wonder how they will get through this phase, those without children may question whether they can attain womanhood if they do not have children and a commitment to a significant other. The Hennig and Jardim study in 1978[23] and the Hardesty and Jacobs study of 1986[24] report similarly that women who had ignored or "given up" such commitments during their earlier years found themselves professionally successful in the corporate ranks, but still feeling "frustration, emptiness, exhaustion, disillusionment, and a sense of personal failure when they realized the personal and interpersonal costs of their professional success."[25] It is at this phase that many women choose to leave Corporate America to find work opportunities that will better facilitate integrating personal and professional life. For example, Taylor[26] found that one-quarter of the women MBAs in the class of 1976 from top business schools left management; and Gallese[27] reported in 1985 that many Harvard MBA graduates found it necessary to trade-off between their career, that of their spouse, and home.

Two studies completed in 1990 reveal that corporate barriers to advancement are increasingly as important as family reasons for women managers to leave at higher rates than men during this phase. Wick & Co., a Wilmington, Delaware, consulting firm, studied 110 male and female professionals from Fortune 500 companies in the Northeast. Of the women leaving jobs, 73% accepted jobs at other companies, 13% became entrepreneurs, 7% stayed home, and 7% were still unemployed. Family concerns were less important for these women than the perception of a "glass ceiling," of being blocked from further promotions.[28] The second study, by Opinion Research Corporation (ORC) in Princeton, New Jersey, combined data from surveys of 26,500 managers, supervisors, and professionals in seven large corporations to address Felice Schwartz's assertions about the need for a "Mommy Track" directly. The study found greater dissatisfaction among women than men with their career development, their employer, and their opportunities for career advancement. Although two-thirds of the women had children, women were less likely than men to indicate their decisions to quit were related to children (9% vs. 26%). The lower tolerance the women managers had for their situations seemed related to the higher price they thought they already were paying to have a career. Loyalty to the company had much less significance to them than it had for men. The ORC study concludes as follows:

> The implications of ORC's findings are quite different than the *Mommy Track* solution proposed by Felice Schwartz. Our work shows that younger managers, regardless of their sex, express much stronger intentions to turnover than do older managers. Overall, age is *six times more important* than sex in predicting turnover intentions. So rather than creating a dual-career track system only for women, organizations should try to address the special needs of younger managers regardless of sex. Of equal importance, organizations need to identify and address those *internal* factors that stifle the growth and development of their female managers.[29]

The *middle adulthood years* (ages 40 to 50) historically have been a time of relatively great potential for women, a period free of child rearing, when they may well have better health and a better sense of well-being than their male counterparts. The increased sense of autonomy and independence often leads to more and improved career options and a more certain, more forceful woman.[30] (Although with more women waiting to have children until their late thirties and early forties, this greater freedom from child rearing might not be so common during this phase in the 1990s and the 21st century.)

The *age 50 and older phase* requires both men and women to face their own and other's mortality, and the need to retire. Women also must deal with menopause. In contrast to men, women must also face the fact that they are likely to live well beyond retirement. If married, they are likely to outlive their spouses and might well become financially and physically dependent on their children, particularly their daughters (who themselves are likely to be seeking to balance work and home commitments). Nonetheless, given women's greater longevity, reduced probability of heart attacks, and fewer or no dependents, this period is potentially a very positive one for women's career development.

These various phases of women's lives obviously intersect with career anchors and career decisions. That the content of these phases is different from that for men has historically led to the conclusion that women are less career-oriented than men. To cite Gallos:

> When women have managed their professional selves over a course of a lifetime in ways that allow for both professional accomplishment and expression of their relationship/family needs, this has not been seen as a unique, women's perspective toward managing a career. Rather these choices are still framed as women "cutting back on career," "dropping off the career path during child-bearing years," "choosing motherhood vs. career," "taking a step down on the career ladder," "accepting less challenging career options," and so on. The implications are clear. Career means work outside the home, but more importantly, career means a specific path toward approaching work that more often fits men's rather than women's options and experiences.[31]

Individual Career Strategies

One way to understand the different ways men and women as groups tend to approach careers is to explore four basic strategies people use to link their individual choices and behavior with work and employment.[32] The *Entrepreneurial Strategy* requires resources so that self-employment is viable; it allows for flexibility, some discontinuous employment once one is established, and some control over life-style. The *Organizational Strategy* requires employment within an organization, usually a bureaucracy. This strategy typically requires not only particular occupational qualifications, but also full-time continuous employment along a particular career path for career advancement to occur. It is this strategy that reflects the notions of a linear career model where an employee either moves "up or out" and the option of "getting to the top." The organization typically represents the hierarchical structure through which the career path flows. The *Occupational Strategy* emphasizes high development of skills and qualifications within a profession or occupation so that moves from employer to employer are readily made and without too much loss of income or status. The fourth category is the *Careerless Approach,* that is, the holding of jobs with no preconceived notion of a career pattern, seeking only the best monetary rewards available for one's personal concerns at each time period.

At this point in history, it might well be that gender differences in the use of these strategies is as much if not more responsible for men's progress *up* the ladder of success (and women's lack of progress) than the investment women make in their own human capital. Historically, women were prohibited from and often chose not to get training beyond high school. This pattern no longer holds in the United States and Western European countries. In England, for example, whereas 32% of the girls in 1982 furthered their training after high school, only 22% of the boys did.[33] Moreover, in the United States in 1990, females comprised nearly half the students in MBA, law, and other professional programs. One-third of MBAs graduating in the United States in 1986 were women.[34] Women students tend to get higher grades on the average than men students,[35] demonstrating that women are committed to investing in themselves.

Although the proportion of women investing in their human capital is increasing, other patterns persist that perpetuate the gendered economic structure. These include the gendered nature of the training received and of the career strategy chosen. Women tend to opt for the Occupational Strategy rather than the Entrepreneurial or the Organizational Strategy. In other words, very high proportions of young women still tend to get their initial training in female-dominated professions or occupations, that is, in education, health (nursing), catering, or some sort of clerical or low-level administrative work (see Chapter 3). Almost all of the occupations related to this training have higher than average amounts of flexibility—summers off, part-time employment options, and reduced penalties for career breaks; mobility—ability to move from place to place with a spouse and pick up a comparable position; and even relatively reasonable prestige for service to society. Women's greater domestic constraints have made it rational for women to choose this Occupational Strategy at a higher rate than the other strategies.

Men are more likely than women to choose and to retain the Organizational Strategy. For example, the 1990 Wick & Co. study of 110 men and women Fortune 500 managers reported that 77% of the men were "highly likely" to stay with their companies whereas only 35% of the women were. The decision to move to another company might lead to more career opportunities, but company loyalty and organizational experience often enter the promotional calculus.[36] Although it is true that occupational certification and investment in human capital is important in the Organizational Strategy, this latter strategy explicitly recognizes that a substantial part of "getting to the top" and breaking through the "glass ceiling" requires obtaining organizational qualifications, the attainment of which indicates to one's organizational superiors that one is promotable. "The bureaucratic career is in essence both full-time and continuous—part-time *bureaucratic* careers are a contradiction in terms—although the organisation [sic] might hire part-time occupational/entrepreneurial 'practitioners.' "[37] In the 1980s, three-fourths of the female pathbreakers with MBAs who entered corporations in the 1960s or 1970s left corporate management, whereas one-half of their male counterparts did.[38]

Even within these strategies gender differences exist. For example, among entrepreneurs in the hairdressing industry, male apprentices are much more likely to aspire to be a stylist/owner/manager of a centrally located, high fee salon, whereas female apprentices are more likely to plan on working in either a local—and low paid—shop, to work out of their own home, and to stop working during childbearing years. Among pharmacists, women are more likely to choose to work in local, community pharmacies and/or to fill in at larger-scale or hospital pharmacies than to own their own store or work full-time/year-round in a national organization.[39]

In the process of making these choices to accommodate life-style preferences and sex-role expectations, women become practitioners of their occupations and professions. Men are more likely to remain in the linear career path of a bureaucratic hierarchy or to launch their own businesses. The enhanced human capital investment made by women, hence, becomes diffused, devalued, and/or lost as they surrender their investment in the organizational strategy more often than male competitors do. This difference in investment strategies is one of the key reasons why women must be better educated, better qualified, and more experienced than men to compete for advancement. Until and unless comparable organizational investments are made by women, women as a group will continue to have reduced chances of "getting to the top."

"Some professions—notably management—only exist within an organizational context."[40] It should also be recognized that a person can have a managerial career without being completely credentialed professionally. A person with both professional and managerial credentials obviously will tend to have better promotion opportunities.

For most individuals, a career strategy is needed if one is going to have a chance of reaching the top of one's organization or profession.

Barney and Lawrence[41] have developed an economic model of individual career strategies (see Table 7.2). They examine the type of career investments that individuals can make from two dimensions: the number of managers who make the investment and the likelihood that organizations will value that particular investment at promotion time. In Table 7.2, investments made of Type IV, the right clothes, the right hair style, and a college education, are made by almost all aspirants. Hence, although they are necessary prerequisites for career advancement, they alone are insufficient to distinguish one candidate from another. Type III investments are made by the fewest aspirants and, hence, they (getting an MBA degree from a prestigious school or performing well on a committee of critical importance to the organization) are what set candidates apart from one another. Individuals determined to succeed in the sense of rising to the top ought to pursue Type IV, then Type III, then Type I, and maybe Type II activities.[42]

The inclusion of "relationship with a mentor" in the Type I, the low-low category, might surprise some people, but on reflection the rationale is evident. A close relationship with one mentor in one time period can help an individual at a time of competition for promotion only if that mentor plays a key role in selection. As often as not, the fortunes of the protegee suffer with those of the mentor. Hence, the likelihood of one's career success advancing on the basis of one particular mentor-mentee relationship is lower than some of the other strategies.

The fact that women represent over 45% of the U.S. labor force in 1990 and that this percentage is likely to rise further indicates that a theory of women's career development is needed. It is also evident that such a theory is likely to be different from those articulated about men. Laurie Larwood and Barbara A. Gutek[43] suggest that such a theory needs to include human capital investment and career preparation, societal opportunities, the impact of the wife/mother roles (of marriage, pregnancy, and children), timing of career moves, and age. Timing is important for women because, in contrast to many men, women are less likely than men to follow a linear model of career development. Women are more likely than men to take "time out" for children, spousal, and parental support activities. Gallos agrees with the elements identified by Larwood and Gutek and adds considering the implication of "women's distinctive developmental needs and voices."[44]

TABLE 7.2 An Economic Model of Individual Career Strategies

Likely Values at Promotion Time[a]	Number of Managers Who Make + the Investment	
	Low	High
Low	Type I Training in a narrow technology Experience in a specialized business function Relationship with a mentor	Type II Membership on a task force or committee Being a good citizen, e.g., arranging social functions, handling bureaucratic details
High	Type III An MBA degree from a prestigious school Membership on a committee of critical importance to the firm	Type IV The right clothes The right hair style A college education

SOURCE: From Jay B. Barney and Barbara S. Lawrence, "Pin Stripes, Power Ties, and Personal Relationships: The Economics of Career Strategy," in Michael B. Arthur, Douglas T. Hall, and Barbara S. Lawrence (Eds.), *Handbook of Career Theory* (Cambridge, UK: Cambridge University Press, 1989), p. 428. Reprinted by permission.
NOTE: a. In the original this label was as follows: "Likelihood of organizationally perceived value at time of promotion decision (t_2)."

Synchronizing Careers and Personal Life

It is clear that being a wife/mother is no longer the dominant career choice for most women. In 1986, about 55% of U.S. women were married. Not having children has become acceptable as well.[45] Nonetheless, at some point in their careers women typically must address whether and/or how they will deal with being a wife, mother, or other traditional role. The decisions made become critical for career development.

Given that over 45 million workers in the United States are spouses in working couple households (and numerous other millions once were or will be), serious attention must be given to alleviating stresses from taking on multiple roles, from diffusion of identity produced by incompatible sex- and work-role expectations, and from the conflicts arising over wanting to start a family while not destroying one's career. To adequately address the career needs of women it is necessary to deal with the various ways home, family, and career can become "out of sync" with each other—for men as well as for women.

Uma Sekaran and Douglas T. Hall define *asynchronism* as follows: it is "a condition under which the person's or the couple's experience is off schedule in relation to some sort of 'timetable' of development. By timetable, we mean a generally accepted understanding about when a person should have attained particular statuses in his or her life or career."[46] The timetables vary from the family, the organization, and society. Each societal role anticipates a different timetable. The timetable for being married and having children is different from that for work and career milestones.

Furthermore, the career timetables for a society and for a particular organization or profession may diverge under certain conditions as well. For example, a high school graduate who was not self-supporting by the age of 25 would be considered behind schedule, whereas a medical student who was not self-supporting at that age would still be on schedule.

Sekaran and Hall[47] identify *organizational asynchronism,* a situation where one's timing is "off" for promotion or for one's occupational and/or chronological age; *couple asynchronism,* a situation where one's career and that of one's spouse are out of synchronization; and *family asynchronism,* a situation where one's timing of having children differs from society's timing expectations about when one should start a family, for example, the age of 15 might be too early whereas the age of 45 might be too old.

Using these concepts of asynchronism, Sekaran and Hall explore how dual career couples typically deal with the potential for asynchronisms in their lives. They identify two basic patterns: a simultaneous model whereby parenthood parallels employment, and a sequential career-family model where parenthood either follows employment, or employment brackets or follows parenthood. In all of the patterns except the one where parenthood follows employment, one of the spouses' careers gets out of sync with organizational and societal norms. Given that the spouse whose career typically is foregone is that of the woman, it is clear that solving asynchronization problems will aid the career development of women considerably.[48]

Suggestions for addressing these dual career problems and the biases they pose for women include "revising transfer and relocation policies, reexamining nepotism policies, spouse relocation assistance, child-care assistance, flexible work scheduling, two-career recruiting, assisting couples in career management, revising travel policies, and career and couple counseling services or referrals."[49] Proctor & Gamble, General

Foods, IBM, Mellon Bank, and General Motors are among the companies that have initiated policies along these lines. In the 1980s, universities also made efforts to recruit dual-career couples.

Other possible approaches to these issues might be to redefine the meaning of success and career development. An important element of this approach would be to rethink the assumption that careers mean "advancement along a hierarchy of power and prestige."[50] As Barley notes, "The notion of vertical mobility is so well entrenched in career research that many of the terms we frequently use to discuss careers make no sense unless hierarchical structures are presumed. . . . for instance, . . . 'up and out,' 'career ladder,' 'plateauing,' 'promotion,' 'demotion,' or even 'lateral transfer.' "[51] "Slow burn" careers or alternative career paths might provide viable options for both men and women who desire a more balanced life style and who want that as their career anchor. Obviously, for these redefinitions to open opportunities rather than foreclose them, the entire society and all organizations would need to adopt them. For women to become competitive with men, the meaning of career would need to change for men as well as women. Otherwise, only a new version of the gendered economy would develop. The "Mommy Track" proposal in 1989 by Felice Schwartz in the *Harvard Business Review* could constitute such a new version.

The External Career

While the internal career conveys the meaning individuals give to their movement within society and its institutions, the external career identifies the institutional forms of such movement within the social structure. Without denying the importance of the individual, an emphasis on the external career suggests that careers are properties of societies and particular organizations. As such, individuals do not have full control over their work lives. They are made by their careers as much as they make a career.

The emphasis on external careers is related to studies showing that human capital theories derived from neoclassical economics cannot adequately account for discrepancies in career attainment and wage differentials. According to these theories, education, training, hard work, ability, overall effort, and productivity should explain most of the differences in individual achievement. Yet, studies consistently show that firms pay "seniority premiums" not based on productivity, and that firms tend to base wages on a predetermined utility of the job, rather than the human capital brought by the individual.[52]

In Chapter 3, the segmented nature of the labor market and the relative position of women as a group within different firms and industries were described. At this point, Jeffery A. Sonnenfeld's typology of career systems,[53] which suggests that career systems will vary depending on differences among firms themselves, is presented (see Figure 7.2). Market control, size, extent of competition, institutional networks, geographical scope, and nature of the business (e.g., manufacturing vs. retail) are among the factors that can affect the nature of the career systems available to employees.

Sonnenfeld[54] suggests using two dimensions to describe models of career systems: cohort competition and openness of the labor market. Figure 7.2 depicts the resulting models and provides examples of firms whose career systems tend to have the characteristics noted. Before describing them, however, it should be noted that openness of the internal labor market assumes that for many firms, such as IBM, competition exists primarily at entry-level jobs. However, for other firms, such as many smaller high-tech firms, competition is more open to external influences throughout the hierarchy. Competition for advancement also depends on turnover, job vacancies, growth, and demographic changes.

The labels placed in each quadrant illustrate the type of competition and career systems offered by each type of firm. The *Baseball Team* label applies to organizational patterns that promote competition among highly talented performers with transferable talents. The "best" talent is sought and interchangeability within an entire industry enhances one's value and career advancement. The *Academy* label reflects a more stable career system where, once admitted, an individual is developed and made a member of a modern guild. Professional growth is sought by individual employees and fostered as a community and institutional obligation of the employer. Since the organization invests heavily in its employees, interchangeability with other organizations is not so highly desired. The *Club* label suggests a fraternal order. Treating members loyally and fairly is highly valued, as is seniority. Club firms often have monopolies or regulatory buffers protecting them from a more competitive environment. They often see themselves as having a special public mission, for example, a public utility or governmental agency. Status attainment, such as education before employment, has high value in this career system. The *Fortress* label conveys the idea of "an institution

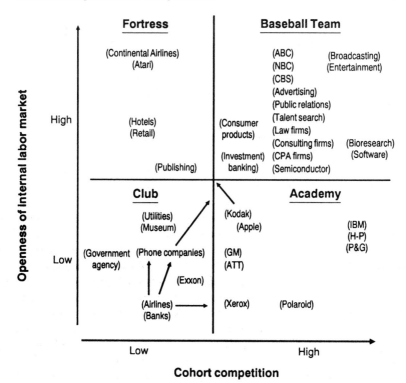

Figure 7.2. Models of Career Systems

SOURCE: From Jeffrey A. Sonnenfeld, "Career System Profiles," in *Handbook of Career Theory*, eds. Michael B. Arthur, Douglas T. Hall, and Barbara S. Lawrence (New York: Cambridge University Press, 1989), p. 215. Copyright 1989 by Cambridge University Press. Reprinted by permission.

under siege, with low commitment to individuals. The larger goal is institutional survival, even at the cost of individual members."[55]

It matters greatly in which of these career systems one attempts to enter and to work. Academy-like firms provide great security[56] but have been notoriously difficult to penetrate. Preferring to make rather than buy mid-career talent, organizational loyalty and continuity are highly valued. If old patterns persist, major academy-like corporations, such as IBM, Dupont, Proctor & Gamble, Johnson & Johnson, General Motors, Merck, Corning Glass, Digital, and Cargill, will require a generation of new entry-level hires before enough female personnel will even be in the queue for high-level positions.

It will be easier for women and minorities to enter the career systems offered by the Team firms, that is, by the most competitive and peripheral to the economy (see Chapter 3). It is also evident that the probability of leaving such an organization through dismissal, job layoffs, or resignation is very high. Threat of layoffs is higher only in the Fortress firms. To have a successful career as traditionally defined, an individual might prefer the reduced risks of jobs in the Academies and Clubs, but it is within these hierarchies that the "glass ceiling" is the most apparent and the hardest to break.

From the perspective of the external career, careers are part of the social structure, and consciously or unconsciously, they will be organized in such a way so as to perpetuate the more essential social stratification features of society. As Barley suggests,

> the temporal structure of vertical careers might operate as a subtle mechanism for reproducing a multiplex stratification system while otherwise appearing to satisfy a philosophy of equal opportunity. Representatives of underprivileged groups would still advance, but at slower rates. Because advancement opportunities appear to decline with age (Lawrence, 1984; Rosenbaum, 1984), a progressively smaller proportion of the minority group would arrive at successively higher strata before their age prohibited further advancement. The upshot would be to ensure that the top positions in a hierarchy remain heavily populated by majority group members but that there are enough minorities in mid-level positions to diffuse charges of blatant discrimination.[57]

It would appear that this collective use of the career system operates to maintain gender stratification as well.

In the 1980s, an increasing number of firms lost their protective buffers to competition when deregulation occurred. For women and minorities deregulation had the effect of opening up the career system, of moving it from an Academy type to a Team type. This opening of doors, however, may have given the illusion of progress. Many women and minorities might have thought they had entered the Academy or Club type of career system where stability and movement through a hierarchy was possible. But, as both men and women are learning, competition has a negative side. More frequent career changes might well be the norm for the 1990s.

These different career systems reflect another significant factor influencing gender differences in careers—the pay one receives. Joyce R. Shackett and John M. Trapani developed a model to assess the effect of government regulation and market structure wage levels.[58] They found that for the men, privately owned, unregulated industries paid less than regulated ones, that nonprofit industries paid below-average wages, and that governmental agencies paid average wages. For women, higher wages were paid by nonprofit, regulated, and governmental organizations. Black women did not benefit as much as white women in these organizations. The more positive pay level for women in these industries was due to regulation and to the higher degrees of occupational stratification.

Conclusion

The ways careers link individuals to the rest of society provide clues for developing individual strategies for career advancement. Knowledge of the internal and external career can help individuals develop strategies of their own.

Studies of the internal career indicate that individuals must be proactive to have successful careers. Being proactive means having career goals, an understanding of one's career anchor, a career plan, and strategies and tactics concerning timing, moves, family, and relationships that will enhance the chances of success. Competence alone is insufficient.

An individual's goals can and do change over time. Nonetheless, a regular time for setting career goals annually and monitoring them monthly or quarterly will facilitate attaining career success and being flexible to changing circumstances, whether they are personal, organizational, societal, or familial. In setting goals, consulting others—peers, parents, teachers, mentors—can be helpful. External supports and awareness of how occupations interrelate with career options will improve the utility of the goal-setting process.

Passive strategies for pursuing a career seldom lead to high levels of success. Working hard and knowing the details alone are insufficient. Enhancing one's skills, appearance, motivational levels, enthusiasm, knowledge of the institutional perspective, climate, management and leadership style, and being able to read the political environment are all critical parts of career development. If career success means reaching the top of a particular organization, maintaining continuous, full-time employment—even if married and with children—is vital. Prerequisites of success are good health, enhancement of the comfort zone for one's co-workers, and a sense of humor. Avoiding unnecessary criticism of colleagues, predecessors, and competitors is as important as being prepared and performing well when giving reports and presentations. One must be willing to take risks, work long hours when needed, travel, develop a strong record of management and leadership performance, and make the record visible. Identifying role models, obtaining mentors, joining networks and professional associations, and obtaining and fine-tuning appropriate skills for the next stage of one's career are all useful, if not fully sufficient, strategies for advancement.[59]

Knowledge of the external career reveals the critical importance employing institutions play in career development and advancement. Business organizations in the United States have had a privileged access to political power, contributing to the national vision of society, and controlling national resources.[60] In 1990, this privileged position remains, and allows businesses to shape and structure societal career options.

Notes

1. C. Brooklyn Derr and Andre Laurent, "The Internal and External Career: A Theoretical and Cross-cultural Perspective," in *Handbook on Career Theory,* eds. Michael B. Arthur, Douglas T. Hall, and Barbara S. Lawrence, 454-474 (Cambridge, UK: Cambridge University Press, 1989).

2. Derr and Laurent, "The Internal and External Career," 466.

3. Edgar H. Schein, *Career Dynamics* (Reading, MA: Addison-Wesley, 1978); and Edgar H. Schein, "Individuals and Careers," in *Handbook of Organizational Behavior,* ed. J. W. Lorsch, 155-171 (Englewood Cliffs, NJ: Prentice-Hall, 1987). See also D. E. Super, *The Psychology of Careers* (New York: Harper & Row, 1957).

4. Super, *The Psychology of Careers,* 155.

5. Super, *The Psychology of Careers,* 158.

6. Super, *The Psychology of Careers,* 158.

7. The concept of a career anchor was developed by Edgar H. Schein as the result of a longitudinal study of managerial careers conducted in the 1960s of 44 alumni of the Sloan School of Management at Massachusetts Institute of Technology. Cf. Edgar H. Schein, "How Career Anchors Hold Executives to Career Paths," *Personnel* 52(3) (1975): 11-24. See also Schein, *Career Dynamics.*

8. Schein, *Career Dynamics,* 169.

9. Schein, *Career Dynamics,* 169.

10. Schein, *Career Dynamics,* 169. Emphasis in the original. See also, Paul Evans and Fernando Bartolome, *Must Success Cost So Much?* (New York: Basic Books, 1981).

11. Schein, *Career Dynamics,* 169.

12. Schein, *Career Dynamics,* 169.

13. Schein, *Career Dynamics,* 170.

14. Joan V. Gallos, "Exploring Women's Development: Implications for Career Theory, Practice, and Research," in *Handbook of Career Theory*, eds. Michael B. Arthur, Douglas T. Hall, and Barbara S. Lawrence, 110-132 (Cambridge, UK: Cambridge University Press, 1989). See also Joan Bardwick, "The Seasons of a Woman's Life," in *Women's Lives: New Theory, Research, and Policy*, ed. D. McGuigan (Ann Arbor: University of Michigan Center for Continuing Education of Women, 1980).

15. Gallos, "Exploring Women's Development," 115.

16. Gallos, "Exploring Women's Development," 120.

17. M. Hennig and A. Jardim, *The Managerial Woman* (New York: Pocket Books, 1978); C. Gilligan, "Restoring the Missing Text of Women's Development to Life Cycle Theories," in *Women's Lives: New Theory, Research, and Policy*, ed. D. McGuigan (Ann Arbor: University of Michigan Center for Continuing Education of Women, 1980); and R. Josselson, *Finding Herself: Pathways to Identity Development in Women* (San Francisco: Jossey-Bass, 1987).

18. Gallos, "Exploring Women's Development," 120. See also L. R. Gallese, *Women Like Us: What Is Happening to the Women of the Harvard Business School, Class of 75—The Women Who Had the First Chance to Make It to the Top?* (New York: William Morrow, 1985); and J. Abramson and B. Franklin, *Where Are They Now?* (New York: Doubleday, 1986).

19. Bardwick, "The Seasons of a Woman's Life."

20. Gallos, "Exploring Women's Development," 121-128.

21. Gallos, "Exploring Women's Development," 120.

22. Gallos, "Exploring Women's Development," 121.

23. Hennig and Jardim, *The Managerial Woman.*

24. Sarah Hardesty and Nehama Jacobs, *Success and Betrayal: The Crisis of Women in Corporate America* (New York: Franklin Watts, 1986).

25. Gallos, "Exploring Women's Development," 121.

26. A. Taylor, "Why Women Managers are Bailing Out," *Fortune* 18 August 1986, 16-23.

27. Gallese, *Women Like Us.*

28. Victoria Tashjian, *Don't Blame the Baby: Why They Leave the Corporation* (Wilmington, DE: Wick & Co., 1990). See also Cathy Trost, "Women Managers Quit Not for Family but to Advance their Corporate Climb," *Wall Street Journal* 2 May 1990, B1.

29. "ORC Research Challenges 'Mommy Track,' " *Organizational Research Practice* (Princeton, NJ: Opinion Research Corporation, n.d. Incidental report which appeared in winter of 1989-90), 3. See also Trost, "Women Managers Quit."

30. Uma Sekaran and Douglas T. Hall, "Asynchronism in Dual-Career and Family Linkages," in *Handbook of Career Theory*, eds. Michael B. Arthur, Douglas T. Hall, and Barbara S. Lawrence, 168 (Cambridge, UK: Cambridge University Press, 1989).

31. Gallos, "Exploring Women's Development," 124.

32. R. Brown, "Work Histories, Career Strategies and Class Structure," in *Social Class and the Division of Labor*, eds. A. Giddens and G. Mackenzie (Cambridge, UK: Cambridge University Press, 1982). See also Rosemary Crompton with Kay Sanderson, "Credentials and Careers: Some Implications of the Increase in Professional Qualifications Amongst Women," *Sociology* 20(1) (1986): 25-41.

33. Crompton and Sanderson, "Credentials and Careers."

34. Sharon Tucker, "Careers of Men and Women MBAs, 1950-1980," *Work and Occupations* 12(2) (May 1985): 166-185.

35. Burton F. Schaffer, Hamid Ahmadi, and D. Ordell Calkins, "Academic Qualifications of Women with Degrees in Business," *Journal of Education for Business* 61(7) (1986): 321-324.

36. Trost, "Women Managers Quit."

37. Crompton and Sanderson, "Credentials and Careers," 32.

38. Tucker, "Careers of Men and Women MBAs."

39. Crompton and Sanderson, "Credentials and Careers," 38.

40. Rosemary Crompton, "Gender, Status, and Professionalism," *Sociology* 21(3) (1987): 413-428, cited from p. 423.

41. Jay B. Barney and Barbara S. Lawrence, "Pin Stripes, Power Ties, and Personal Relationships: The Economics of Career Strategy," in *Handbook of Career Theory,* eds. Michael B. Arthur, Douglas T. Hall, and Barbara S. Lawrence, 417-436 (Cambridge, UK: Cambridge University Press, 1989).

42. Barney and Lawrence, "Pin Stripes," 430.

43. Laurie Larwood and Barbara A. Gutek, "Working Toward a Theory of Women's Career Development," in *Women's Career Development,* eds. B. A. Gutek and L. Larwood (Newbury Park, CA: Sage, 1987).

44. Gallos, "Exploring Women's Development," 127.

45. Rena Bartos, "The New Woman—Going Beyond Derived Status," *Marketing Communications* 11(3) (1986): 35-38.

46. Sekaran and Hall, "Asynchronism in Dual-Career," 164.

47. Sekaran and Hall, "Asynchronism in Dual-Career," 165.

48. See, for example, P. Daniels and K. Weingarten, *Sooner or Later: The Timing of Parenthood in Adult Lives* (New York: W. W. Norton, 1982); and Uma Sekaran, *Dual-Career Families: Contemporary Organizational and Counseling Issues* (San Francisco, CA: Jossey-Bass, 1986).

49. Sekaran and Hall, "Asynchronism in Dual-Career," 164. (See Chapter 5 in this volume for more details.)

50. Stephen R. Barley, "Careers, Identities, and Institutions: The Legacy of the Chicago School of Sociology," in *Handbook of Career Theory,* eds. Michael B. Arthur, Douglas T. Hall, and Barbara S. Lawrence, 48, 41-65 (Cambridge, UK: Cambridge University Press, 1989).

51. Barley, "Careers, Identities, and Institutions," 148.

52. J. A. Sonnenfeld, "Career System Profiles and Strategic Staffing," in *Handbook of Career Theory,* eds. Michael B. Arthur, Douglas T. Hall, and Barbara S. Lawrence, 208-209 (Cambridge, UK: Cambridge University Press, 1989).

53. Sonnenfeld, "Career System Profiles," 202-226.

54. Sonnenfeld, "Career System Profiles," 214-217.

55. Sonnenfeld, "Career System Profiles," 216.

56. Sonnenfeld, "Career System Profiles," 216-217.

57. Barley, "Careers, Identities and Institutions," 58-59.

58. Joyce R. Shackett and John M. Trapani, "Earnings Differentials and Market Structure," *Journal of Human Resources* 22(4) (1987): 518-531.

59. For more discussion of career tactics and strategies, see, among others, Lee Gardenswartz and Anita Rowe, "Getting to the Top: The 5 Success Secrets of Women Who Have Made It," *Executive Female* (November/December 1987): 34-35; Hennig and Jardim, *The Managerial Woman;* Gary N. Powell, *Men and Women in Management* (Newbury Park, CA: Sage, 1988), 201ff.; Eleanor Smith, "Upward Mobility: Black and

White Women Administrators," *Journal of National Association of NAWDAC* [Women, Deans, Administrators, and Counselors] 48(3) (1985): 28-32; Lynda A. Kuyper, "Career Development of Women in the Administration of Higher Education: Contributing Factors," *Journal of NAWDAC* (Summer 1987): 3-4.

60. Charles Lindblom, *Politics and Markets* (New York: Basic Books, 1977).

PART III

Alternatives for Change

Part III considers policies that could be enacted to facilitate women's success, not only in advancing their careers, but also in integrating their personal, economic, and public lives.

Chapter 8 explores the roles government and business play in shaping women's career options. Chapter 9 describes a variety of alternative frameworks that have been proposed to address the issues raised as women seek equality in the U.S. labor force.

8

The Role of Government and Business

Individuals make career decisions within the constraints imposed by employing institutions and governmental policies. They also make such decisions to accommodate needs they perceive in their daily lives. No one acts in a vacuum. The personal options women have depend on the collective decisions made by business and government. The first part of this chapter examines the role government plays in promoting affirmative action, equal opportunity, positive women's employment, pay equity, and child-care policies. The last half reviews alternative strategies that employing organizations can adopt to enable women to break through the various "glass ceilings."

Affirmative Action and Equal Opportunity

Title VII of the Civil Rights Act of 1964 and the Equal Pay Act of 1963 laid the foundation for affirmative action and equal opportunity for women. Even now, however, the commitment of organizations to the spirit of these laws varies considerably. Powell[1] identifies three categories of organizational responses: (1) proactive recruitment and promotion of women and minorities before the federal laws required it; (2) minimal compliance to federal affirmative action requirements, the hiring of women only after prolonged pressure and legal action from the government or women's groups; and (3) refusal to address sex discrimination with the hope that the emphasis on equal opportunity

AUTHOR'S NOTE: This chapter was written and researched with Kimberly Fisher.

159

will recede with time and changing political winds. Different strategies and tactics are needed to deal with each form of response.

Senior personnel executives of large corporations surveyed by the Conference Board in 1979 indicated that awareness of federal laws and regulations ranked first in the 10 factors most encouraging their companies to hire women.[2] The other factors included commitment on the part of the chief executive officer; establishment of organizational goals and timetables; development of an Equal Employment Opportunity (EEO) policy; analyses of women's positions within the company; awareness of large back-pay awards in class-action suits; monitoring of EEO results against plans; dissemination of EEO policy; identification of special problem areas in utilizing women; and changes in personnel practices on special programs to improve opportunities for women.[3] This Conference Board survey emphasized the importance of further federal legislation.

The critical impact that federal action has on employees lead many strategists to believe that more federal involvement would be helpful. As a consequence, in addition to affirmative action and equal opportunity policies, some efforts have been made to develop a more comprehensive national women's employment policy. According to advocates, such a policy would rest on several components: (1) knowledge of historical trends and the problems women face in the U.S. segmented labor force; (2) multilevel programs addressing the overall economic structure, its underlying labor market mechanisms, and women's mobility within that structure; (3) programs that address the interrelationship between women's labor force work and house/home/family work; (4) evaluations of previous policies and strategies, such as unionization, affirmative action, and comparable worth; and (5) a political action plan so policies will be implemented.[4] The components for such a policy are obviously still being constructed. A recent thrust has been made in component (3) in the child-care area.

Child-Care Policies

Child-care policies affect individual careers as well as efforts to change the national sex-role ideology. In 1986, over 70% of women age 20 to 44 were in the U.S. labor force. Most of these women must address child care along with other career issues. In the 1990s all levels of government in the United States—federal, state, and local—are seeking new policy options to meet the child-care needs of the labor force.

Federal

The U.S. government provided limited child-care assistance for the first time with the Lanham Act, adopted during World War II. In the 1960s, President Richard Nixon vetoed the first proposal for a national child-care policy. In the 1988 presidential campaign, child care became a major issue. Attention was drawn to the fact that the United States is the only major industrial country that has not developed a national child-care policy. The 100th Congress considered close to 150 bills on the subject, but none have become law.

The Bush administration and many Senate leaders in 1990 sought a minimalist approach to child-care policies. President Bush has repeatedly expressed support of income tax breaks for the working poor and his opposition to subsidies and parental-leave policies.[5] Such policies, although an advance over previous ones, unfortunately do not open many day-care choices for poor women. Even so, supporters of the tax-break initiatives gained sufficient power in the U.S. House of Representatives to craft the child-care bill passed in April 1990 that focuses primarily on earned-income tax breaks.[6]

The Senate has also modified requests from religious groups to preserve church day care in a revision of the Senate's 1989 version of the Act for Better Child Care (A.B.C. bill). Unlike the 1988 child-care bill, the 1990 version provides federal funding for day-care centers run by religious institutions. This funding requires such centers to meet three criteria: religious principles may not be taught at the center; centers may not limit potential enrollment exclusively to members of the religious group; and centers that receive more than 80% of their funds from government agencies may not give preference to children from families associated with the institution.[7]

The general popularity of child-care legislation ensured that some version of day care legislation would pass in 1990. Such groups as the Children's Defense Fund considered day care a main test of the decade for House Democratic leaders.[8] Nevertheless, the bill that did pass has been described by critics as more of an anti-poverty bill than a child-care bill.[9] The bill phases out dependent-care tax credits for people in higher income brackets, expands funds for Head Start, offers states incentives to encourage day care at schools, establishes a grant and voucher system that states will distribute to low-income parents for day care, and requires states to set loose standards for child care. The main portion of the bill, three-fifths of its $5 billion cost, will come from earned-income tax breaks.[10] This legislation, while providing minimal relief, nevertheless increases the burden on states to address child-care issues.

State

State response to the need for day care has varied widely. The New Jersey legislature has encountered little difficulty convincing businesses to build day-care centers since developers in that state have begun using day-care facilities as a marketing tool. In May 1990, the New Jersey Family Leave Act went into effect, establishing the most generous family-leave policy in the country. The law requires businesses with over 100 employees to give 12 weeks of unpaid leave with benefits every two years for employees having or adopting a child or having a serious illness in the immediate family. On returning to work, the same or an equal job with the same pay must be given to the employee. By 1992, the law will be extended to companies with 50 or more employees, encompassing about half of all employed New Jerseyites. Violators will be fined $5,000 and are subject to being sued.[11]

By 1990, most states were considering some form of day-care policy. The Women's Legal Defense Fund reports that 25 states and Puerto Rico have family-leave laws, and four of these states, Connecticut, Maine, Pennsylvania, and Wisconsin, guarantee leave for both newborn care and family illness.[12] Many states are also offering tax incentives for employers who provide day care assistance. Table 8.1 presents a brief overview of the type of tax incentives selected states provide for employer-sponsored child-care programs.

The tax incentive programs are relatively new, and comprehensive studies of their effectiveness have not yet been completed. Nonetheless, at the state level, tax incentive legislation remains the most popular means of addressing child-care issues.[13] Progressive states like California, Connecticut, and Oregon extend a variety of tax credit options to corporate taxpayers offering financial assistance in (1) the building, start up, or operating costs of child-care centers; (2) employee child-care benefits; and (3) information and referral services for child care. Since 1984, child-care legislation for Arizona has resulted in strengthening the licensing and regulation of day-care providers, and amortization of construction and start-up costs of day-care facilities.[14]

TABLE 8.1 Tax Incentives for Employer Sponsored Child-Care Programs

State	Type of Incentive	Activity Covered	Cap	Tracking Mechanism	Participation Rates	Cost	Enactment Date
Arizona	Amortization of child care facility	Start-up expenses	None	No	Unknown	Unknown	1984
California	30% credit	Financial assistance R&Rs	$600/year full-time; $300/year part-time	Yes	Unknown	Unknown	1988
	50% credit[a]	Start-up expenses	$30,000	Yes	Unknown	Unknown	1988
Connecticut	Tax Credit	Financial assistance	$75,000	Yes	1986-22 businesses 1987-34 businesses 1988-36 businesses	$ 97,000 $263,433 $406,411	1986
	40%	Operating expenses	$20,000	Yes	1986-4 businesses	Unknown	1986
Florida	100% deduction	Start-up costs	None	No	Unknown	Unknown	1985
Maine	Tax credit	Financial assistance ex-AFDC employees	Lower of $5,000; 20% of costs; or $100 per child	No	Unknown	Unknown	1987
Maryland (local)	Property tax credit	Property improvement	None	No	Unknown	Unknown	1986

(continued)

TABLE 8.1 Continued

State	Type of Incentive	Activity Covered	Cap	Tracking Mechanism	Participation Rates	Cost	Enactment Date
New Mexico	30% tax credit	Financial assistance/operating expenses	$30,000	Yes	One claimant	$2,000	1983
Ohio	Tax credit	Financial assistance for qualified employees	$300/child/year up to 2 years	No	Unknown	Unknown	1982
Oregon	50% credit	Financial assistance R&Rs Start-up costs	$2,500/year employee $100,000	Yes	Less than 10 businesses 25-30 businesses 2 businesses	Unknown	1987
Pennsylvania	Employment incentive assistance	Financial assistance for ex-AFDC employees	$600/employee during first year of employment	No	Unknown	Unknown	1985
Rhode Island	30% tax credit	Financial assistance	$30,000 per year	Yes	3 businesses 2 in progress	Unknown	1988

SOURCE: Reprinted from Cate Sonnier, "States Offer Incentives for Child Care Programs," *The Fiscal Letter*, (March/April 1989) (Denver, CO: National Conference of State Legislatures), pp. 5, 6, 11. Reprinted by permission.
NOTE: a. Estimated.

State governments have not only been saddled with the burden of enticing businesses to support child care, but they also have the responsibility for regulating day-care facilities. State regulations range from statutes requiring workers to wash their hands at regular intervals to bans on corporal punishment to limitations on the number of children who can be attended by a single caregiver. A 1990 study found that most regulations do not significantly affect the availability of child care.[15]

Municipalities

Some of the most creative initiatives occur at the municipal level. In Sacramento, California, zoning and planning ordinances are used to expand the supply of child care.[16] Developers who include a child-care center in a commercial complex receive priority consideration. In Hartford, Connecticut, a developer gets six additional square feet of floor area for each square foot of child-care space that is provided. In Phoenix, Arizona, similar attempts are being made to create a partnership between the city and its developers in increasing the number of day-care centers.[17]

Strategies for Employing Institutions

Tokenism and Company Policy

Employing institutions can have considerable influence over social attitudes of the general population, not just their immediate employees. Studies consistently show that tokenism (having fewer than 15% of women or minorities) in a work group exaggerates gender differences.[18] Workers tend to focus on gender differences and sex roles of a female employee when she is the only woman at a particular level. Small numbers of women in an organization are expected to represent all women. Hence, the mistakes of one or a few individuals are projected onto the entire group. In addition, small numbers of women in work groups appear to be more difficult to integrate into the system than larger numbers. Additionally, sexual harassment appears to stem from "skewed sex ratios favoring men."[19] These findings suggest that increasing the numbers of women in each occupational, professional, and managerial position beyond the token level offers an effective strategy for breaking glass ceilings. This strategy would require having more than 15% and preferably a minimum of 35% of women in each category. At this point, sex and gender differences in interaction, behavior, and promotion become less significant.[20] A minimum of 15% (or more than one in small groups) is essential for the worst effects of tokenism to be addressed; yet, this 15% level also triggers overt resistance to women managers.[21]

Studies show that women administrators/managers who are tokens often feel stigmatized. They are neither "normal women" nor "normal administrators/managers." This stigma pushes the token to take drastic action to resolve this dilemma. Ultimately, organizations must accept responsibility for helping to change the sex-role ideology that produces the stigmatization and tokenism.[22] The organization must eliminate incentives for managers and, to the extent possible, clients to discriminate against women and minorities. The simplest solution may be promoting more women and minorities in top line management positions.[23]

Systematically Addressing Sexism

Studies in the mid-1980s[24] found that male graduate business students at several universities had substantially more negative attitudes toward women as executives than women did. No changes in the level of negativity had occurred from 1975 to 1983. Such results indicate that organizational policies and firm leadership from upper-level administration will be essential for women to receive equal opportunities. Given that many of these students will be among the top managers/leaders in the 1990s, attention needs to be paid to how their personal biases can be neutralized, if not converted to a more positive stance.

Male and female managers have different perceptions of women's opportunities in the work place. A 1985 Administrative Management Society Committee survey found that close to 7 of 10 women believed advancement was harder for females; whereas close to 6 of 10 men believed it was no harder for women than for men to advance.[25] The *Harvard Business Review* reported in 1985 that women saw less opportunity within their companies than women in comparable positions had perceived in 1965![26] Men in the survey were more inclined to view women as executive material, but both sexes thought women preferred not to work for another woman. Another survey of undergraduates in the early 1980s found that women students in a personnel management course were as likely to stereotype women managerial aspirants in a negative fashion as the men students.[27] The fact that students of both sexes had just completed courses dealing with federal fair employment practices, Title VII, The Equal Pay Act, and related topics suggests even less progress toward gender neutrality than anticipated. Recognition of differing perceptions of male and female managers may become an important part of this behavioral modification process.

Several specific steps can be taken to address sexism systematically. First, the organization can reaffirm its commitment to affirmative action goals. Second, managers' bonuses can be tied as incentive compensation to affirmative action and equal opportunity goals. Third, a woman's rotating advisory panel can meet regularly (at least quarterly) with the CEO to discuss interests, aspirations, and issues and to monitor progress. Fourth, women's progress can be tracked on a specific timetable. Merck used this procedure and increased female managerial staff by 40%.[28] Fifth, affirmative action and equal opportunity goals can be merged with productivity efforts to highlight female competencies and contributions. Sixth, organizational (company/corporate) support can be given for a women's network of entry-, middle-, and upper-level managers. Seventh, both male and female high-level officers can explore ways of moving "women's issues" into the human resource arena so that appropriate policies will become the organizational norm. Specifically, this means reassessing what factors constitute "disabilities" for career advancement and success. Eighth, the CEO's spouse and children can be asked to help advance affirmative action and equal opportunity. Ninth, equal pay, participatory management, and day care can be featured company policies.

Clarifying Career Investment Decisions

Certain types of career investments raise the probability of promotion more than others, and organizations can help women and minorities by identifying what those investments are in that organization. Managers can also develop appropriate reward structures to make the particular investments visible to aspirants.[29] Once the human resource managers have isolated the types of career investments valuable to an organization, surveys of employees can be conducted to ascertain the extent to which employees accurately perceive the nature of these investments. Career investments promoted within an organization should coincide to a high degree with the perceptions of the employees

about the investments they personally need to make. In addition, organizations can provide financial support to women and minorities seeking to make these types of investments.

Providing Mentors

Mentors promote the professional and organizational development of
other, usually less experienced, employees. Although, as noted in Chapter 7, having a mentor does not gurantee success, it can help. Both men
and women in mentor relationships tend to have more job success and
job satisfaction. Women who work with mentors report significantly
more often that their careers are on a fast track than women without
such mentors.[30]

Mentoring might well be more effective as a career strategy for
women than it has been for men.[31] In addition to helping women
develop the contacts, credentials, and skills necessary for success,
mentors facilitate refocusing attitudes and personality characteristics
toward the corporate/organizational managerial role.

Characteristics of helpful mentors include: "(1) willingness of the
mentor to share his/her knowledge and understanding, (2) knowledge
of the organization and its people, (3) being of high rank, (4) peer
respect, (5) knowledge of the use of power, (6) upward mobility,
and (7) organizational power."[32] Mentors help overcome such problems as tokenism, inadequate access to appropriate networks, sex-role
stereotyping, male-biased socialization practices, negative norms about
cross-gender relationships at work, and dependence on an inappropriate
power base, which can impede career advancement for women.[33] Although mentors tend to work with junior employees who have similar
social styles, women can attract the attention of potential mentors by
visibly demonstrating the potential to excel.[34]

Providing Female Role Models

Although male mentors are valuable, males cannot substitute for
female role models.[35] For this reason, organizations should strive to
increase the visibility of female leadership and accomplishments. Female role models can be particularly important guides to help new
employees learn to cope with sex-role conflicts.[36] Female role models
can assist younger women in avoiding structural constraints within the
organization, industry, and occupation. Males might not even be aware
of these obstacles to female aspirants. Women are also more likely to

be aware of and be willing to address issues of sexual harassment and subtle forms of sex discrimination.[37]

Enhancing Women's Positions of Power

Promotion requires competence. It also requires promotees to learn to acquire, hold, and use power to the benefit of both themselves and the organization. Promotion additionally requires demonstrating leadership ability. Organizations can facilitate the career and managerial success of its female employees by moving them into positions of authority, but, more importantly, they can counsel women to seek elective offices in professional associations, to take some risks on task forces, and to serve in highly visible positions to enhance this power image.[38]

Promoting Colleagueship Among Company Peers

Peers are those in a similar position on an organizational chart. Colleagues are those we accept as equal to us in competence, expertise, and personal attributes—those we trust, accept, and feel comfortable with. It has been difficult for women to become "one of us" rather than "one of them." According to Helen H. Solomons and Aubrey Cramer, women must pass three hurdles to become colleagues: gaining the trust of peers and senior officials, convincing these people to depend on women employees, and developing patterns of office behavior that reduce the physical and social distance.[39] Although individual employees must play a major role in overcoming these barriers, management training and development programs can assist in promoting colleagueship for females as well. Case studies of the issues involved in the transition from peer to colleague can be included in training programs. Mentors and role models can focus on the topic. Networking within and outside the organization can provide reality testing, ideas, and support during the transition. Attention can be paid to pitfalls created for women by clothing expectations, travel circumstances, and social functions in business contexts that establish both colleagueship and power bases in the organization and within the industry.[40]

Providing Child Care and a Positive Family/Work Relationship

Organizations seeking to open doors for women must systematically address the conflict between family and work responsibilities.[41]

Although employers generally perceive that child care increases productivity and improves employee morale, only 14% of U.S. corporations offer child-care benefits to their employees—arguing that the
bottom line costs outweigh the benefits.[42] Nevertheless, the number of
day-care centers built in or near the workplace has increased from
110 in 1979 to 4,000 in 1989.[43] While the growth of business involvement is encouraging, it is far from sufficient. In 1988, only 2% of
employers sponsored on-site or near-site child care.[44]

Companies at the forefront of this issue project that their long-term
savings will more than compensate for start-up costs. AT&T has created two funds totaling $10 million to support child- and elder-care
efforts in the community. In addition, AT&T employees needing to care
for elderly parents or born or adopted children may take up to one year
of leave with guaranteed reinstatement.[45] Employees can also contribute up to $5,000 per year to a pre-tax fund for child or elder care. The
chairman of the board of AT&T, Robert Allen defended his company's
program by noting that the program meets a vital need in the changed
workplace. It publicly acknowledges that children and the elderly exist
and that work life and personal life must accommodate each other.[46]
Programs such as this recognize the diverse nature of family care needs
and the importance of business accommodation of these needs.

Similar changes in business attitudes have occurred in America's
northern neighbor, Canada. Canadian unions now routinely negotiate
for both weekday and weekend shifts. Addition of the new shifts, they
note, will enable two-income families to better coordinate schedules so
that one parent can be at home with the children while the other works.[47]
A contract developed during negotiations between the Canadian Auto
Workers' Union and Canada's "Big Three" auto companies requires the
corporations to contribute five cents per worker per hour to a fund that
provides child care.[48] Again, these policies allow men to play a role in
child care by opening benefits to all workers, not just women.

Such programs are gaining support among American workers. A
recent survey conducted by the Gallup Organization for the Employee
Benefit Research Institute found that 81% of Americans surveyed
support legislation mandating leave for care of newborns and newly
adopted children and for family illness, and 53% additionally supported provisions requiring employers to continue to pay workers on
such leave.[49] Moreover, 77% believe that employees on paid or unpaid leave should continue to receive health-care benefits.[50]

Nevertheless, businesses have failed to account for one growing group of workers: relocated employees. As modern society becomes more mobile, workers require new day-care options during the relocation process. A 1988 study conducted by management consulting firm Moran, Stahl, and Boyes found that 60% of relocated employees report that the lack of company sensitivity to the absence of transitional child-care and spouse relocation programs posed the most difficult problems during their move.[51]

Conclusion

Both government and business will need to address the multitude of issues facing women and minorities if progress toward equality is to occur. A wide variety of options can and must be taken to redress inequalities in the work force. Citizens need to encourage their employers and all levels of government to pursue these and other yet-to-be created strategies.

Notes

1. Gary N. Powell, *Women & Men in Management* (Newbury Park, CA: Sage, 1988), 216-220.

2. Powell, *Women & Men in Management,* 226.

3. Powell, *Women & Men in Management,* 226, taken almost verbatim from Table 7.1, Factors Contributing to the Overall Success of EEO Efforts.

4. For a more detailed discussion see Christine Bose and Glenna Spitze, eds., *Ingredients for Women's Employment Policy* (Albany: State University of New York Press, 1987). See also Linda Tarr-Whelan and Lynne Crofton Isensee, eds., *The Women's Economic Justice Agenda: Ideas for the State* (Washington, DC: The National Center for Policy Alternatives, 1987).

5. Cathy Trost, "House Approves Bill Expanding Child-Care Aid: Legislation Faces Reshaping with Senate Conferees, and Bush's Opposition," *Wall Street Journal* 6 October 1989, A12.

6. "A Good Child Care Bill," *Washington Post Weekly Edition* 9-15 April 1990, 27.

7. Robert P. Hey, "Coalition Sought on Day-Care Bill: Compromise to Meld Two Federal Funding Bills Still Might Be Derailed by Church-State Concerns," *Arizona Republic* 5 June 1989, 8.

8. Frank Swoboda, "Baby-Sitting the Child Care Bill: Rival House Committees Are at Odds over Financing," *Washington Post Weekly Edition* 29 January-4 February 1990, 34.

9. "A Good Child Care Bill," *Washington Post Weekly Edition,* 27.

10. "A Good Child Care Bill," *Washington Post Weekly Edition,* 27.

11. Milo Geyelin, "States Try to Balance Job, Family," *Wall Street Journal* 4 May 1990, B1.

12. Frank Swoboda, "Parental Leave Goes on the Fast Track: House Gets Ready to Vote on Family Time Off," *Washington Post Weekly Edition* 25 February 1990, 35.

13. Phoebe Stambaugh, "Report to the Governor on Child Care Tax Incentive Programs," unpublished report for the Arizona Governor's Office of Women's Services (1989), 5, Phoenix, Arizona.

14. Stambaugh, "Report to the Governor," 5.

15. William T. Gormley, Jr. and the Robert La Follette Institute of Public Affairs, "State Regulations and the Supply of Day Care Services," paper presented at the Midwest Political Science Association Annual Meeting, Chicago, IL, 5-7 April 1990, 15.

16. Stambaugh, "Report to the Governor."

17. Karen Berney, "Public-Private Initiatives," *Nation's Business* 76 (May 1988): 22.

18. Rosabeth Kanter, *Men and Women of the Corporation* (New York: Basic Books, 1977); Jennifer Crocker and Kathleen M. McGraw, "What's Good for the Goose Is Not Good for the Gander," *American Behavioral Scientist* 27(3) (1984): 357-369.

19. Ann M. Morrison and Mary Ann Von Glinow, "Women and Minorities in Management," *American Psychologist* 45(2) (1990): 200-208; and Barbara A. Gutek, *Sex and the Workplace* (San Francisco, CA: Jossey-Bass, 1985).

20. Gutek, *Sex and the Workplace.*

21. Susan Fraker, "Why Women Aren't Getting to the Top," *Fortune* 16 (April 1984): 40-45.

22. Catherine Marshall, "The Stigmatized Woman: The Professional Woman in a Male Sex-Types Career," *Journal of Educational Administration* 22(2) (1985): 131-151.

23. Cf. Laurie Larwood, Barbara Gutek, and Urs E. Gattiker, "Perspectives on Institutional Discrimination and Resistance to Change," *Groups and Organization Studies* 9(3) (1984): 333-352; and Laurie Larwood, Eugene Szwajkowski, and Suzanna Rose, "Sex and Race Discrimination Resulting from Manager-Client Relationships: Applying the Rational Bias Theory of Managerial Discrimination," *Sex Roles* 18(1-2) (1988): 9-29.

24. Peter Dubno, "Attitudes Toward Women Executives: A Longitudinal Approach," *Academy of Management Journal* 28(1) (March 1985): 235-239.

25. Janet Mason, "Opportunities for Women," *Management World* 14(9) (October 1985), 16-17.

26. Charlotte Decker Sutton and Kris K. Moore, "Executive Women—20 Years Later," *Harvard Business Review* 63(5) (September/October 1985): 42-66.

27. Kenneth A. Kovach, "Sex Stereotyping by Tomorrow's Executives," *Personnel* 62(12) (1985): 14-20.

28. Sarah Hardesty and Nehama Jacobs, *Success and Betrayal: The Crisis of Women in Corporate America* (New York: Franklin Watts, 1986), 42.

29. Jay B. Barney and Barbara S. Lawrence, "The Economics of Career Strategy," in *Handbook of Career Theory,* eds. Michael B. Arthur, Douglas T. Hall, and Barbara S. Lawrence (Cambridge, UK: Cambridge University Press, 1989), 430.

30. Don W. Brown, "Were Men Meant to Mentor Women?" *Training Development Journal* (February 1985): 30-34.

31. Laura Vertz, "Women, Occupational Advancement, and Mentoring: An Analysis of One Public Organization," *Public Administration Review* 45(3) (May/June 1985): 415-423.

32. Carol M. Michael and David M. Hunt, "Women and Organizations: A Study of Mentorship," in *Preparing Professional Women for the Future: Resources for Teachers and Trainers,* ed. V. Jean Ramsey, 177-190 (Ann Arbor: University of Michigan Press, 1985), especially p. 182.

33. Raymond A. Noe, "Women and Mentoring: A Review and Research Agenda," *Academy of Management Review* 13(1) (1988): 65-78.

34. Michael and Hunt, "Women and Organizations," 182. See also Rosabeth Kanter, *Men and Women of the Corporation* (New York: Basic Books, 1977).

35. Vertz, "Women, Occupational Advancement, and Mentoring," 415-423.

36. Cf. Felice N. Schwartz, "Don't Write Women Off as Leaders," *Fortune* 8 June 1987, 185, 188.

37. Gary N. Powell, "The Effects of Sex and Gender on Recruitment," *Academy of Management Review* 12(4) (1987): 731-741.

38. See Barbara A. Ivey, "Identity, Power, and Hiring in a Feminized Profession," *Library Trends* 34(2) (1985): 291-307.

39. Helen H. Solomons and Aubrey Cramer, "When the Differences Don't Make a Difference: Women and Men as Colleagues," *Management Education and Development* 16(2) (1985): 155-168.

40. Solomons and Cramer, "When the Differences Don't Make a Difference," 167.

41. See Hardesty and Jacobs, *Success and Betrayal,* 420-421.

42. R. Garbarine, "Building Workplace Centers to Reduce Turnover," *New York Times* 15 October 1989, 32.

43. Garbarine, "Building Workplace Centers."

44. Elizabeth Ehrlich, "Child Care, the Private Sector Can't Do It Alone," *Business Week* 6 October 1986, 52-53.

45. Robert E. Allen, "It Pays to Invest in Tomorrow's Work Force," *Wall Street Journal* 6 November 1989, A16(W).

46. Allen, "It Pays to Invest," A16(W).

47. Robert White, "Changing Needs of Work and Family: A Union Response," *Canadian Business Review* 16(3) (Autumn 1989): 31-33.

48. White, "Changing Needs of Work and Family," 31-33.

49. Swoboda, "Parental Leave Goes on the Fast Track," 35.

50. Swoboda, "Parental Leave Goes on the Fast Track," 35.

51. Loretta D. Foxman and Walter L. Polsky, "Family Relocation Is Company Business," *Personnel Journal* 19 September 1989, 30-35.

9

Balancing the Scales of Justice: Alternatives for Integrating Women's Personal Lives into the U.S. Economy

Traditional sex-role ideologies and traditional career models inhibit working women from integrating their personal and economic lives. Reconceptualization of women's position in the economy is in order. First, we examine alternative frameworks that challenge the traditional ideology typically adopted by the U.S. government. Particular attention is focused on public policies suggested by these alternatives which may yield an economic system more receptive to women. Second, we evaluate the effects of the traditional framework in the modern workplace.

Alternate Conceptual Frameworks

Why do women encounter difficulty combining the roles of wife, mother, and worker? Presumably, the answer does *not* lie in a male conspiracy to keep women in the home. The United States has made numerous attempts, albeit somewhat unsuccessfully, to address the problems of gender inequality in the economy. Congress has passed legislation such as the Equal Pay Act of 1963 (requiring employers to pay workers equal pay for equal work, regardless of sex) and Title VII of the Civil Rights Act of 1964 (prohibiting employers from discriminating on the basis of sex in hiring, promoting, or firing practices).

AUTHOR'S NOTE: This chapter was researched and written with Deborah De Paoli.

These laws have enabled women to make some advances in the labor market; however, governmental actions remain inadequate.

Since the 1970s, feminists of various ideological persuasions have offered alternative frameworks that reconceptualize U.S. law, public policies, and the economy. One underlying goal appears, either implicitly or explicitly, throughout these frameworks: Achievement of a balanced system in which women's differences from, as well as similarities to, men are taken into consideration in the ideological and institutional organization of the United States. The change advocated within each position depends on the explanation given for the failure of traditional structures and laws to protect women as they enter labor markets. Although feminists have offered many different methods to achieve a balanced system, the analyses generally revolve around two general theses: (1) the need to expand our understanding of "equality" and (2) the need to expand our understanding of "human" nature. Table 9.1 provides a brief overview of some of the more recent feminist approaches to critiquing the gender basis of traditional U.S. jurisprudence and the alternatives they proposed.

Definitions of Equality

The first general category of frameworks in Table 9.1 identifies the use of a one-sided definition of equality as the reason for current structural inadequacies with respect to women's issues.[1] Traditional U.S. jurisprudence defines equality according to the Aristotelian tradition, which, in turn, defines equality as similar treatment for those similarly situated.[2] This definition of equality pervades the U.S. Supreme Court's analysis of issues concerning sex discrimination and inequality in the workplace. The equal protection analysis of the Fourteenth Amendment, the equal treatment and disparate impact analysis of Title VII, and the equal pay analysis of the Equal Pay Act all are based on this definition of equality.

The implications of this definition are threefold. First, the definition requires a comparison of the treatment of women in relation to men instead of focusing on the treatment of women in their own right. Second, the traditional model of equality establishes men as the standard of comparison. Third, this comparison assumes a certain degree of similarity between the sexes; however, as we have seen with the empirical data summarized herein, men and women are often not similarly

TABLE 9.1 Frameworks for Critiquing Traditional U.S. Jurisprudence

Counter Models	Traditional Position	Critique of Traditional Position	The Alternative
Critiques of Male-Biased Understandings of Equality			
Eliminating Disadvantages Model	Equality = similar treatment for similarly situated people.	Achieving equality is futile. Males are standards for comparison. Female differences require "special" treatment.	Standards of comparison should consider: historical, social, and economic differences so we can identify and change those disadvantaging women.
Achieving Full Participation Model	Equal participation is defined by a male standard.	Women cannot participate as fully as males in this framework.	Full participation should be based on individual's capacity rather than on the present male standard.
Achieving Acceptance Model	A difference between men and women is only perceived as "real" if it can be analogized to the male's experience.	Discussions on sex discrimination focus on the question "what are true gender differences?"	Differences should be accepted and not limit one's choices in life.
Critiques of Male-Biased Understandings of Human Nature			
Socialized-Contextualized Individual Framework	Humans are self-determining, atomistic, with equal opportunities to succeed.	Individuals are socialized to roles, values, relationships, and customs that give men entitlements and rights women do not have.	Society's understanding of human nature should emphasize social forces and contextual environment acting on individuals so that constraints of traditional roles, values, relationships, and customs can be identified and removed.

The Connectedness Model	Humans are separate, autonomous, with fear of annihilation and violence being of greatest concern.	This understanding of humanness does not apply to women who are continually connected to others who are socialized to an ethic of care, and who need protection from invasion more than from annihilation and violence. Liberal law protects the autonomous male but ignores the connectedness of females.	Protection from invasion should be equally valued with the right to autonomy.

situated with respect to the ability to integrate multiple roles. When a difference between the sexes does exist, such as pregnancy, women's needs or problems are inadequately addressed within a framework founded on men's needs and problems. Any need or attribute that differs from the male standard is considered "special." Any law that attempts to address a "special" need or attribute is labeled "special treatment." Thus, "It is always woman's characteristics—her pregnancy, her child-rearing responsibilities, her physical or sexual vulnerability—that appear 'special.' "[3]

In general terms, women activists in the 1980s increasingly turned to shifting the focus away from an abstract and universalistic value of "equality," as defined by Aristotelian traditions, toward a value that is based on the daily and historical experiences of women, with the aim of (1) eliminating disadvantages, (2) achieving full participation, and (3) achieving acceptance of differences. Using the established rhetoric of disadvantage, full participation, and acceptance already common to other groups in the United States, these activists and scholars analyze the treatment of women in terms of results (i.e., eliminating disadvantage); they also seek to develop public policies more receptive to women's issues, especially women's efforts to integrate their personal and economic lives.

The "Eliminating Disadvantages Model" would focus on the historical, social, and economic foundations of problems faced by women and then build theoretical and policy alternatives to address them. The key question in this model is "whether legal recognition of sex-based differences is more likely to reduce or to reinforce sex-based disparities in political power, social status and economic diversity."[4] The "Full Participation Model" requires concluding that any treatment that restricts women's choice of social roles or prevents them from entering the public sphere is unconstitutional.[5] The "Achieving Acceptance Model"[6] would change the "equality" norm to make gender differences cost less. This model shifts the focus away from "the question of whether *women* are different" vis-à-vis men to the "question of how the social fact of gender asymmetry can be dealt with so as to create some symmetry in the lived-out experience of equal membership in the community."[7] What should matter is not gender difference but the "difference that gender makes."[8] The objective of all three models is to end the current societal patterns whereby female multiple sex-roles are punished in political and economic life whereas male roles are rewarded.

The Atomistic Understanding of "Human" Nature

The understanding of human nature typically implicit in decisions made by Congress and the U.S. Supreme Court presupposes that a "human" being is an autonomous individual essentially separate from other individuals. This individualistic presupposition about "human nature" guides policy decisions concerning the economy generally, and women's place within the economy specifically. Scholars in the second general category of Table 9.1 criticize this atomistic understanding of "human" nature on the grounds that it excludes the realities of women's lives.[9]

The feminists in this category—those adopting the "Socialized-Contextualized Individual Approach" and the "Connectedness Approach"—offer an understanding of "human" nature that takes into account the daily experiences of women's lives. Their analysis parallels the critique of the Aristotelian definition of equality in one central respect: both criticize the use of an abstract, universalistic theory adopted by and for men that excludes the realities of women's lives but is nevertheless applied to women's issues. Indeed, most feminist scholars in the 1980s had adopted the Socialized-Contextualized Individual understanding of human nature.[10] This worldview emphasizes the connections of the individual with others and with the community. Human beings are seen as constituted by social relationships. Mutuality, interrelationships, responsibility to others and of others to oneself are highlighted. Individuality is not denied; rather social bonds are stressed and self-interest is downplayed.

Mary Hawkesworth rejects the atomistic presupposition that all individuals have equal opportunities to succeed, and, hence, that success is determined by "individual initiative and effort, and is consequently deserved."[11] She also rejects the notion that governmental and market actions are objective, external, and "impersonal" forces.[12]

Scholars such as Hawkesworth, using a "Socialized Individual" understanding of human nature, perceive society as a "complex web of values, norms, roles, relationships and customs" that shape an individual's self-understanding and understanding of others.[13] Individuals act upon their understanding of these roles and norms. As a result, certain individuals have opportunities to succeed because of their membership in a particular group and not because of any individual talent or ability.[14] In addition, human action based on established roles and norms may underlie what has been assumed to be "impersonal objective forces."

From within this framework "neither the [hiring or promotion] criteria adopted nor the employing institutions are neutral or impersonal. Objective forces do not determine individual applicants' merit and prospects for success—the decisions of fallible administrators do."[15] To change the conditions of women as a group, feminists using the Socialized-Contextualized Individual framework focus on reconceptualizing society's understanding of human nature so as to emphasize the social forces and contextual environment acting upon the individual. Support for affirmative action is clearly more likely among those who follow this understanding of human nature than among those who adopt the atomistic understanding.

The Connectedness Model, as offered by Robin West,[16] also rests on the notion that humans are socialized, not atomistic, individuals. West begins with the assertion that the atomistic understanding of human nature is "essentially and irretrievably masculine," and that law and public policy, operating within society, primarily address "rights" from the male perspective of separateness and autonomy. West identifies those male "rights" as the right to be protected against physical violence and annihilation. Autonomy and separateness from others creates an intense physical vulnerability. An individual's actions may conflict with another person's actions while both individuals are exercising their right to freely pursue their own ends. This conflict is a threat to the autonomy of each and may result in physical violence or, in the extreme case, killing (or annihilating) the individual in one's way. U.S. laws are aimed to protect this value of autonomy while at the same time preventing, or at least minimizing, the threat that one's autonomy presents to others.

West asserts that, in contrast to men, women are connected; they are not autonomous, separate individuals. Rather, women are biologically, emotionally, and socially connected to life in ways significantly different from men. Women are physiologically connected to life during pregnancy, heterosexual intercourse, menstruation (potential for pregnancy), and breast-feeding. Women more than men are socially connected to life through their roles as child-rearer, wife, and general caretaker of others. According to West, everyday physiological and social experiences create in women the ethic of care, the value of intimacy, and a capacity to bond and nurture.[17]

These positive experiences of women also have a counter side of negative experiences, such as sexual invasion (rape), fetal invasion (unwanted pregnancy), and invasion, generally, caused by social structures that define and limit women's experiences (e.g., sexual harassment in the workplace). This argument is based on an assumption that the same capacity to become pregnant and bear children also makes women biologically suited to be invaded by others. Moreover, the positive values of connectedness also can lead to a loss of identity vis-à-vis oneself rather than vis-à-vis others. According to West, these "invasions" and loss of identity are what women most fear and for which they most desire protection.

West proposes that women's experiences and human needs be translated into human and civil rights that will reveal rather than conceal the origin of women's "distinctive existential and material" state of being. A new understanding of "human" nature, which includes the female perspective, will lead to a more balanced understanding of human rights, and thus, facilitate resolving the integration of personal, political and economic life for everyone.

These alternatives provide us with new conceptual tools for addressing typical problems faced by women attempting to integrate their personal and workplace lives. We turn now to illustrate how the alternative frameworks might address women's multiple-sex-roles dilemmas. Table 9.2 summarizes selected issues raised in this volume, the current legislative and legal approaches to these issues, and new strategies suggested by these various models.

The Problem of Being a Wife/Mother as Well as a Worker

In 1970, a woman was refused employment because she had a preschool-age child. The employer's hiring practice was not to hire women with preschool-age children although fathers with preschool-age children were hired by this employer. Believing this gender-specific hiring practice was sex discrimination, the woman brought her case (*Philips v. Marietta Corporation*, 1971)[18] before the U.S. Supreme Court. This case prompted the Court to define a violation of Title VII's prohibition against sex discrimination. The Court held that Title VII requires persons with like qualifications be given equal employment opportunities regardless of their respective sex.

TABLE 9.2 Applying the Alternatives to Women's Workplace Problems

Problem	Current Approach	Alternative Reconceptualization
Being a mother and a worker	Pregnancy Disability Leave Act—views pregnancy as a "disability" so that it can be analogized to men's reasons for requiring leave from work.	Women's attributes should not be compared to men's attributes if the standard for comparison is the male norm; women's reproductive choices should have same status as men's reproductive choices.
Being historically excluded from particular types of work due to protected wife/daughter roles	Title VII—equality requires similar treatment for similarly situated individuals.	Move from the male-based standard toward a standard that equally considers women's issues; consider economic, social, and historical factors unique to women.
Being segregated into low status positions	Title VII is sufficient to ensure equality of opportunity; sex-segrated occupations are caused by social factors beyond the scope of legitimate governmental interference.	Comparable worth analysis of institutional bias.
Being assigned role of sex object to the workplace	Thanks to feminists, Title VII added sexual harassment as a violation of civil rights.	Sexual harassment is an invasion and should be criminalized.

The Court's opinion is one example of the contradictory analysis employed by the Supreme Court in the area of sex-based discrimination relying on traditional definitions of equality. On the one hand, the Court believes that some sex-based differences do exist, are justified, and thus can constitute a "bona fide occupational qualification." On the other hand, the Court refuses to find sex-based discrimination if men do not have the same attribute or some comparable attribute as women.

The Court's opinion has posed problems for pregnant workers. Prior to 1978, it was not uncommon for employers to offer their employees insurance policies that would *not* pay medical expenses or unemployment benefits for pregnancy-related "disabilities." These same policies, however, did cover almost any other disability, including disabilities affecting only men, such as, prostate surgery. Two cases were brought before the Supreme Court to determine whether such insurance policies constituted sex discrimination.[19]

The Court was faced with a "real" difference between the sexes. Male workers do not become pregnant. The traditional framework's equality analysis requires similar treatment for those similarly situated. In order for the Court to apply the equality analysis, it had to fit pregnancy into the traditional model of the worker (i.e., a man who is the breadwinner, father, and husband). Therefore, the Court had to label pregnancy as a "disability" that required "sick" leave like any other male disability.[20]

Once pregnancy was labeled as a disability, pregnancy became like any other disability affecting men. Thus, the Court could conclude that the differential treatment of these insurance policies was no longer a difference between men and women but rather a difference between "pregnant and nonpregnant *persons*."

Only in the traditional model of the workplace, designed by and for men, would such a natural and common event affecting women be considered an additional risk and significantly different from the typical benefits provided to workers. According to this traditional model, women are allowed to enter the public realm of work if they are willing to adapt this already extinct model of the "worker"—a man who is the breadwinner, father, and husband.

The Court's application of the Aristotelian equality analysis failed to challenge this male-centered model and failed to address the unique employment problems faced by women who desire to work and to have children. Although the Court did acknowledge biological differences between the sexes, men's biological ailments and diseases set the standard for an employer's disability coverage. And consequently, a "disability" unique to women, such as pregnancy, was an "additional risk" beyond the scope required by any employer's coverage.

In another pre-1978 case concerning pregnancy-based discrimination, the Court further reinforced the traditional male model of the workplace and failed to address the unique experiences and needs of women in their reproductive role of mother. In this case, *Nashville Gas Co. v. Satty* (1977),[21] the Court was asked to consider whether an employer's policy of requiring pregnant employees to take a formal leave of absence without receiving sick pay or accumulating job seniority violated Title VII. The Court held that the employer's refusal to provide accumulated seniority violated Title VII because it acted to deprive pregnant women of "employment opportunities and to adversely affect [their] status as an employee." However, the Court held that the employer's refusal to provide sick leave did not violate Title VII. The Court could not conceptualize that the absence of sick leave would disadvantage women as much, if not more than, the employer's refusal to provide accumulated seniority. Nor was the Court willing to entertain the argument that the absence of sick leave decreased working women's reproductive choices in a way that working men's reproductive choices were not affected. The average worker, male or female, financially cannot afford to take off work for three or four weeks without pay. Pregnancy leave usually requires at a minimum three weeks of leave from work. The male bias of the workplace along with the traditional legal framework served to frustrate women's ability to combine their roles as worker and child-bearer.

In response to these pre-1978 cases, Congress enacted the Pregnancy Disability Act (PDA) of 1978.[22] This act defines a pregnancy-based classification as a sex-based classification subject to Title VII's prohibitions against sex discrimination. Although this act states pregnancy discrimination is sex-based discrimination, it goes no further. The United States still lacks adequate laws that require employers to provide pregnancy and/or parental leave for working women. Until such time, women will continue to face the difficulty of combining their roles as workers and mothers.

California attempted to expand the PDA by eliminating the disparate impact that inadequate leave policies have on working women's decision to have children. This state adopted a statute that required employers to grant reasonable leave to female employees "temporarily disabled" by pregnancy, childbirth, or related medical conditions. In *California Federal Savings and Loan Association v. Guerra* (1987),[23] this statute was challenged as violating Title VII and the PDA because it gave "preferential treatment" to women. The Court, however, found no violation of Title VII or the PDA. The Court reasoned that Congress intended the PDA to be "a floor beneath which pregnancy disability benefits may not drop—not a ceiling above which they may not rise."[24]

The celebration over the *Guerra* decision was short-lived. That same year a unanimous Supreme Court, in *Wimberly v. Labor and Industrial Relations Commission of Missouri* (1987),[25] found no violation of the Federal Unemployment Tax Act (FUTA) for a state to deny unemployment benefits to a woman who lost her job after temporarily leaving her work to have a child. FUTA prohibited states from denying unemployment benefits "solely on the basis of pregnancy or termination of pregnancy." The state statute was written in neutral language that denied benefits to any person who left his or her job "voluntarily" and "without good cause attributable to his work or to his employer." Pregnancy leave was classified by the state as "voluntarily leaving the job without good cause" and thus not covered under the state's unemployment benefits program.

In reaching its decision that this statute did not violate FUTA, the Court reasoned that pregnancy was not the "sole basis" for the state policy. According to the Court, the intent was to deny benefits to all persons who stopped working voluntarily and without good cause. Concluding that temporary leave on the basis of pregnancy was not a good cause for leaving work was never thought to be discrimination or reflective of a subjective, male-centered worldview. Nor was the Court concerned that this woman, like many women, lost her job in the first instance because she desired to have children. Once again, traditional sex-role ideology merged with jurisprudence to perpetuate a male assimilationist model of the workplace.

In 1990 the California State Supreme Court heard a challenge to the Johnson Controls, Inc. policy barring women potentially capable of pregnancy from jobs which exposed them to hazardous substances. The California Court ruled that this policy discriminated against women. The 4th District Court of Appeals upheld this conclusion, noting that Johnson Controls could not demonstrate that sex constituted a bona fide occupational qualification. The U.S. Supreme Court applied a broader standard to the case. Lead exposure at the Johnson plants created fertility risks for both men and women. The Court ruled that the company could not deny a choice of employment to women which it extended to men.[26]

The Aristotelian approach to equality embedded in U.S. Court opinions clearly has not—up to this point—facilitated combining roles of mother/wife with worker. When confronted with a "real" difference between the sexes, the equality analysis of being similarly situated failed to balance the scales of justice so that women's choice to work and have children would be equal to men's choice to work and have children. Instead, women are placed in a position that requires female assimilation to male norms rather than fair recognition of women's separate abilities and commitments.

As an alternative to this stark reality imposed by the equality analysis, the "Achieving Full Participation," "Achieving Acceptance," and

"Eliminating Disadvantage" models all would require a different outcome. Economic institutions and ideological assumptions about the workplace would be restructured to prevent women's differences (pregnancy) from becoming excuses for discrimination against women. The Connectedness and Socialized Individual frameworks would also require society to restructure its presuppositions about life and human needs so that women's voices may be fully represented in our society's ideological and institutional structures.

The Problem of Exclusion Stemming from the Protected Wife/Daughter Role

The problem of the historical exclusion of women from particular types of work and its impact on women in the 1990s can be illustrated by two examples of discrimination: (1) hiring practices in the private employment sector and (2) hiring practices in the public sector based on veteran status. In the private sector in 1973, the Supreme Court established explicit criteria for determining when hiring practices are discriminatory in violation of Title VII.[27] The claimant must establish that she is a member of a protected class—gender; that she applied for the job and was qualified for it; that despite her qualifications, she was rejected; and finally, that after her rejection, the employer continued to consider other applicants for the job.

Nowhere in this test does the Court consider whether the "qualities" or "requirements" of the job may themselves be sex-biased, and hence discriminatory toward female applicants. Feminists would require an analysis of how a business is already structured and whether the job qualifications already established are male-biased. Present hiring discrimination based on the historical exclusion of wives and daughters from certain jobs and public roles can only be eliminated if we analyze discrimination from this perspective. Otherwise, employers will continue to justify not hiring women because it is "job-related" or "necessary to the employer's business" when in reality it is only a customary way of doing things. The alternative frameworks in Table 9.1 would challenge this defense to discrimination, which is formally called the "bona fide occupational qualification" (BFOQ) defense.

A very specific hiring policy based on traditional sex-roles that discriminates against women is the veterans' preference policy. In the mid-1970s, a woman sued the State of Massachusetts because

Massachusetts had enacted a statute that required hiring veterans over nonveterans for state civil service jobs (*Personnel Administrator of Massachusetts v. Feeney,* 1979).[28] The Supreme Court was asked to determine whether Massachusetts' facially gender-neutral hiring statute violated the Equal Protection Clause of the Fourteenth Amendment. The test for whether a facially gender-neutral statute violates the Equal Protection Clause requires a showing of "purposeful discrimination" and a showing of disparate impact. The woman who brought this dispute before the Supreme Court claimed that the statute had a substantially disparate impact on women. Ninety-eight percent of veterans were men and 60% of the available public jobs were classified as "civil service jobs." In response to these charges, Massachusetts claimed that the statute was designed to "reward veterans for the sacrifice of military service," not to discriminate against women.

Despite the obvious disparate impact on women, the Court did not find a violation of the Equal Protection Clause. The Court acknowledged that this statute disproportionately affected women, but concluded that, to find purposeful discrimination, the legislature must have adopted this statute "because of" not merely "in spite of" its adverse effects on women.

The Court assumes discriminatory *intent* rather than discriminatory *impact* is what most offends the Constitution. This focus on intent shifts the Court's analysis away from the impact this statute has on women seeking employment in state jobs. Moreover, this intent-oriented analysis misunderstands the "dynamics of gender prejudice."[29] Sex biases, insensitivities, and stereotyped assumptions often are subconscious rather than consciously intended. Even if a bias is conscious and the disparate impact is intentional, it is still difficult to prove this intent. Nonetheless, the Court states that the Fourteenth Amendment guarantees "equal" laws. Logically, a law that benefits men to the disadvantage of women can hardly be considered equal. Rhode states:

> Given the state's wide variety of means to assist veterans, its choice of policies that reserve the upper echelons of state employment exclusively for men can scarcely be regarded as gender-neutral. Rather, that choice reflects insensitivity to women's opportunities for economic advancement and political influence.[30]

As in the area of pregnancy, the Court avoided the deeper issues: women constitute only 2% of all veterans because of a male-bias against women in the military, and now society is rewarding these male veterans at the expense of women.

The alternative models in Table 9.1 directly challenge the rationale of this policy and of the Court's decision. They would focus first on whether a policy has a disproportionate impact on women. Second, they would determine whether the policy reflects past discrimination and "reinforces current gender disadvantage." Even if a policy was not enacted "because of" its adverse impact on women, it would be struck-down if it prevented women's full participation, or hindered their equal acceptance in the market place.

Subordinate Status and Comparable Worth

The Supreme Court has not ruled on the issue of comparable worth. In *County of Washington v. Gunther* (1981),[31] the issue raised was whether paying female guards in the female section of the county jail less money than male guards in the male section of the same county jail constituted sex-based discrimination. The female guards alleged that their work was substantially equal to the male guards' work. This position of the female guards appears to involve a simple comparable worth argument—my job has substantially the same responsibilities and pressures as your job, so my job should be paid the same as your job. Although the Supreme Court ruled in favor of the female guards, it was careful to emphasize that this case was not concerned with the "controversial concepts of 'comparable worth.' "

Numerous federal circuit courts have ruled on this issue, and these rulings tend not to favor women's interests. The circuit courts seem to be in agreement that wage discrimination in violation of Title VII will not be found if the cases are based on comparable worth. Their decisions are based on the argument that Title VII requires a comparison of equal or substantially equal work and was not designed to "abrogate fundamental economic principles such as 'supply and demand' or to prevent employers from competing in the labor market."[32]

The question has been posed: "Didn't Congress 'abrogate' an earlier instance of 'laws of supply and demand' by enacting the Equal Pay Act, which prevents the employer from taking advantage of market conditions that set lower wages for women performing equal work to that performed by men?" (Hill, supplement at 200). The answer to this question is "Yes." However, the Court has refused to see the interrelationship between the Equal Pay Act and Title VII. Title VII, as the Court has said, allows discrimination on the basis of sex if sex is a bona fide occupational qualification; however, whether women are allowed into these sex-specific jobs has often determined the job's pay scale. For example, male-dominated jobs frequently draw better pay than female-dominated jobs or jobs that include both men and women. The Court, however, has said that the Equal Pay Act allows only a comparison between the wages of men and women who are currently employed in the same occupation or substantially similar occupations. The Equal Pay Act does not require an analysis of what an employer might have paid employees if men were hired.

Some states and political subdivisions have attempted to "abrogate" sex-segregated occupations that result in lower wages for women by establishing affirmative action programs. For such programs, the Court determines the importance of the governmental objective in its "Manifest Imbalance Test." This test requires determining whether consideration of sex as a hiring factor was justified by the "existence of a manifest imbalance that reflected underrepresentation of women in traditionally segregated job categories."

The affirmative action plan of Santa Clara County, California, was the most recent action plan aimed at redressing sex discrimination to be upheld by the Supreme Court.[33] In *Johnson v. Transportation Agency, Santa Clara County,* the Court ruled in favor of the affirmative action plan on the grounds that a *manifest imbalance* did exist in Santa Clara's public jobs. The dissenters to *Johnson* (Chief Justice Rehnquist and Justices White and Scalia) were sharply critical of the decision to allow affirmative action. The dissenters argued that the occupation targeted for affirmative action was not a traditionally segregated job category in the sense of conscious, exclusionary discrimination. They believed that women chose not to apply for the job as a road maintenance crew worker, the necessary position before one could be promoted to road dispatcher. Relying on many of the presumptions of the atomistic individualism, they wrote:

It is absurd to think that the nationwide failure of road maintenance crews . . . [to employ women] is attributable primarily, if even substantially, to systematic exclusion of women eager to shoulder pick and shovel. [Rather *this is a case of*] *longstanding social attitudes,* it has not been regarded by women themselves as desirable work. . . . And *it is the alteration of social attitudes rather than the elimination of discrimination that this decision justifies.*[34] (Emphasis added.)

In contrast, the alternative frameworks in Table 9.1 would require an analysis of institutional and ideological biases. Particular focus would be placed on the evaluation criteria. Why was the job as maintenance crew worker (manual labor job) necessary for the job as road dispatcher? The woman who eventually was hired had experience as a road dispatcher in the nongovernmental sector. Why should private employment experience not be considered sufficient for the public sector? A second example of biases is illustrated by the actions of one of the evaluators who had been the female applicant's supervisor. He took actions to make her job purposely unpleasant because he objected to her presence as the first woman hired for the job as crew worker. His actions only stopped after she filed a sexual harassment grievance.

The Socialized Individual framework criticizes the atomistic understanding of individuals because the latter presupposes that impersonal social and biological forces, not individuals, cause the underrepresentation or underpayment of women. It is from within this framework that affirmative action imposes responsibility for a collective problem on specific individuals. In the Atomistic framework, affirmative action is viewed as preferential treatment and as imposing reverse discrimination against the "best qualified candidates who just happen to be nonminority men."[35]

The Socialized-Contextualized Individual framework begins with an understanding that men, as a group rather than as individuals, receive many advantages merely because they are men, and that previous decisions about economic structures, jobs, and wages were made within a male-biased frame of reference. These past decisions can be changed. "Thus, it is not blind social processes which affirmative action must remedy, but rather the particular decisions of specific individuals who serve as gate-keepers to the positions of power and privilege in contemporary society."[36] Justifying sex-segregation in industries and occupations on the grounds of gender-"neutral" hiring criteria, and the perpetuation of gender pay inequities on the grounds of market-based pay criteria, simply glosses over the powerful role that patriarchal sex-role ideology continues to play in the economy, the courts, politics, and the personal life of all Americans.

The Problem of Being a Sex-Object in the Workplace

Sexual harassment has existed as long as women have been in the workplace. Until 1986, sexual harassment was not considered a serious issue warranting judicial redress until the victim suffered a negative economic effect on her employment (i.e., was fired or denied promotion). In 1986, the U.S. Supreme Court accepted, for the first time, the argument that sexual advances as well as a "hostile environment based on discriminatory sexual harassment" violated Title VII's prohibition against sex-based discrimination.[37] The Court established in the *Vinson* case the modern standard of review for sexual harassment: "For sexual harassment to be actionable, it must be sufficiently severe or pervasive 'to alter the conditions' of [the victim's] employment and create an abusive environment.' " In *Vinson,* the Court rejected the traditional defense to sexual harassment, that the victim's sexual encounters with the harasser were "voluntary." This defense was based on the fallacy that the victim failed to claim or prove such encounters were physically forced upon her (i.e., rape). The Court rejected this line of reasoning and held that the proper judicial inquiry was whether the sexual advances or encounters were "unwelcome," not whether they were physically "voluntary."

The "Connectedness Model" requires a reconceptualization of sexual harassment. The traditional framework classifies sexual harassment as sex "discrimination." This classification defines sexual harassment in terms of rights that men can understand. In contrast, the Connectedness Model would redefine sexual harassment into rights that women, who are the primary targets of sexual harassment, can understand. According to Robin West, "invasion" is what women most fear and for which they most desire protection.[38] From this perspective, sexual harassment is a form of invasion. Therefore, this model would require the *criminalization* of sexual harassment as a form of invasion as well as a violation of women's human rights.

Conclusion

Establishing a successful career in any field requires integrating one's private and public identity. This work makes it clear that the successful integration of women's personal and workplace lives is much more than an individual or even an organizational matter. It involves a reconceptualization of sex-role ideology within the legal and political systems and the implementation of that reconceptualization within not only the men and women of the United States but also within its political and economic institutions. The traditional framework has institutionalized and perpetuated abstract, universalistic theories about equality, human nature, and civil rights that do not adequately reflect the qualities and experiences unique to women. Consequently, these abstract theories do not redress the special employment problems arising out of women's need to combine multiple sex-roles. U.S. jurisprudence, business and governmental institutions, and individual men and women must recognize the impact these multiple sex-roles have and how they contribute to producing our gendered economy. Individual men must be expected to participate fully in child-rearing and household work. Business, government, jurisprudence, and the national ideology must be reshaped to facilitate these changes.

Notes

1. Stephanie M. Wildman, "The Legitimation of Sex Discrimination: A Critical Response to Supreme Court Jurisprudence," *Oregon Law Review* 63 (1984), 265; Deborah L. Rhode, *Justice and Gender: Sex Discrimination and the Law* (Cambridge, MA: Harvard University Press, 1989); Carrie Menkel-Meadow, "Excluded Voices: New Voices in the Legal Profession Making New Voices in the Law," *University of Minnesota Law Review* 19 (1989): 42; and Christine A. Littleton, "Restructuring Sexual Equality," *California Law Review* 75 (1987): 1279.

2. Deborah L. Rhode, "Gender Difference and Gender Disadvantage," *Women & Politics* 10(2) (1990): 121.

3. Rhode, *Justice and Gender,* 318.

4. Rhode, *Justice and Gender,* 318.

5. Wildman, "Legitimation of Sex Discrimination," 317.

6. Littleton, "Restructuring Sexual Equality."

7. Littleton, "Restructuring Sexual Equality," 1297.

8. Littleton, "Restructuring Sexual Equality," 1332.

9. Robin West, "Jurisprudence and Gender," *University of Chicago Law Review* 55(1) (Winter 1988): 1, 4; and Mary E. Hawkesworth, *Theoretical Issues in Policy Analysis* (Albany: State University of New York University Press, 1988). For further reading, see also Suzanna Sherry, "Civic Virtue and the Feminine Voice in Constitutional Adjudication," *Virginia Law Review,* 543 (1986): 72; Catherine A. MacKinnon, *Feminism Unmodified* (Cambridge, MA: Harvard University Press, 1987); and Christine A. Littleton, "Feminist Jurisprudence: The Difference Method Makes," *Stanford Law Review* 41 (1989): 751-784.

10. Rosemarie Tong, *Feminist Thought* (Boulder, CO: Westview Press, 1989), 11-37.

11. Hawkesworth, *Theoretical Issues,* 98.

12. Hawkesworth, *Theoretical Issues,* 98.

13. Hawkesworth, *Theoretical Issues,* 99.

14. Hawkesworth, *Theoretical Issues,* 112-113.

15. Hawkesworth, *Theoretical Issues,* 112-113.

16. West, "Jurisprudence and Gender."

17. See also Nancy Chodorow, *The Reproduction of Mothering: Psychoanalysis and the Sociology of Gender* (Berkeley: University of California Press, 1978); Dorothy Dinnerstein, *The Mermaid and the Minotaur* (New York: Harper & Row, 1983); and Carol Gilligan, *In a Different Voice: Psychological Theory and Women's Development* (Cambridge, MA: Harvard University Press, 1982).

18. *Philips v. Marietta Corporation,* 400 U.S. 542, 91 S.Ct. 496, 27 L.Ed. 2d 613 (1971).

19. *Geduldig v. Aiello,* 417 U.S. 484, 94 S.Ct. 2485, 41 L.Ed. 2d 256 (1974); and *General Electric Co. v. Gilbert* 429 U.S. 125, 97 S.Ct. 401, 50 L.Ed. 2d 343 (1976).

20. For a discussion of the consequences of categorizing pregnancy as a "disability" rather than as an "ability" for society, see Herma Hill Kay, "Equality and Difference: The Case of Pregnancy," *Berkeley Women's Law Journal* 1 (1985): 1; and the Brief *Amici Curiae* for the Coalition for Reproductive Equality in the Workplace in *California Federal Savings and Loan Association v. Guerra,* 479 U.S. 272 (1987).

21. *Nashville Gas Co. v. Satty,* 434 U.S. 136, 98 S.Ct. 347 54 L.Ed. 2d 356 (1977).

22. Pregnancy Disability Act of 1978.

23. *California Federal Savings and Loan Association v. Guerra,* 479 U.S. 272 (1987).

24. Rhode, *Justice and Gender,* 121. Interestingly, feminists were sharply divided on the issue raised in *California Federal Savings and Loan Association v. Guerra* (1987). The National Organization for Women (NOW) joined forces with President Reagan and the ACLU to oppose the statute. They viewed the statute as "preferential treatment" of women equivalent to the protective legislation of the 19th century.

25. *Wimberly v. Labor and Industrial Relations Commission of Missouri,* 479 U.S. 511, 107 S.Ct. 821, 93 L.Ed. 2d. 909 (1987).

26. *International Union, United Automobile, Aerospace and Agricultural Implement Workers of America, UAW, et al. v. Johnson Controls, Inc.,* 51 CCH S. Ct. Bull. pp. B1162-B1183.

27. *McDonnell Douglas v. Green,* 411 U.S. 792, 93 S.Ct. 1817, 36 L.Ed. 2d 668 (1973).

28. *Personnel Administrator of Massachusetts v. Feeney,* 442 U.S. 256, 99 S.Ct. 2282, 60 L.Ed. 2d. 870 (1979).

29. Rhode, *Justice and Gender,* 177.

30. Rhode, *Justice and Gender,* 179.

31. *County of Washington v. Gunther,* 452 U.S. 161, 101 S.Ct. 2242, 68 L.Ed. 2d 751 (1981).

32. *AFSME v. State of Washington,* 770 F.2d 1401 (9C 1985), p. 1407.

33. *Johnson v. Transportation Agency, Santa Clara County, California,* 480 U.S. 616, 107 S.Ct. 1442, 94 L.Ed. 2d 615 (1987).

34. *Johnson v. Transportation Agency, Santa Clara County, California,* 480 U.S. 616, 107 S.Ct. 1442, 94 L.Ed. 2d 615 (1987).

35. Hawkesworth, *Theoretical Issues,* 103.

36. Hawkesworth, *Theoretical Issues,* 103.

37. *Meritor Savings Bank v. Vinson,* 477 U.S. 57, 106 S.Ct. 2399, 91 L.Ed. 2d 49 (1986).

38. West, "Jurisprudence and Gender."

PART IV

A Case Study: Women and the Economy in Arizona

Women have enjoyed many particular opportunities when entering the work force in Arizona. They have also faced particular constraints. Chapter 10 reviews the legal and economic status of women in Arizona. In Chapter 11, Arizona women, the participants in the Fifth Arizona Town Hall, present their reactions, consensus statements, and recommendations to the materials presented in Chapters 1-10.

10

Women, Work, and Careers in Arizona

Women constitute a very substantial and growing force in the Arizona economy. In 1989, women accounted for 50.9% of the state's population[1] and 41.7% of the civilian labor force.[2] Interestingly, Arizona law has facilitated women's business success. This chapter examines women's legal advantages in this state, reviews trends in Arizona's female labor force participation, and then profiles some of Arizona's more influential women entrepreneurs. Throughout, attention is paid to the unique situation of minority women.

Women and Arizona Law

When the Territory of Arizona held a Constitutional Convention in 1910, the question of women's suffrage sparked one of the most heated debates.[3] Anti-prohibition delegates most strongly opposed granting women the right to vote,[4] believing that women might introduce prohibition into the Arizona Constitution. When 3,200 women submitted a prohibition petition to the convention,[5] anti-prohibitionists felt that their worst fears had been confirmed.

The Arizona Constitution proposed by the delegates ultimately included neither women's suffrage nor prohibition.[6] Nevertheless, supporters of these issues successfully lobbied for inclusion of provisions allowing the constitution to be amended by "initiative." Any group

AUTHOR'S NOTE: This chapter was written and researched with Marcia Cech-Soucy, Deborah De Paoli, and Kimberly Fisher.

gathering sufficient signatures could place a constitutional amendment on the ballot so that Arizona voters could decide the issues. This initiative provision was used in 1912 during the first post-statehood election by supporters of women's suffrage. By over a two-to-one margin, Article VII, Section 2 of the constitution was amended to give women the right to vote and hold public office.[7] (The national government did not give women the right to vote in federal elections until 1920.) Women lost no time entering state politics. In 1915, the first election in which women could vote, Rachael Berry, a Democrat from St. Johns, won a seat in the state house, and Frances Lillian Willard Munds, a Democrat from Yavapai County, won a seat in the state senate.[8]

Surprisingly, the organizers of the women's suffrage initiative failed to amend Article V, Section 2 of the Constitution, which allows only "male persons" to hold the offices of governor, secretary of state, state treasurer, attorney general, and superintendent of public instruction. Even more surprisingly, voters did not approve removal of this provision until 1988. In spite of Article V, Section 2, however, a number of women have held executive-level positions, including Carolyn Warner, former superintendent of public instruction; C. Diane Bishop, superintendent of public instruction; and Rose Mofford, former secretary of state and later governor from 1988 to 1991.

Although the original Arizona Constitution did not grant women full voting rights, Article VII, Section 8 permitted women to vote in school elections. Some historians believe that women were given this voting right because, at that time, 80% of normal school teachers (12 out of 17) and three-fourths of the normal school students were female.[9]

Pay equity was a central issue of both the U.S. and Arizona women's movements in the early 1960s. Arizona passed the Arizona Equal Wage Act in 1962.[10] One year later, the United States enacted the U.S. Equal Pay Act. In 1973, Arizona amended its state act to allow an employee to recover three times the amount of unpaid wages if the employee was a victim of wage discrimination.[11]

The Arizona Civil Rights Act of 1965, modeled after the U.S. Civil Rights Act of 1964, has remained essentially unchanged.[12] The original act provided that discrimination in voting and employment was unlawful when based on race, color, religion, sex, national origin, or ancestry.[13] In 1974, discrimination in employment advertising based on these same factors was made unlawful, unless employers could demonstrate that such factors constituted a bona fide occupational qualification.[14]

Two additional forms of discrimination have since been included under the act: age, added in 1980, and handicap, added in 1985.[15]

Strangely, the act's provision prohibiting discrimination in public accommodations permitted such discrimination on the basis of sex.[16] Though the Arizona act's wording remains unchanged, two U.S. Supreme Court cases have rectified this problem. In *Roberts v. United States Jaycees,*[17] and *Board of Directors of Rotary International v. Rotary Clubs of Duarte,*[18] the Court ruled that the clubs in question could not restrict their membership on the basis of gender. Presumably, a woman in Arizona could bring suit based on federal civil rights laws and these two decisions.

Most of the 1970s' sex discrimination cases involving Arizona female employees were brought in federal court and used federal law to decide the issue. Even so, in *Davis v. Jobs for Progress, Inc.* (1976), the Federal District Court of Arizona combined a number of federal statutes and Arizona's pay equity statute (A.R.S. section 23-355) to award a female employee who had suffered wage discrimination triple the amount of unpaid wages that were due her.[19]

Nathalie Norris of Scottsdale challenged Arizona's deferred compensation pension plan in the U.S. District Courts (in *Norris v. Arizona Governing Committee,* 1980). This plan permitted smaller monthly annuity payments to female employees contributing the same amount to the plan. The courts held that such payment differentials violated the Civil Rights Act. As the result of the *Norris* case, women throughout the United States now receive more equitable pension payments.

Arizona courts often are more favorable to sex discrimination claims based on the Arizona Civil Rights Act than the U.S. Supreme Court has been on sex discrimination claims based on the U.S. Civil Rights Act. In 1989, the U.S. Supreme Court decided in *Wards Cove Packing Co., Inc. v. Antonio*[20] that *the person suing for discrimination had the burden* of proving that his or her employer lacked business justification for the business practices that had a statistically disadvantageous effect. Although *Wards Cove* was brought by a person claiming racial discrimination, it applied to all discrimination cases brought under the Civil Rights Act of 1964, including sex discrimination cases. In response, Congress passed the U.S. Civil Rights Act of 1990, which overturns the *Wards Cove* decision and shifts the burden of proof back on the employer. It was vetoed by President Bush on October 24, 1990.

The Arizona courts have not adopted the *Wards Cove* approach.[21] In *Arizona Department of Law v. Amphitheater School District,*[22] a female applicant for a high school biology teaching position was denied a teaching job because the job required all applicants to have the ability to coach varsity football. In reaching its decision that sex discrimination existed, the court clearly placed the burden of proof on the defendant-employer after the plaintiff-employee had shown discriminatory effect:

> In disparate impact suits, the burden is placed on the defendant to establish the defense of business necessity and it is a much heavier burden than merely articulating a legitimate nondiscriminatory reason for hiring decisions.

Arizona courts have also been more willing than the U.S. Supreme Court to find pregnancy discrimination as a form of sex discrimination. Despite the U.S. Supreme Court ruling in 1976 that pregnancy discrimination was not sex discrimination within the meaning of the U.S. Civil Rights Act of 1964,[23] the Civil Rights division of the Arizona Department of Law generally has succeeded in convincing superior court judges that Arizona's Civil Rights Act prohibited discrimination based on pregnancy. In 1989, the Arizona Supreme Court reviewed and let stand a lower court's decision concerning an employee who was terminated from her employment because of her pregnancy.[24] The pregnant woman was placed by an employment service to work for a physician. The physician contended that the employment service was her employer, thus he was not liable for terminating her work at his office. The Court of Appeals held that the Arizona Civil Rights Act should be broadly construed so as to include "any individual charged with the responsibility for making or contributing to an employment decision for an employer."[25] Therefore, the physician was liable for the wrongful discharge of this pregnant woman.

Additionally, Arizona courts tend to analyze employers' job classifications critically. For example, in the case of *Arizona Civil Rights Division, Department of Law v. Olson,* the court held that the Yavapai County Police Office could not pay female "matrons" less than male "jailers," because their work was essentially equal. The court reasoned that job content, not description or title, determines the existence of "discrimination in pay on the basis of sex."[26]

In the area of sexual harassment, the Arizona Supreme Court has recently ruled on two cases. In *Ford v. Revlon, Inc.* (1987), the Arizona Supreme Court held that a manager who sexually harasses a female employee is liable for assault and battery. The court also ruled that the Revlon Company was liable for intentionally inflicting emotional distress because it knowingly neglected to address the abusive behavior of its manager, even after being notified on numerous occasions.[27] In a sexual harassment case in which a male court official forcibly hugged a female attorney, swore, and used language with sexual overtones, the Arizona Supreme Court initially decided to publicly censure him.[28] Years later, after a second incident, the official was removed from office.

The General Demographic Picture

Arizona's population grew 33.2% in the 1980s—to 3,619,660 people. Over half (50.9%) are female.[29] The median age for these 1,845,451 females in July of 1989 was 32.9 years; the median age for males was 30.6 years. As Table 10.1 shows, the female median age has been rising steadily from its 21.7 years level in 1910.

The proportion of minority women in the state is also rising. In 1910, 17.7% of Arizona females were nonwhite. In 1989, the Arizona Department of Economic Security, Research Administration, reported that this figure had risen to 25.1% (see Table 10.1): 16.1% of Arizona females were Hispanic, 5.4% were native American, 2.5% were black, and 1.1% were Asian or other.[30]

The median age of the different female populations varies considerably. In 1989, 34.7% of Hispanic females were under 16 years of age. Comparatively, 29.6% of black females, 14.8% of native American females, 19.4% of Asian females, and 18.6% of white females were in this age group. In 1986, Hispanics, on the average, were eight years younger than other Arizona ethnic/racial groups. Hispanic women between the ages of 15 and 44 have two-thirds more children than non-Hispanic women in the state.[31] Consequently, child-care issues are likely to affect Hispanic and black workers the most strongly, whereas elder care might be of greater concern to the white population. Financial needs for education and training might well also vary by ethnic/race grouping due to the differential ages and numbers of children needing care and resources.

The proportion of women in the labor force has tended to increase with the percentage of single, divorced, and widowed women in the society. In 1980, about 60% of white and Hispanic women in Arizona were married, whereas 41% of black women and 67% of American Indian women had married. More than 15% of Arizona families in the early 1980s were female-headed.[32]

TABLE 10.1 Some Characteristics of Arizona Women, 1910-1989

Date	% of Total Population Female	Female Median Age	% of Female Population That Are Nonwhite and Other Races[a]
1910	42.0	21.7	17.7
1920	45.1	22.2	12.3
1930	46.9	23.0	12.9
1940	48.3	24.6	14.2
1950	49.4	26.7	12.5
1960	49.7	26.0	10.1
1970	50.8	27.3	9.3
1980	50.8	30.1	17.3
July 1989	50.9	32.9	25.1

SOURCES: U.S. Department of Commerce, Bureau of the Census: Table 21 of 1970 Census and Table 17 of 1980 Census; Arizona Department of Economic Security, Summary 1983; U.S. Department of Commerce, Bureau of the Census, *Current Population Reports*, Table 8; State Population Estimates, by Age and Sex: April 1, 1980-July 1, 1989, p. 23; and Arizona Department of Economic Security, Research Administration, January 1989, Table 1. Arizona Total Population by Sex and Minority Status.
NOTE: a. Did not include Hispanic women until 1980, the large majority of whom were considered white for purposes of racial classification. In 1980, when Hispanic figures were reported, 15.9% of the female population was Hispanic. In 1989, Arizona Department of Economic Security data in Table 10.1 indicated that 16.1% of the female population was Hispanic. Between 1910 and 1989, the Native American (proportion of the female) population declined markedly, from 16.5% in 1910 to 5.4% in 1989.

Education levels are also related to work and career success. In 1980, 73.1% of males and 71.1% of females over the age of 25 in Arizona were high school graduates, placing Arizona men 5.8 and Arizona women 5.3 percentage points above the national average. By 1987 the national percentages had risen to 76.0% for males and 75.0% for females. In 1987, in the United States as a whole, about one-sixth of all white females over the age of 25 had completed four or more years of college compared to one-fourth of all white males over 25. Among blacks about 11% of each sex had attained this level of education; among Hispanics only 7.5% of the women and 9.7% of the men had four or more years of college.[33]

Female Participation in the Labor Force

In 1989, 1,705,999 individuals were in the Arizona civilian labor force. A substantial number (712,076 or 41.7%) were women. White women constituted 33.1% of the total labor force, whereas Hispanic, native American, and black women constituted 5.5%, 1.6%, and 1.1%

respectively (see Note 1). The proportions of working women within each racial/ethnic group has remained stable since 1980.[34] The proportion of minority women in the civilian labor force is 8.6%, their proportion of the total population is 12.9% (see Note 2) while calculations of the labor force participation of Arizona women over the age of 15 ranges from 49.7% to 53.1%. Though discrepancies in the findings of government studies exist, these studies do conclude that Arizona women's labor force participation rate is slightly below the national average of 56.6%.[35]

Variations in female participation in the labor force exist by ethnic/racial grouping. Smaller percentages of native American (41.6%) and white (45.7%) women participate in the Arizona labor force than women of other groups. Hispanic (48.0%), Asian (53.6%), and black (58.1%) women have higher participation rates.[36] These latter groups also have a higher proportion of children under the age of 16.[37]

Women's Participation by Industrial Sector

In Arizona, as in the rest of the United States, women are, on the average, employed in different industries and in different occupations than are men. In 1983, the percentage of all Arizona women working in construction was 0.9%; in agriculture 1.0%; in transportation, communications, and utilities 3.7%; finance 10.1%; manufacturing 10.3%; government 17.3%; wholesale and retail trade 22.1%; and services 25.0%.[38] State minority women follow a similar pattern with a higher proportion, Hispanic women in particular, falling in the services (38.2%) and manufacturing of nondurable goods (18.4%) categories including food, apparel, and printing products.[39]

The industries in which women work in disproportionate numbers compared to men tend to have substantially lower annual wages. Table 10.2, Average Annual Wage Payments to Covered Employees in Arizona, regroups the industries to reflect those where more than 15% of all Arizona women are employed. The average annual wage payments to employees in these industries in 1988 was $19,741. This wage is 80.5% of the average annual wage of $24,521 paid to employees in industries where males predominate. This differential in employment by industry accounts for a substantial portion of the gender pay gap that exists in Arizona, as it does for the United States as a whole.

As women become employed in the industrial sectors offering higher wages, the pay gap will likely decrease. For example, in the 1980s

TABLE 10.2 Average Annual Wage Payments to Covered Employees in Arizona[a]

Industry	1982	1984	1986	1988
Male-Dominated Industries				
Agriculture & Forestry	$10,277	$11,056	$11,421	$11,963
Manufacturing	20,593	22,650	24,787	27,441
Mining	28,197	29,825	30,217	35,890
Construction	19,658	19,210	20,598	21,175
Transportation & Utilities	21,645	23,113	24,594	26,290
Wholesale Trade	19,110	21,010	22,846	24,642
Finance, Ins. & Real Estate	16,526	19,376	22,582	24,249
All Other	NA	NA	16,006	12,819
Mean Annual Wage				$24,521
Female-Dominated Industries				
Retail Trade	$ 9,775	$10,818	$11,493	$12,058
Services	13,588	14,941	16,338	18,516
State & Local Government	16,776	18,380	20,957	22,022
Federal Government	20,708	23,396	24,082	26,367
Mean Annual Wage				$19,741
Arizona Average	$16,001	$17,341	$18,870	$20,353

SOURCE: Developed from data in *Arizona Statistical Review*, Valley National Bank, September 1985, Economic Planning Division, Phoenix, Arizona.
NOTE: a. Covered employees are nonpolitical appointees whose employment conditions, pay, and terms must conform to Arizona's civil service rules and procedures.

women moved increasingly into finance, insurance, and real estate. The average annual wage in 1988 for this sector was $24,249. "The fact that this industry is heavily concentrated in major urban areas, particularly Maricopa County, suggests one source of increasing disparity between income-earning potential for women in metropolitan and nonmetropolitan Arizona."[40]

Compared to women throughout the nation, relatively higher percentages of Arizona women are employed in services, finance, and trade. The recession and cutbacks hitting Arizona banks, savings and loan corporations, and other financial institutions in 1989 and 1990 do not bode well for Arizona women. Although unemployment for both men and women dropped by a whole percentage point between 1980 and 1989 (for women 5.1% versus 6.1%).[41] Arizona women, as well as all U.S. women, tend to work part-time rather than full-time. Shifts to part-time work conceal some of the loss of income that occurs among women during such cutbacks.

Reductions in the defense and electronics manufacturing industries (where about 22% of all Arizona manufacturing workers are employed) would directly impact more men than women. Nevertheless, these cuts will hurt service industries that do business with defense and electronic firms. Women thus will face the indirect impact of these cuts.

National trends toward moving the manufacturing of both durable and nondurable goods to developing countries with lower wages have affected Arizona women as well. The apparel and food processing industries in Arizona, for example, employ large percentages of minority women, especially Hispanic women.

Tourism has grown substantially in the 1980s, becoming the second largest industry in the state with a substantial service component. Tourism employs many low-skilled individuals and creates opportunities for small businesses. The growth of retirement cities (e.g., Sun City and Sun Lakes) and special entertainment communities (e.g., Lake Havasu and Laughlin) have created both retail sales and service jobs throughout the 1970s and 1980s for women. The potential of these jobs to provide viable career options for women (or men) is not high, however.

Women's employment in the public sector in Arizona has been substantial. The numerous military bases offer many clerical and service jobs. Between 1975 and 1984, women constituted nearly 83% of all state employees in the lower grades of government service.[42] With more than 17% of Arizona employed women working for a level of government, it is clear that local, state, and federal expenditures are important to their well-being.

Women's Participation by Occupational Categories

Figure 10.1 compares the proportion of males and females in specific occupational categories. The data reveal that, in Arizona, 12.3% of all employed women work as executives or managers. Another 14.2% of Arizona women are employed in the professional category. As is the case nationally, the highest proportion of women are employed in the administrative support/clerical category (28.1% in 1988), in the service occupations category (16.5%), and in sales (15.0%). Four percent or fewer Arizona women are employed in craft and repair work, farming, forestry, or fishing. These percentages do not differ markedly from the national ones.

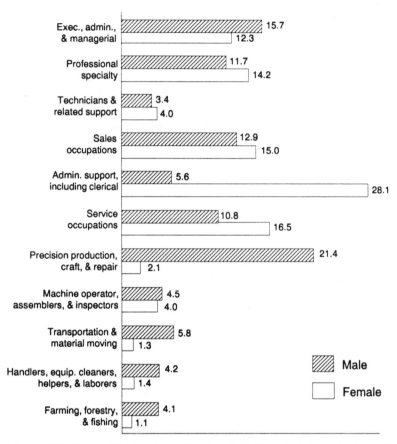

Figure 10.1. Percent Distribution of Employed Civilians in Arizona by Sex and
Occupation, 1988 Annual Averages

SOURCE: U.S. Department of Labor, *Geographic Profile of Employment and Unemployment*
(Washington, DC: Government Printing Office, 1988), p. 58, 59.

Table 10.3 recalculates these figures to depict the percentage of
women compared to men holding jobs in each of these categories. That
is, these data answer the question, "What proportion of individuals in
each occupational category are women?" The data for 1988 are generally comparable to the national percentages depicted in Table 3.4. The
percentage for female employment in the services category is lower in
Arizona than nationally, undoubtedly because the Arizona data group
protective and household services together. In Arizona, as nationally,

TABLE 10.3 Arizona Female Civilian Labor Force Employed in Specific Occupational Categories, 1980, 1985, 1988 (in percentages).

Occupational Categories	1980[a]	1985[b]	1988[c]
Executive, Administrative, Managerial	25.7	35.2	39.2
Professional/Technical	44.0	49.1	50.1
Sales	46.6	42.5	48.8
Administrative Support/Clerical	83.1	82.8	80.4
Services (Household, Protective, Other)	61.8	56.4	55.6
Crafts	6.5	11.8	7.4
Operators	38.0	44.3	42.0
Transportation, Communication, Utilities	5.9	12.5	15.4
Laborers	14.7	15.7	31.0
Farm	12.1	15.3	18.4

SOURCES: a. U.S. Bureau of Labor Statistics, *Geographic Profile of Employment and Unemployment, 1980,* Bulletin No. 2111 (March 1982), Table 4 (Washington, DC: Department of Labor); b. U.S. Bureau of Labor Statistics, *Geographic Profile of Employment and Unemployment, 1985,* Bulletin No. 2236 (September 1986), Table 15 (Washington, DC: Department of Labor); c. U.S. Bureau of Labor Statistics, *Geographic Profile of Employment and Unemployment, 1988,* Bulletin No. 2327 (May 1989), Table 15 (Washington, DC: Department of Labor).

most household service work is performed by females and most protective service work is performed by males. A slightly higher percentage of Arizona women work in the transportation and laborer categories than the national average as well. Both variations might be due to the importance of tourism in the state, increasing employment in food processing and handling as well as in transportation.

Some ethnic/racial differences that exist nationally among employed women also occur in Arizona. Non-Hispanic women hold more jobs as executives and administrators (10.1% for non-Hispanics as compared to 6.6% for Hispanics) and work in professional specialty occupations (15.4% for non-Hispanics as compared to 8.0% for Hispanics).[43]

Employer's Efforts to Address Women's Workplace Issues

Arizona employers have similar options for addressing women's workplace issues as employers in other parts of the nation (see Chapter 8). As the Arizona data reveal, tokenism and sexism are still prevalent in the 1990s, albeit reduced from previous years. Some Arizona employers are seeking to deal with the family-work dilemmas that many women face. In conjunction with the state legislature, steps are being taken to address employer responsibility for child care. Arizona

Revised Statute 43-1032, enacted in 1984, allows employers operating child care facilities to depreciate the cost of the facility over a two-year period. For-profit operations can be amortized over a five-year period. A 1990 state Senate bill, No. 1357, would give immunity from liability to an employer who subsidizes child care to its employees in a licensed day care center, so long as the employer is not guilty of gross negligence. In the Phoenix metropolitan area, near or on-site child care centers were supported in 1990 by the employers listed in Table 10.4.

Women as High-Level Executives

In Arizona, the general occupational distribution within the core and peripheral firms described in Chapter 3 seems comparable to the national pattern; however, Arizona had fewer branches of the multinational corporations than other states. In 1988, only seven of the Fortune 500 companies had their national headquarters in the Phoenix metropolitan area. In 1988, none of the chief executive officers of the top 100 privately held companies in Arizona were women.[44] In addition, only one of thirty executives who received the highest salaries in 1989 was a woman, Judy Wischer of American Continental Corporation.[45] Although her pay of $816,216 as president was the fourth highest on the list, three other men, including two senior vice presidents at American Continental, earned more than she did. The listing of the chief executives of the top 87 Arizona public companies revealed only one woman at the very top, Kathleen R. Loback at Continental Homes Holding Corporation. Wischer was not on this list because, although she is president, she is not the CEO.

Women have fared better as top executives in the governmental sector than in the private sector. In 1990, Arizona has a female governor, Democrat Rose Mofford, and a female Speaker of the House of Representatives, Republican Jane Hull. The whip of the Democratic party was a woman as were numerous committee chairs. In 1990, 30% of the Arizona legislators were women, making Arizona one of the top states in the nation for female political participation at the state level of government. Locally, in 1985 almost three of ten (28.8%) elected county seats and slightly less than one of six (17.6%) elected seats in Arizona's incorporated cities were held by women. Although Arizona women may not hold as many offices as men do, they have made gains that are higher than the national figures (only 13% of local elected

TABLE 10.4 Employers Who Support Child Care in Arizona

On-Site or Near-Site Center

American West Airlines	Phoenix Children's Hospital
Boswell Hospital	St. Joseph's Hospital
Circle K Corporation	State of Arizona
Maricopa County Community Colleges	The Point Tapatio Resort
Phoenix Memorial Hospital	

Home Day Care Systems

American West Airlines	Arizona Public Service

Resource and Referral Services

Allstate Insurance	NCR
American Express	Streitch, Lang, Weeks & Cardon
ASM Lithography	Tandem Computers
First Interstate Bank (Tucson & Phoenix)	Tucson Medical Center
IBM	Tucson General Hospital
Mitre Corporation (Phoenix)	

Sick Child Care Programs

Bilby, Shoehair (Attorneys)	JNC Companies
Burr Brown (Tucson)	O'Connell, Wezelman, Poston, Bosse (Attnys)
City of Tucson	Tucson Electric Power Co.

Voucher Programs

Arizona Bank	

Contributions to Initiate or Maintain Child Care Programs

American Express	Federal Express
Arizona Public Service	Honeywell
AT&T	Mervyn's
Basha's Markets	Salt River Project

positions went to women in 1985 nationally).[46] Margaret Hance, the mayor of Phoenix from 1976 to 1983, was among the first woman mayors of a major U.S. city.

Arizona women have also been leaders in holding significant judicial positions at the state and national levels.[47] In 1965, Arizona's Lorna E. Lockwood became the first woman ever to serve as a chief justice of a state supreme court. Sandra Day O'Connor, another Arizonan, became the first woman ever to become a U.S. Supreme Court justice in 1981. Jean Williams, the first black woman to practice law and be a judge in Arizona (appointed a Phoenix City Court judge in 1977), was also the first black woman to ever be an assistant attorney general for Cook County, Illinois (in the 1950s). Gloria G. Ybarra in 1977 became the fifth Hispanic ever to be a Maricopa County Superior Court judge, the second female Hispanic judge in Arizona. Lena Rodrigues, who served on the Pima County Superior Court, was the first Hispanic woman to serve in this capacity. In the summer of 1990, Linda Akers became the first woman U.S. attorney for the District of Arizona. Although Arizona women have been leaders in the legal field, the state still has fewer women lawyers than the national average: "In 1985, women made up 12.6 percent of the total of 7,535 lawyers in Arizona—a significant increase from 1980 [when it was 7.5 percent] but below the national rate of 15 percent."[48]

Women have enjoyed mixed degrees of success in the Arizona university system. Molly Broad holds the position of executive director of the Arizona Board of Regents and Edith Auslander serves as the 1990 president of this board. Nevertheless women are still underrepresented in line positions at the universities themselves. Arizona State University (ASU) has a better record than either the University of Arizona or Northern Arizona University, but its record also leaves much to be desired. One woman, Betty Asher, has been a vice-president (of Student Affairs); she left in 1988 to become president of the University of South Dakota. Another, Christine Wilkinson, an Asian-American, became director of Student Affairs in June 1990. Several women have been assistants to the president and assistant vice presidents (of personnel, academic programs, and business affairs). By 1990, ASU had three female deans, the highest number to date: Janelle Krueger of the College of Nursing, Anne Schneider of the College of Public Programs, and Gladys Johnston of the College of Education. Less than one-sixth of the chairs of the various ASU departments and schools are women. In part, this low percentage stems from the relatively small numbers of senior women faculty in the Arizona university system—less than 4% of all the professors are female full professors.[49]

Tokenism also hampers women's participation in the Arizona executive branch of government, but some progress has been made. Only 13% of Arizona's top public administrators (those in grades 23-30) were women in 1986. Nonetheless, between 1980 and 1985, Arizona ranked fifth in the nation in the numbers of women appointed to cabinet-level offices, with three of ten positions held by women (Betsey Bayless as head of the Department of Administration, Kathy Ferris as head of the Department of Water Resources, and Beth Jarman, and then Rita Carillo, the first Hispanic woman to hold a cabinet office, as head of the Department of Commerce). Under Governor Bruce Babbitt,

Mary C. Short also served as the state superintendent of banking. In 1988, during the governorship of Evan Mecham, Arizona's position fell to 35th of 38 states for which data were available on cabinet-level appointments of women.[50] In 1990, under Rose Mofford, the numbers of women in elected and appointed high-level positions rose again, with Catherine Eden serving as head of the Department of Administration, Linda Moore Cannon as head of the Department of Economic Security, Susan Gallinger as director of the Department of Insurance, Joyce Geyser as deputy chief of staff, and eight other women serving on the governor's executive staff. Under Mofford, Rhonda Davis has become the first black woman to serve as the registrar of contractors, and C. Diane Bishop was elected as superintendent of public instruction. Women are also making some inroads in the regional national governmental offices in Arizona. In 1984, Phoenician Ruth Anne Myers became the first woman district director in the United States in the Immigration and Naturalization Service.[51]

Profiles

Although statistics indicate the progress women have made in the Arizona economy, they only tell part of the story. Many individual women have overcome formidable barriers to create successful careers. During Arizona's first years as a state, such businesswomen as Mary E. J. Colter, the architect who designed the Bright Angel Lodge, seven other structures at the Grand Canyon, and the La Posada Hotel in Winslow, earned distinction in traditionally male fields. In the early 1970s, some Arizona women had risen to the upper rungs of management. By 1979, to name a few examples, Pamela Grant had been promoted to president of Goldwater's department stores; Shirley Agnos had become executive director of the Arizona Academy; Jeanne Herberger had become the first woman president of the Phoenix Symphony Association; and Helen Rogers and Roberta Ball had each developed successful modeling agencies (Plaza Three, Inc., and Bobby Ball Agency, respectively).[52] These women executives have received little media coverage. The next section of this chapter briefly documents the accomplishments of a few of these women executives who have had the greatest impact in this state.

Women in Real Estate and Finance

From the first years of statehood, Arizona women have advanced to positions of high authority in the real estate and financial sectors. One of the state's most influential politicians was Ana Frohmiller, who served as the elected state auditor from 1926 until 1950. Frohmiller began her political career with appointments as deputy county treasurer for Coconino County then, later, as Coconino County treasurer. Founder of the Business and Professional Women's Club, Frohmiller was the first woman state auditor in the United States.[53] In the 1980s, Bette Rambo proved that Arizona women are equally competitive in the private sector. Rambo, who is now retired, rose to the level of vice president and assistant secretary of United Bank (now Citibank).[54]

Affiliation with the government or a large corporation is not essential to women's investing success; some of Arizona's top women investors have built fortunes with their own small businesses. Trudy Connor began her career in 1970 by investing in Tucson real estate. After building a small fortune, she joined Denton Realty. In just six months, she had become the top listing agent of Denton's 125 agents.[55] Following the motto "Everything must make money: if it does not, it makes no sense," Connor later founded her own real estate investment company, Southwinds Realty, which has earned sales of over $14 million.[56] Sally Goodale, whose credits include founding the Valley of the Sun chapter of the Northwood Institute National Women's Board, past membership in the Phoenix and Scottsdale Chambers of Commerce (and knighthood granted by Prince Robert of Malta!), also earns her living by real estate investments. In the early 1980s, Goodale served as a member of the National Million Dollar Real Estate Club board of directors and as the founder and the first president of the Arizona branch of the American Chapter of the International Real Estate Federation.[57]

Arizona women have also become effective charity fund raisers. Dana Jirauch is one distinguished example. One of Phoenix's top charitable fund raisers, Jirauch helped to raise over $250,000 for the American Heart Association at the 1986 Arizona Heart Ball—the highest total raised of all of the Heart Balls held around the country in that year.[58] Jirauch's other primary interests have included: Arizona Kidney Foundation, Friends of Crisis Nursery, Gompers Women's Guild, and the Junior League of Phoenix.[59] Together, these women have provided exemplary role models for those women now beginning their financial careers.

Women in Technology and Medicine

Until recent years, Americans generally considered most technological and medical occupations to be appropriate only for men. Arizona women like Bance Hom have helped to shatter this misconception. When her family first moved to Arizona, Hom spoke only her native Chinese. By age 10, however, Hom had not only mastered the English language, she had also begun dabbling in real estate investment.[60] Hom later graduated from Arizona State University with a degree in chemical engineering, then perfected her skills in semiconductor tin-plating. In a 1987 interview with *Arizona Trend,* Hom's colleague Scott Voss, then-president of the California firm Mesa Technology, described her as "absolutely the best semi-conductor tin-plating engineer in the world."[61] Many in the business share his assessment. Hom has worked on projects with the leading American semiconductor companies and has managed plants in several Southeast Asian nations, an accomplishment achieved by few women.[62] Although her business has taken her around the world, Hom has continued her real estate investment activity in Arizona.

Another woman whose administrative skills have earned national attention is Alethea Caldwell, a chief executive officer of the University Medical Center hospital, the training hospital for the University of Arizona medical school. When Caldwell assumed her post in 1984, the Medical Center was losing $20 million a year and was on the verge of financial collapse.[63] Concluding that state regulation of the hospital encouraged inefficiency, she persuaded the state legislature to change the hospital into a nonprofit corporation whose teaching functions remained under the control of the university. Her tough management style initially alienated many, but, as the hospital's financial health improved, she has built coalitions with faculty members and doctors.[64]

Women in Education

Arizona women have also found management opportunities in education fields. One of the state's leading Democrats and gubernatorial candidate for the Democratic party in 1986, Carolyn Warner was first elected as the superintendent of public instruction in 1974, a position she held until 1986. In that year C. Diane Bishop, another Democrat, was elected to replace her. Bishop was reelected in 1990. Indeed, superintendent of public instruction is one of two elected state political offices for which the most Arizona women candidates have sought and won (secretary of state is the other).[65]

Louise Yellowman has balanced her teaching career with political service. She has been elected as both a member of the Tuba City School Board and Coconino County supervisor, but her teaching accomplishments prompted the staff of *MAAZO Magazine* to honor her as one of the most successful Navajo women of 1985.[66] Few women better represent the achievements of Arizona women in education than Betty M. Greathouse. During her years as an associate professor in the ASU College of Education, Greathouse held numerous administrative posts "including director of the Division of Curriculum and Instruction; assistant dean of admissions and minority affairs in the Graduate College; and assistant chair of the Department of Elementary Education."[67] This Arizona native, who received her college degrees at Phoenix College and ASU, has additionally served on the Advisory Council of the Arizona Department of Economic Security; the Arizona Black Women's Task Force; Booker T. Washington Child Development Center Board; Governor's Council on Children, Youth and Families; and the board of the NAACP. Her commitment to her students prompted the ASU Black Graduate Student's Association to present her with its first faculty service award, which Greathouse lists as "the highlight of my ASU career."[68] Though she accepted an appointment to serve as dean of the School of Education at California State University at Bakersfield in July 1990, Greathouse notes that "Arizona will always be one of my homes."[69]

Women in the Arts

The Arizona arts community owes a great debt to such women administrators as Jinx Patterson, creator of the "Art in the Workplace" project, and Dr. Collice Portnoff, a former chair of the Arizona State University English Department. Patterson, who is also a member of the arts council for the Maricopa Community College District and the East Valley Partnership Art Committee, developed the workplace project to persuade business leaders and building managers to coordinate arts displays in corporate buildings, thus making art more accessible to more Arizonans.[70] Portnoff's activities have included working as the book review editor for both the *Arizona Republic* and the *Scottsdale Progress* and serving as a founding member of the Valley Shakespeare Festival, the Arizona Cello Society, the Mount Claret Cursillo Center, and the Paradise Valley Country Club.[71]

Women Entrepreneurs

Previous chapters in this book have noted that some businesswomen have fared better by starting their own companies rather than working their way up existing corporate ladders. From 1980 to 1983, women-owned businesses in Arizona grew 43%; nationwide, the growth was 28%.[72] Arizona has fielded many successful women entrepreneurs. Vicki Piña, a Nogales native and founder of Metro Printing Services, was honored as the state's Business Woman of the Year - 1982.[73] A sense for style and atmosphere enabled Carol Steele to launch the popular C. Steele & Co. gourmet food stores and bakeries,[74] which, in 1990, had grown to be among the most profitable food companies in the state. By George, which started as a small boutique and has since grown to a respected chain, vaulted Pam Del Duca to the top three small business owners in the United States in 1986.[75] In the same year, Del Duca became the first woman president of the Scottsdale Chamber of Commerce.[76]

These businesses often develop from simple product lines. Dot Nez and her husband Jerry, who is also her business partner, began their business careers in video rentals. This Navajo couple initially sought the help of their tribe's Commerce Department to acquire their first business lease in Fort Defiance and purchased controlling interests in a Rent-A-Flik franchise. The couple later expanded their business to include television and video equipment sales. In 1990, they owned two additional Rent-A-Flik franchises in Chinle and Kayenta.[77]

Kathy Kolbe found that entrepreneurial success can lead to greater political power.[78] Kolbe was born with dyslexia and dysgraphia, which not only caused her to read and write backward, but also made it extremely difficult for her to learn from the standard methods of teaching. She overcame these handicaps by developing creative solutions to problems in school and in everyday life. As a mother of two exceptionally bright children, Kolbe saw a need for educational material to teach gifted students and started Kolbe Concepts, Inc., to fill this need. By 1987, over 250,000 teachers, parents, and schools from around the world were using her materials. In 1982, the Small Business Administration named her Arizona Small Business Person of the Year. In 1985, she was also honored in *Time* magazine's Man [sic] of the Year Issue.

Kolbe is the first woman to be named to the Phoenix 40, a politically influential group in the metropolitan Phoenix area.

Many women have created profitable businesses, but few in Arizona, or the rest of the nation, can match the success of Linda Brock Nelson. When she first moved to Arizona in 1969, Brock teamed up with Gus Demas. The two formed a 50-50 business partnership to start Demas Volkswagen. Brock was, and still is, one of the few women car dealers in the country.[79] Until she threatened court action, banks refused to lend Brock money without her father's approval. When Demas retired in 1979, the Volkswagen corporation initially refused to recognize Brock as a legitimate sole owner and dealer—even though she had been successful in the business for 10 years![80] Volkswagen put Brock on three months trial probation before renewing its contracts with her company. Even her employees initially threatened to leave, fearing that a woman could not handle the dealership. Brock, however, soon captured the respect of her doubters, and by 1986, owned the largest BMW and Volkswagen dealership in the state.[81] Today, Linda Brock owns four dealerships (she has added Oldsmobile and Jeep to her entourage), all of which are housed in the Linda Brock Automotive Plaza that she designed and had constructed in 1986.

Referral Networks and Professional Organizations

As women have made greater strides in the Arizona economy, some enterprising women have developed professional networks to further advance the economic power of Arizona women. "The single most important women's community-building organization in the first half of the 20th century was the Arizona Federation of Women's Clubs," started in Phoenix in 1901.[82] The Federation assisted local women's clubs with community improvement efforts and coordinated state-wide efforts to increase the political education and activities of women. In the 1990s, such professional organizations as Women in Construction, Women in Communications, Arizona Women Lawyers Association, and the Arizona Women's Initiative are helping Arizona women to continue their economic progress.

1990 marks the fifteenth year of operation for the Women's Yellow Pages, a directory and referral service now owned and published by Charlotte White. The Women's Yellow Pages semi-annual directory enables women to locate businesswomen around the state and also provides a calendar of upcoming seminars, trade shows, and other women's business events. During the first five months of 1990, White has more than doubled the circulation of her service. The January/ June 1990 edition listed 1,512 businesses and professionals. The July/ December issue will contain between 3,500 and 4,000 listings.[83]

Conclusion

The role of women in the Arizona economy is generally comparable to that of women in the rest of the United States. Compared to women in other states, Arizona women have a slight advantage in rising to high-level political office and gaining entrepreneurial success. Whether or not these advantages will be used to advance women to more significant leadership roles and executive position in the 1990s is yet to be determined.

Notes

1. Sources: 1980 Figures—Census of Population, 1980; 1989 Figures—Arizona Department of Economic Security, Research Administration, February 1990. *Arizona Labor Market Information: Affirmative Action Planning Information* (Phoenix: Arizona Department of Economic Security, Research Administration, 1990).

2. Sources: 1980 Figures—Census of Population, 1980; 1989 Figures—Arizona Department of Economic Security, Research Administration, February 1990; *Arizona Labor Market Information: Affirmative Action Planning Information* (Phoenix: Arizona Department of Economic Security, Research Administration, 1989).

3. While suffrage was an issue during the Convention, it did not become an issue during the selection of the all-male delegation to the Convention. See C. Brice, "The Constitutional Convention of 1910," cited in John D. Leshy, "The Making of the Arizona Constitution," *Arizona State Law Journal* 20 (Spring 1988), 1, 47.

4. An anti-prohibitionist yelled, "You should be shot. . . ." to a delegate who merely proposed that the issue of suffrage be put to a vote of the people. Leshy, "The Making of the Arizona Constitution," 47.

5. Leshy, "The Making of the Arizona Constitution," 47.

6. The word "proposed" is used because Congress and the president would have to approve Arizona's Constitution prior to Arizona's admittance into statehood.

7. Leshy, "The Making of the Arizona Constitution," 47, 67.

8. Leshy, "The Making of the Arizona Constitution," 67, citing to, *Arizona Legislative Blue Book: 1915-1916,* 6-7, 34-35.

9. Leshy, "The Making of the Arizona Constitution," 67. (Although very few women, nearly the reverse percentage, worked at the university level.)

10. See Arizona Revised Statutes (A.R.S.) section 23-340 et seq.

11. See A.R.S. section 23-355.

12. See 42 United States Code, Annotated, section 2000e et seq.; See A.R.S., section 41-1401 et seq.

13. See A.R.S. section 41-1421; A.R.S. section 41-1463.

14. See A.R.S. section 41-1464.

15. A.R.S. section 41-1465 limits age discrimination to individuals who are at least 40 years of age, but less than 70 years of age.

16. See A.R.S. section 41-1442.

17. *Roberts v. United States Jaycees,* 468 U.S. 609 (1984).

18. *Board of Directors of Rotary International v. Rotary Clubs of Duarte,* 107 S. Ct. 1940 (1987).

19. *Davis v. Jobs for Progress, Inc.,* 427 F. supp. 479 (1976). Citing two other judicial decisions, the Court held that this female employee was not entitled to triple damages. The Court awarded her actual damages, plus 6% interest.

20. *Wards Cove Packing Co., Inc. v. Antonio,* 109 St.C. 2115 (1989).

21. See *Higdon v. Evergreen International Airlines, Inc.* 138 Ariz. 163 (1983).

22. *Arizona Department of Law v. Amphitheater School District,* 140 Ariz. 83, 680 P.2d 517 (App. 1983).

23. *General Electric v. Gilbert,* 429 U.S. 125 (1976).

24. Attorney General's Office, *1988-1989 Annual Report,* at 117.

25. Attorney General's Office, 117.

26. *Arizona Civil Rights Division, Department of Law v. Olson,* 132 Ariz. at 26.

27. *Ford v. Revlon, Inc.,* 153 Ariz. 38, 734 P.2d 580 (1987).

28. Matter of Ackel, 155 Ariz. 34, 745 P.2d 92 (1987).

29. U.S. Bureau of the Census, *Current Population Reports,* Table 8, State Population Estimates, by Age and Sex: April 1, 1980-July 1, 1989 (Washington, DC: Government Printing Office), 23.

30. Calculated from data provided in *Arizona Labor Market Information: Affirmative Action Planning Information,* (Phoenix: Arizona Department of Economic Security, Research Administration, February, 1990), Table 1: Arizona Total Population by Sex and Minority Status, 1.

31. *Arizona Labor Market Information.* See also, "Hispanics in Transition" *Report to Governor Bruce Babbitt* (Phoenix: Arizona Department of Economic Security, 1986), 9.

32. Ray Marshall, *Work & Women in the 1980s: A Perspective on Basic Trends Affecting Women's Job Opportunities* (Washington, DC: Women's Research & Education Institute, 1983).

33. The 1980 data are from the U.S. Bureau of the Census, *Current Population Reports,* Tables 3, 17, 86, 107, 231, 239, 240, and 244 (Washington, DC: Department of Commerce, 1981). The 1987 data are from the U.S. Bureau of the Census, *Current Population Reports: Population Characteristics,* Series P-20, No. 415. Educational Attainment in the United States (Washington, DC: Department of Commerce, March 1987), 74-75.

34. Arizona Department of Economic Security, Research Administration, February 1990. "Table 2, Employment Status by Sex and Minority Status."

35. U.S. Bureau of Labor Statistics, *Handbook of Labor Statistics,* Bulletin 2340 (Washington, DC: Department of Labor, August 1989), Table 5. Civilian Labor Force Participation Rates by Sex, Race, Hispanic Origin, and Age, 1948-88, p. 27. See also, U.S. Bureau of Labor Statistics, *Geographic Profile of Employment and Unemployment, 1988,* Bulletin 2327 (Washington, DC: Department of Labor, May 1989). It might well

be that the Arizona data include all individuals over the age of 16 regardless of institutionalization status, raising the population base. Although this explanation works for the male data, it does not for the female data. The Arizona Department of Economic Security had a smaller number of women employed, 712,076, in 1989 than the U.S. Bureau of Labor Statistics, which had 714,000 in 1987. See U.S. Bureau of Labor Statistics, *Geographic Profile of Employment and Unemployment, 1987,* Bulletin 2305 (Washington, DC: Department of Commerce, April 1988), p. 41.

36. These figures are calculated from tables in the sources cited in Note 1 and Note 2. For example, the white female labor participation rate is calculated by dividing the number of white women listed as participating in the 1989 civilian labor force (565,181) by the total number of females 16 years old and over in the Arizona population in 1989 (1,237,064), which equals 45.7%.

37. U.S. Department of Commerce, Bureau of the Census: Tables 52, 67, 83, and 86 from the 1960 Census; and Tables 56, 67, 71, 176, and 180 from the 1980 Census.

38. From Figure 1. Women's Employment by Sector, 1983. Susan Christopherson, "Women in the Arizona Economy: Recent Trends and Future Prospects," in *Women and the Arizona Economy: The First Arizona Women's Town Hall,* eds. Janice Monk and Alice Schlegel (Tucson: University of Arizona, Southwest Institute for Research on Women, 1986), 197.

39. Arizona Department of Economic Security, "Hispanics in Transition," *Report to Governor Bruce Babbitt* (Phoenix, AZ: Author, 1986), 9.

40. Christopherson, "Women in the Arizona Economy," 203.

41. See Note 2, this chapter.

42. Mary M. Hale and Rita Mae Kelly, "Women in Arizona Government," *Gender, Bureaucracy, and Democracy* (Westport, CT: Greenwood, 1989), 46.

43. U.S. Bureau of the Census, "The Hispanic Population in the United States: March 1986-1987," *Current Population Reports: Population Characteristics.* Series P-20, No. 434 (1988); see Table 12.

44. Karen Kolbe, "Private Companies: A Glimpse into the Affairs of 100 of the State's Top Private Corporations," *Arizona Trend* August 1988, 51-55.

45. "Arizona Public Companies: A Look at How They Rank," *Arizona Trend* June 1989, 42-49.

46. For details, see Rita Mae Kelly, ed., *Women and the Arizona Political Process* (Lanham, MD: University Press of America, 1988).

47. The following information is taken from Ria Hermann and Rita Mae Kelly, "Women in the Judiciary," in *Women and the Arizona Political Process,* ed. Rita Mae Kelly (Lanham, MD: University Press of America, 1988), Ch. 6, pp. 84-108.

48. Hermann and Kelly, "Women in the Judiciary," 91.

49. Kristie Young, "Education College Aiming for Quality," *State Press* 5 March 1990, 2.

50. Hale and Kelly, *Gender, Bureaucracy, and Democracy,* 41-64.

51. Helen Ferger, "Ruth Anne Myers: Finally It's Illegal to Hire Illegal Aliens," *Arizona Trend* June 1987, 17.

52. William K. Bare, "Mary E. J. Colter: Architect and Designer," *Arizona Highways Magazine* 60 (May 1984): 16-17. See also Carol Osman Brown, "Women Executives— Phoenix' Greatest Resource," *Phoenix Metro Magazine* 14 (April 1979), 82-87ff.

53. Mary Aickin Rothschild and Pamela Claire Hronek, "A History of Arizona Women's Politics," in *Women and the Arizona Political Process,* ed. Rita Mae Kelly (Lanham, MD: University Press of America, 1988), 13.

54. "Reaching for the Stars," *Phoenix Metro Magazine* 19 (May 1984), 70.

55. Beverly Gary Kempton, "Passionate Investors: Putting Your Money Where Your Heart Is," *Working Woman* 11(2) (February 1986), 35.

56. Kempton, "Passionate Investors," 35-36.

57. "Juggling Act," *Phoenix Metro Magazine* 19 (May 1984), 70.

58. Catherine Czagany, "Rising Stars: Charity, Dana Jirauch," *Phoenix Metro Magazine* 22 (September 1987), 69.

59. Czagany, "Rising Stars . . . Dana Jirauch," 69.

60. Ellie Winninghoff, "Bance Hom: An Engineer Who Knows How to Play Her Chips," *Arizona Trend* 1 (August 1987), 22.

61. Winninghoff, "Bance Hom," 22.

62. Winninghoff, "Bance Hom," 24.

63. John Craddock, "Alethea Caldwell: Tough Operator in a Life-or-Death Business," *Arizona Trend* 1 (January 1987), 30.

64. Craddock, "Alethea Caldwell," 30-32.

65. Barbara J. Burt-Way, "Women in the Electoral Process: As Voters, Candidates, and Municipal Officeholders," in *Women and the Arizona Political Process,* ed. Rita Mae Kelly (Lanham, MD: University Press of America, 1988), 27.

66. "MAAZO's Selections: Successful Navajo Women, 1985," *MAAZO Magazine* 1(4) (Winter 1986), 36.

67. John Mathews, "Greathouse Named Education Dean at Cal State Bakersfield," *ASU Insight* 7 May 1990, 11.

68. Mathews, "Greathouse Named Education Dean," 11.

69. Mathews, "Greathouse Named Education Dean," 11.

70. Czagany, "Rising Stars: Arts, Jinx Patterson," *Phoenix Metro Magazine* 22 (September 1987), 69.

71. Nick Salerno, "The Remarkable Collice Portnoff," *Phoenix Metro Magazine* 19 (May 1984), 67-68.

72. M. Christine Prentice, "Women in the Arizona Economy," in *Arizona's Changing Economy,* ed. Bernard Ronan (Phoenix, AZ: Commerce Press, 1986), 249-262. See also, Bernard Ronan and Christine Prentice (with Mary Melcher and Rita Michalak), "Private Sector and Nonprofit Sector Women and the Political Process: Women and Contemporary Institutional Structures," in *Women and the Arizona Political Process,* ed. Rita Mae Kelly (Lanham, MD: University Press of America, 1988), 109-128.

73. *En Arizona, Quien es Quien: In Arizona, Who's Who* (Phoenix, AZ: Fiesta Productions, 1983), 230.

74. Carrie Sears, "Carol Steele's Delectable Digestibles," *Phoenix Metro Magazine* 18 (October 1983), 51, 137.

75. Ronan and Prentice, "Private Sector and Nonprofit Sector," 124.

76. Ronan and Prentice, "Private Sector and Nonprofit Sector," 124.

77. "Starting Out: Jerry Nez and Dot Nez, Partners in Business," *MAAZO Magazine* 1(3) (1985), 12.

78. Ronan and Prentice, "Private Sector and Nonprofit Sector," 123.

79. Judy Schriener, "Linda Brock: Green Light in the Fast Lane," *Arizona Trend* 1 (October 1986), 60.

80. Schriener, "Linda Brock," 27.

81. Schriener, "Linda Brock," 25.

82. Rothschild and Hronek, "A History of Arizona Women's Politics," 15-16.

83. Kimberly Fisher, telephone interview with Charlotte White, May 23, 1990.

11

Consensus Statements and Recommendations of the Fifth Arizona Women's Town Hall

Approximately 450 women from throughout the state have now participated in this Arizona Women's Town Hall—an event best characterized as public participation in a consensus process. The process annually revolves around an issue of particular importance to women as individuals, as Arizona residents, and as U.S. citizens.

A broad cross-section of statewide nominations provides a powerful source of potential participants. Applicants are selected with the intent of providing a comprehensive balance of knowledge and experience by achieving diversity in race, occupation, income, educational background, and urban versus rural lifestyles. (See Appendix for a list of the 1990 participants.)

Consensus is basic to Town Hall, beginning each year with a research document produced at one of the state's universities. This document provides the focus of panel discussions that seek the group's collective viewpoint. As each panel reaches consensus on identical discussion questions (see Appendix), their statements are merged into one report. The last half day is spent in a plenary session during which each paragraph of the final Town Hall report is discussed, amended as necessary, and ultimately approved by all participants. Because personal enrichment, sensitization to issues, and new ideas have spurred many to action following past Town Halls, it is the hope of the Executive Committee that this report will provide a basis for further discussion and action regarding public policy on this issue.

The "glass ceiling" has been researched and explored in such diverse fields as religion, medicine, education, the public sector, and the corporate world. The consensus and recommendations that follow are the achievements of participants in the Fifth Arizona Women's Town Hall: "Windows of Opportunity or Locked Doors? Women, Work and Success." Provocative in scope yet nonadversarial in process, "Windows of Opportunity" promises to be a Town Hall of far-reaching impact for some time to come.

To set goals for Arizona women for the next year and the next decade, 150 Arizona women were selected from the pool of nominees. They met for the Fifth Annual Arizona Women's Town Hall, sponsored by Soroptimist International of Phoenix, September 13-16, 1990, in Chandler, Arizona. The research document they considered consisted of the first ten chapters of this book. The final conclusions of these Town Hall participants are enumerated in the remainder of this chapter. The report highlights the Town Hall's consensus about desired goals for Arizona women and their reactions to the research document's major themes: (1) sex-role ideology, the U.S. Constitution, and gender equality in the labor force; (2) sex, gender, stereotypes, and success; (3) the role of government and business; and (4) women, work, and careers in Arizona.

Goals for Arizona Women: Next Year and Next Decade

Setting goals and priorities for Arizona women over the next decade requires clear determination of where Arizona women should be in the year 2000. These goals should include:

A. More female candidates for governor, the legislature, other state and local offices, and Congress.
B. Female CEO positions in no less than ten major Arizona companies.
C. Fifty percent female management positions.
D. A female president of a major university.
E. Doubling female small business ownership.
F. Seventy-five percent turnout of women voters in elections.
G. Obtaining necessary changes in Arizona statutes to permit and encourage flexible work hour arrangements.
H. Affordable housing.
I. Child and elderly care.
J. Health care for all Arizona citizens.

Partnership with the Arizona legislature and the Arizona private and public sectors is required to accomplish results.

Strategies to achieve such goals include:

1. *Political*
   a. Organize to influence candidates campaigning for office.
   b. Support, with both money and time, women candidates who are supportive of women's issues, nationally and locally.
   c. Support elected officials and candidates advocating women and family issues even if this results in increased taxes.
   d. Develop working relationships with legislators to improve communication.
   e. Work to increase women's appointments to influential boards and commissions, public and private.
   f. Monitor decisions by judges on family and job issues and use that information to influence retention of judges.
   g. Establish and permanently fund the Office of Women and Office of Children through legislation rather than by executive order.

2. *Business and Community*
   a. Encourage government and business partnerships to implement new initiatives supportive of the family.
   b. Establish a "watch dog committee" with the following purposes: to monitor the commitment to women's issues of businesses, agencies, legislators, and the judicial system; to disseminate resultant information; and to enhance women's economic power through the effective utilization of our roles as consumers and voters.
   c. Encourage women to use their economic power.
   d. Address issues of staff training in the workplace.
   e. Exert economic pressure on companies that purport to support women but do not.
   f. Encourage business and community organizations to provide scholarships for women.
   g. Recognize agencies and employers which implement and enforce policies which support women and family issues.
   h. Create "800" numbers for women throughout the state to access information and services.
   i. Increase media support for women.
   j. Expand hours and establish appointment schedules to make government agencies more accessible to working employees.

3. *Education*
   a. Monitor educational policies and institutions to ensure that stereotyping is eliminated and that encouragement is provided for student entry into non-traditional fields.
   b. Ensure that school boards support girls' participation in science and math, nonacademic curricula, technical training and athletics.
   c. Promote school/community efforts which recognize and reward academic achievement in all children.

    d. Ensure that community colleges and universities provide services and support for young women and for women reentering the education process.

    e. Ensure appropriate and consistent regulation of private education to reduce exploitation of women.

    f. Ensure the availability of sex education for grades K-12.

4. *Personal*

    a. Be a mentor.

    b. Network.

    c. Volunteer to serve on commissions and boards.

    d. Run for elective office and support policies that benefit women and families.

    e. Become politically active at all levels (city, county, state, federal).

    f. Be informed.

    g. Communicate with elected and appointed officials.

    h. VOTE!

To achieve these long-range goals, Arizona women must pursue them on three fronts: awareness, advocacy, and action. The strategies cited are necessary if change is to be obvious by the year 2000. Advocacy and action are the responsibility of each woman within her own sphere. In addition, existing women's organizations must mobilize as coalitions to enhance their influence and resources, and to capitalize on each group's expertise.

Sex Role Ideology, the Constitution, and Gender Equality in the Labor Force

Women have entered the labor force in large numbers in the last decade. Factors fostering the growth of women in the work force and in management include the impact of World War II, the women's and civil rights movements, increased education, access to birth control, limited day care improvements, and legislative and judicial developments.

Labor force entry has occurred primarily at the lower levels of income and power, with modest participation in mid-management. Representation at top levels of management and in critical policy- and decision-making positions remains minimal. Although women hold management positions in increasing numbers, they have not made significant advances in positions of authority or salary levels and remain largely absent from the policy- and decision-making processes. In addition, women's progress into management fields has been isolated to particular segments of the economy (e.g., service, technical, or professional), and progress in the "core industries"[1] has been very limited. Women tend to advance in the service and public sectors, in small businesses in which they have become entrepreneurs, and in those sectors of the economy in which competence is critical and gender differences are irrelevant.

A number of factors slows the admission of women into the management power structure and their progression within that structure. Women do not use networking effectively and may not have the support systems typically available to men. Women bring different management perspectives to the workplace. Few successful career role models exist for women. Women are perceived as not supporting other women and as unable to provide leadership in a team mode. The actions of one woman, regardless of race or age, are perceived as typical of all women.

For the mind-set of society to change, continued emphasis must remain on affirmative action, equal pay for equal or comparable work, and policies and processes that support the "family." (In this document, the concept of family is broadly defined, recognizing the real changes in our culture.) As the critical agent of cultural change, family must not be characterized as a liability. Rather, the family and its support must become a priority. The marketplace must allow greater accommodation of important personal demands by provisions for child care, family care, parental leave, elderly care, and health care. Moving the marketplace into the home by ascribing economic value to care-giving is one way to do this.

The Legal System

Numerous myths about women pervade the legal system and work to the detriment of both women and men. The legal system operates on the fundamental assumption that women are weak physically, intellectually, and emotionally and, therefore, need protection. In effect, the assumption of weakness is used to remove options for women rather than to protect them. The law assumes that women always rear children better; thus, men may also suffer when courts award custody in a divorce. The move to no-fault divorce in most states has had the unexpected result of the "feminization" of poverty. Child support awards alone cannot replace equal responsibility for children, particularly when payments are not forthcoming. Such myths cannot be overcome by tinkering with particular laws. Basic cultural structures reflected in those laws must be addressed.

To foster change that will benefit society, women must become involved with the legal system in greater numbers. Women must become aware of their rights and work to remove antiquated laws that impose legal barriers. Women must encourage the administrative, legislative, and judicial branches of government to support positive solutions to issues inaccurately stereotyped as "women's issues." These issues are more appropriately called "human issues" and "family issues" and include, but are not limited to, affirmative action, prenatal care, parental leave, and day care for children or elderly dependents. Existing laws must be adequately and fairly enforced. Women must take advantage of their important opportunity to exercise their strength in numbers in the political process through voting, lobbying, contributing to and working in political campaigns, and running for elective office. Women must continue to move into leadership roles in the legal system.

Women's Involvement in the Economy

Historically, women have been employed in segments of the economy that are vulnerable to economic fluctuations and change. Cultural bias, lack of recognition of skills that are transferable to the workplace, and role expectations partially explain why women gravitated toward less secure service industry jobs and other jobs with lower pay and prestige. Often, these were not jobs of choice; they were simply the jobs that women could get.

Women raised with goals of safety and security gravitate by default toward vulnerable segments of the economy. Low self-esteem or low self-concept may cause women to self-select jobs in vulnerable economic areas. Women's role as caregivers draws them to service-oriented occupations such as teaching and nursing. Most women assumed the primary obligation of family, limiting their ability and opportunities necessary for promotions.

The education system currently perpetuates cultural bias and gender-based expectations; this must change to both accommodate and emphasize early awareness and exploration of options for girls (including math, science, and technical areas). Education must provide women with the background to position themselves for advancement within or reentry into the work force. At the same time, the status of traditional "women's work" must be improved to command salaries commensurate with male-dominated positions. We must all break down our traditional notions of what boys and girls will grow up to do in the family and workplace. Family planning and sex education curricula in the schools will assist in this process.

Barriers in the Workplace

Women face many barriers in the workplace, and these barriers vary across occupations. Women's primary responsibility for family concerns creates conflicting demands that the workplace does not often accommodate. Women in small businesses have difficulty getting financing. Few support systems exist for women in either traditional or nontraditional working environments and particularly for women who work alone. The traditional attitudes inherent in the "good ol' boy" network operate to prevent the full involvement of women. Discrimination interferes with the promotion of women. Traditional professions often are more rigid than the newer entrepreneurial fields. Often women are not taken seriously, and women and men do not support each other in the workplace. Men sometimes relate to women as sex objects, wives, and daughters.

Overcoming these barriers requires conviction that they constitute temporary stumbling blocks and are not insurmountable. Women should network, supporting each other to make fundamental changes in the workplace. Discrimination on the basis of sex, race, age, religion, or physical and mental disability must not be tolerated.

Society must acknowledge that different occupations require different family planning strategies and career path timing. Women must have freedom to plan their careers accordingly. Positive female role models are critically important if we are to impart a full awareness of options and opportunities to both girls and boys at an early age. The impact of education on the home, community, and workplace cannot be underestimated.

Women need opportunities to participate in leadership education so that they may learn management and leadership strategies. As women reach positions of power, they must exert their power in such a way that both women and men benefit. Women must recognize and use their potential, their ability to manage power, and their ability to manage multiple demands on their lives. As women more clearly define their long-term goals and balance them with the lifestyle of their choice, they must map out strategies. Mentors and mentoring are essential to achieve this goal.

Women can make a positive difference for themselves and for future generations by spearheading the effort to ensure that action will be taken. Barriers will erode by increasing the number of women in the work force and by full use of their economic power for positive change. The majority of this nation's population is women; to fail to foster, consciously or unconsciously, their full participation in the growth and development of a dynamic society limits that growth and development.

Sex, Gender, Stereotypes, and Success

As women of all ethnic backgrounds enter the work force in greater numbers and seek career success, they encounter conflict between their socialization and the behavior expected in the traditional workplace. Because males and females are socialized differently, personal and organizational role conflicts are created as women try to advance in their chosen occupational fields. This may be true even though women may have the same career aspirations as men.

Role Expectations

When the Town Hall participants considered what roles women are expected to play, the consensus was, "Women are expected to be everything but quarterback."

Different institutions influence women's perceptions of their ability to succeed in business and occupations. The family is most influential on women's perceptions of their role in society. Many women are expected to fulfill all of the traditional family roles including wife, mother, caregiver of elderly dependents, and chauffeur—leading to the imposition of "super women" standards. However, it was recognized that these expectations are often self-imposed. Creation of new and realistic expectations for all family members is critical to the success of women in their multiple roles. Family members influence these expectations by the example they set in the division of family responsibilities.

The media can assist in reformulating traditional gender-specific roles. It must portray effective, realistic role models and excise stereotypes from routine programming, news coverage, and advertisements.

The educational system can influence role expectations by directing and encouraging students on the basis of capability rather than gender. Recent legislation improved access to nontraditional career paths for girls, including increased participation in athletics.

Government can promote equality or destroy it. Women must work to keep government open and responsive. Government should foster women's rights to choose career fields, including the choice to be a full-time mother and homemaker.

Workplace structures influence women's perceptions of their ability to succeed. Research documents the small number of women in high-level positions and the existence of the "glass ceiling." Employers must provide opportunities for women to achieve high positions and move beyond the use of female managers as mere tokens.

All institutions have a responsibility to positively influence women's perceptions of their ability to succeed. Without change, women will remain trapped in the "super woman" syndrome. Women and men must develop the concept of joint responsibility for what happens in the home, as well as what happens in the workplace. Support systems that will open opportunities and foster the growth and development of women must be implemented. Women must also come together and share, compare notes, and form coalitions to create an awareness of the need for change.

Necessary Workplace Policies

The workplace must change to appreciate the value of all work and not define jobs and careers by gender. Efforts must increase to insure women's and men's participation in nontraditional occupations. In addition, employers must consider how to support the changing demands of their workers' families. Both large and small employers will gain a more productive work force by adopting policies that address the issues of care for newborn or newly adopted children, sick children, and elderly dependents. Although in the past these concerns have been predominantly those of women, all workers must deal with these pressures. Business and government both must cooperate as neither can implement these policies alone. In order for employers to move in this direction, creative and flexible incentives must be found and such benefits must be available to all workers, both male and female.

Numerous strategies and benefit options have been considered and implemented throughout the country. These options include flextime, job sharing, cafeteria-style benefit programs, tax incentives and tax credits, work-at-home options, and the availability of care centers at the workplace. These strategies, however, often place undue burdens on small employers or those that operate in rural communities. Strategies and laws that foster cooperation and pooling of resources must be encouraged. Government assistance must not be hampered by bureaucracy, red tape, or processes demeaning and frustrating to recipients.

Opportunities for Promotion

Women do not enjoy the same promotional opportunities as men even though they accomplish the same tasks as effectively as men. Women are isolated from the informal power structure and from unspoken rules that affect opportunities for advancement.

Inequities must be addressed by education and training. The initial responsibility rests with women; however, the workplace must provide opportunities for learning and advancement. Women need to focus on the goals they want to attain and identify strategies to achieve those goals. They must shed their reluctance to step forward and take advantage of opportunities as they surface, accepting the accompanying risks. Rather than molding themselves to traditional behavioral norms, women must develop the confidence to maintain their individuality so that those norms will change.

Networking, mentoring, and sponsoring are critical in the sharing of experiences so that women and men may expand their understanding of workplace culture and share strategies for success. Successful women who share their knowledge help to generate success in others. Women must lead and promote other women's advancement within the workplace by hiring and promoting other qualified women whenever possible.

The Role of Government and Business

In our society, individuals believe they can make free and open decisions. In reality, their decisions are constrained by employing institutions and governmental policy.

Spheres of Family and Work

Personal and workplace responsibilities inevitably overlap; they cannot and should not remain separate. Sharing work experiences with family is important so that they understand the worker's job.

Numerous strategies are available in the workplace to reduce conflicts between work and the home: alternative work arrangements such as flex-time, telecommuting, and job sharing; employee assistance programs; and education and staff development options to assist employees with changes in the workplace and at home. Consortium and pooling of resources may assist small businesses in providing such programs. Employers must recognize that these strategies improve workers' productivity, job satisfaction, and longevity and minimize costs associated with employee absenteeism and turnover.

Recent legislation encourages school districts to establish pre-school and extended day-care programs. Although this action is wholeheartedly supported, guidelines and regulations must be implemented to assure quality care.

In the future, new entrants to the labor pool will be primarily women and minorities. To maximize this new human resource, employers and employees must cooperate and recognize their interdependence. The employee's challenge is to achieve a balance between work and personal lives. Employers need to be flexible and respect workers' familial responsibilities. When the interrelationship of work and home is acknowledged, both employee and employer benefit.

Affirmative Action and Other Options

Affirmative action is a necessary means for integrating the work force. The misperception that affirmative action is for the "unqualified" affects the success of its programs and creates potential for backlash. Some employers merely pay lip service to affirmative action programs; many employers are not bound by current affirmative action and EEO constraints; government monitoring has been inconsistent. There must be measures to enforce affirmative action. Moreover, changing demographics require employers to better implement and understand affirmative action and to provide opportunities in addition to those mandated by affirmative action.

Women must develop options to bring about systematic change and diversity in the workplace. Educational programs can assist employers and employees in this regard. Multiple hiring criteria should be used to identify and tap potential from a broader pool of applicants. Early recognition and development of women's and minorities' potential can be accomplished through specialized programs, including educational scholarships and internships in the workplace. Employer outreach programs can bring women and minorities into the workplace at younger ages; grade school programs, youth programs, and "adopt-a-school" efforts are important strategies. Employers and employees must recognize the value of mentoring; those who mentor should be rewarded. Although the U.S. Supreme Court is eroding concepts of affirmative action, employers must be aware that benefits accrue and profits are enhanced by a diverse work force.

Concepts of Equality

Traditional male-defined concepts of equality do not value the circumstances and attributes of women. Indeed, traditional concepts of equality are limiting, presenting only one model for conduct. A new paradigm of human equality and equity that does not preclude diversity must be established.

Many women, particularly women of color, are forced to sacrifice cultural identity for career advancement. Non-gender-specific performance standards need to be developed and accepted. Women must have access to all economic resources, credit, and business financing. Economic equality for women will exist in the workplace when women and men are chosen for positions based on objective job-related criteria. Progress toward economic equality can be measured by parity in the paycheck and equal access to the highest paid positions.

Women must have the confidence to attach a higher value to their services and arm themselves with data to support their value. Women must educate themselves and take responsibility for their economic existence, and they must make the decisions that define their economic life.

Understanding of Human Nature by the Legal System

The legal system reflects the autonomous male model, unresponsive to the needs of women as crime victims, primary caregivers, and workers. The legal system must address human issues arising from the interdependence of women and men, family and workplace. Even today, domestic violence is not treated seriously; sexual harassment is not completely understood nor are concepts of equal pay for equal work and comparable work recognized. Failure to pay child support is largely ignored, and payment remains unenforced.

The legal system must be more accessible. Judges must be made more accountable through an impartial tracking system. The courts and legislatures must play a more active role in making the system more responsive to human issues and integrating family and work.

Women, Work, and Careers in Arizona

Economic Power

Arizona women have tremendous economic power at their disposal. Women use economic resources daily but do not use these transactions to exercise their economic influence. Because women's economic power is not highly visible, institutions do not consider traditional women's issues important in making policy.

This power could be exercised through many avenues including: increased base of contributions and support of political candidates who support women and family issues; support of businesses concerned with family and issues related to the employment of women; and boycotts of businesses that do not. Education can help women to use their economic power and control their assets more effectively. This education should begin when children are first introduced to money. Whether their funds are the result of earned income or public assistance, women of all ages must learn how to manage their money, exercise their buying power, negotiate, and understand that money talks.

Collective efforts that take advantage of the power in numbers provide economic power that individuals lack. Coordination with and education from groups not necessarily identified as "women's" groups can assist women in exercising and expanding their economic power.

Disadvantages and Opportunities for Arizona Women

Many characteristics of our state create unique disadvantages for women. Arizona's "good ol' boy" network is strong. The state's large geographic area and low population density perpetuate a "frontier" mentality of macho individualism. The transient nature of our population makes the development of lasting relationships and networks difficult. Women in isolated rural areas and in transient and migrant populations suffer a lack of educational and economic opportunities. Sprawling urban areas deprive cities of a sense of community, foster isolation that hinders collective efforts, and suffer from lack of adequate public transportation. Arizona's current political climate reflects traditional male values and is neither conducive to women or family issues, nor supportive of issues affecting minorities and women.

Arizona lacks educational opportunities, and available educational institutions are concentrated in urban areas. Social welfare, medical, and mental health programs are seriously behind those of other states. Labor laws, domestic relations laws, property laws, and their enforcement inadequately support Arizona women.

At the same time, Arizona's open and informal atmosphere creates unique opportunities in which women can excel. The diverse origins and transient nature of our population bring new ideas to Arizona, and our variety of cultures sensitizes us to world markets. As a young state, a growth state, and a sun belt state, Arizona offers women the opportunity to participate in all institutions and effect change.

Model Programs and Policies in the Private Sector and in Government

Numerous programs exist in Arizona that increase productivity while also benefitting women and children. These models should be explored in depth and considered for replication by other workplace entities. These models include, but are not limited to:

1. *Workplace Programs*
   a. Day and evening dependent care.
   b. Adoption benefits.
   c. Pretax child care payroll deductions.
   d. Child care subsidies and sick care leaves.
   e. Referral services for child care, including participant discounts.
   f. Flextime, job sharing, cafeteria-style benefits, and telecommuting.
   g. Employee assistance programs.
   h. On-site medical services, child care, and emergency care.
   i. Value difference/pluralism programs.
   j. Tuition reimbursement programs.
   k. In-service career counseling.
   l. Literacy and English-as-a-Second-Language programs.
2. *Business/Education/Government Partnerships*
   a. Training, retraining, and internship programs.
   b. "Adopt-a-school" projects.
   c. High school outreach programs.
   d. Displaced homemakers programs.
   e. Job training for women receiving public assistance.
   f. Literacy programs.
   g. Junior Achievement.
   h. The Job Training Partnership Act.
   i. Programs utilizing retired persons' skills.
   j. Grants and scholarships.

    k. Small business loans and incentives.

    l. Housing assistance programs.

    m. Women business enterprise and minority business enterprise programs.

3. *Community Programs*

    a. Community leadership programs.

    b. Big Brother and Big Sister programs.

    c. Leadership training programs for women in rural communities.

    d. Outreach programs for economically disadvantaged.

    e. Community college and university leadership academies.

    f. Community college, university, and other community-based child care programs.

    g. Literacy and English-as-a-Second-Language programs.

    h. Mentoring and internship programs for women.

    i. Women's commissions and issues committees.

    j. Chambers of Commerce.

    k. Arizona Women's Town Hall.

    l. Education and support programs to prevent teen pregnancies and assist pregnant teens and teenage mothers.

    m. Housing assistance programs.

    n. "Women's Yellow Pages" directory.

    o. Women's professional organizations.

    p. Outreach programs for prenatal and postnatal care.

Tomorrow's workplace will be very different from the workplace of today. More women and more minorities will be present; in fact, they are the majority of new workers. These model options are proven strategies that enable all workers, but particularly women, to be more productive, to contribute to the extent of their ability, and to use their talents for the benefit of Arizona's economy and society. These are our "Windows of Opportunity"; Arizona must face this challenge.

    CARPE DIEM!

Note

1. *Core industries* are defined here as those that have sufficient demand for goods and/or services, profit, and cash flow to enable employment of workers on a full-time, year-round basis at a higher level than other industries.

Appendix

1990 Arizona Women's Town Hall Panel Discussion Questions

Part I: Sex-Role Ideology, U.S. Constitution, and
Gender Equality in the Labor Force (Morning Session)

1. Have women made significant advances into management fields over the last decade? What factors best explain women's progress or lack thereof?

2. What myths about women still pervade the legal system? How can these myths be overcome? At what point do laws protecting women discriminate against men? Should women encourage future administrations, congresses, and courts to support women's issues? If so, how, and what issues should be supported?

3. Why have women filtered into more vulnerable segments of the U.S. economy? Are economic factors alone primarily responsible for this problem?

4. Do women still face barriers when working toward upper management or small business success? If so, identify the primary barriers. Do barriers vary over different kinds of occupations? What must be done to ensure that women will succeed in business and occupations?

Part II: Sex, Gender, Stereotypes, and Success (Afternoon Session)

1. What roles are U.S. women expected to play today? To what extent, if any, do each of the following institutions influence women's perceptions of their ability to succeed in business and occupations: family, media, schools, government, corporate structures? How can these institutions best prepare women for careers? What roles should men and women play?

2. Should business adopt policies to address the following issues: day care for children and elderly parents, care of sick children, care of newborn or newly adopted children? If so, what should the policies be, and what other policy issues should businesses address?

3. Do men and women manage differently? If so, how could businesses capitalize on that difference?

4. Do women and men have the same opportunities to be promoted? If general inequities still exist, what can women and businesses do to correct these inequities? What options for career development should women pursue to move into leadership positions? What can individual women who have succeeded do to help other women make it to the top?

Part III: The Role of Government and Business (Morning Session)

1. Should family and work remain separate spheres of workers' lives? How can businesses reduce conflicts between careers and family responsibility?

2. Is affirmative action the most appropriate option to integrate women and minorities into the work force? What other options could replace or compliment affirmative action programs?

3. Have traditional concepts of equality helped or hindered women's entrance into management positions? How should equality for women in economic leadership be defined? How should progress toward this definition be measured?

4. Do women and men have different understandings of human nature? If so, how can these differences be reconciled in the legal system? If not, how can the legal system be made more responsive to women's needs? Should courts and legislatures play a more active role in reducing the conflict between women's roles as employees and their roles as mothers, spouses, daughters, etc.?

Part IV: Women, Work, and Careers in Arizona (Morning Session)

1. How much economic power do Arizona women have today? In what ways is that power, or lack of power, manifested?
2. Do Arizona women face any unique disadvantages? If so, identify. How can these disadvantages be handled? Do Arizona women enjoy any unique business opportunities? If so, identify. How can these opportunities be increased?
3. Identify Arizona private sector business policies and programs which could serve as models to help women. Identify Arizona laws and government programs which could serve as models.
4. What goals should Arizona women pursue over the next year? What goals should they pursue over the next decade? What action should be taken to attain these goals by: state government, city and county governments, large businesses, small businesses, Arizona women?

1990 Arizona Women's Town Hall Executive Committee

Sharon Arnold, Scottsdale. Director of Donor Relations, ASU Office of Development.

Mildred Bulpitt, Phoenix. Retired, formerly Dean, National Institute for Leadership Development, Rio Salado Community College; Assistant to the Chancellor, Maricopa Community Colleges; Dean, Continuing Education and Community Service, Phoenix College.

Susan J. Cypert, Phoenix. Director, Governor's Office of Women's Services.

Sondra F. Davis, Phoenix. Payroll Audit Manager, State Compensation Fund.

Julia E. Ellegood, Phoenix. Technical Writer; Environmental Coordinator.

Janet G. Elsea, Phoenix. President, Communications Skills.

Jenny Erwin, Phoenix. Vocational Equity Specialist, Arizona Department of Education.

Jessica Gifford Funkhouser, Phoenix. Chief Counsel, Criminal Division; Arizona Attorney General.

Carol A. Hebert, Phoenix. Adjunct Faculty, Rio Salado Community College.

Emma Hedlund, Phoenix. President and Owner, Hedlund Fabric & Supply Co.

Toby Jalowsky, Phoenix. Owner and Operator, Academy of Business.

Mindy Korth, Scottsdale. Financial Specialist, Trammel Crow Company.

Deborah Larkins, Phoenix. Owner, Larkins and Associates Advertising.

Althea C. Long, Phoenix. Public Relations and Marketing Manager, Scottsdale Community College.

Kathie P. Lucas, Phoenix. Senior Government Affairs Representative, Salt River Project.

Kay A. Martin, Scottsdale. Assistant State Supervisor, Health Occupations Education, Arizona Department of Education.

Elizabeth McNamee, Phoenix. Vice President of Administration (Northern Region), Intergroup of Arizona.

Barbara L'Ecuyer Nordlund, Scottsdale. Education Program Specialist, Arizona Department of Education.

Judy M. Numbers, Phoenix. Executive Director, YWCA of Maricopa County.

Suzanne Nystrom, Phoenix. Executive Director, American Red Cross, Central Arizona Chapter.

Vicki Piña, Phoenix. Owner, Chroma Copy and Metro Copying & Printing.

Marni Pingree, Glendale. Media Consultant.

Harriet Redwine, Phoenix. Architectural Specifications Consultant.

Jadel L. Roe, Phoenix. Deputy Chief, Special Services Bureau, Maricopa County Sheriff's Office.

Marjorie Schmidt, Phoenix. Marketing and Media Consultant, MS Marketing.

Gail Thackeray, Phoenix. Assistant Attorney General, Organized Crime Division, Arizona Attorney General's Office.

Town Hall Speakers

Keynote Address

Janet Guthrie. Race Car Driver, Aerospace Engineer, Pilot, and Flight Instructor.

Speakers

Carol Fannin: "Women in the Power Position"

Joan Ingalls. Vice President, Compensation and Benefits, Greyhound Dial Corporation.

Panel Discussion—Arizona [S]heroes

Charlene Caro. President, Kezia Contracting Company.

Leona Kakar. Executive Director, Ak Chin Indian Community Council.

Gloria Weimerskirch. Operations Manager, Kwik Kopy.

Chairs and Recorders

Plenary Session Chair: Susan Bolton, Phoenix, Judge, Superior Court of Arizona.

Report Chair: Joyce Elsner, Phoenix, Dean of Administrative Services, Glendale Community College.

Panel Chairs: Marilyn Evans Hawker, Deborah Karr King, Ruth McGregor, Ruth Anne Myers, Vivienne Williams (Panel chairs are also listed under participants, where their affiliations may be found.)

Panel Recorders: Loral Deatherage, Phoenix, Attorney, Fennemore Craig PC; Vicki Gotkin-Adler, Phoenix, Assistant Attorney General, Arizona Attorney General's Office; Mariannina Preston, Phoenix, Assistant Attorney General, Arizona Attorney General's Office; Diana Wilkes, Phoenix, Law Student, Arizona State University; Marty Woelfle, Phoenix, Assistant Attorney General, Arizona Attorney General's Office.

Consensus Processor: David Flowers.

1990 Arizona Women's Town Hall Participants

Vicki Gotkin-Adler, Phoenix. Assistant Attorney General Criminal Division, Arizona Attorney General's Office.

Marilyn Alexander, Phoenix. Teacher, Madison School District.

Sharon Arnold, Scottsdale. Director of Donor Relations, Office of Development, Arizona State University.

Carolyn J. Baecker, Mesa. Partner, The Evans Investment Company.

Marilyn Bagwell, Scottsdale. Associate Professor, College of Nursing, Arizona State University.

Georgianne Baker, Scottsdale. Associate Professor of Family Studies and Women's Studies, Arizona State University.

Joan Barry, Phoenix. President, Facilities Development, Inc.

Josephine E. Bates, Globe. Retired, Past Educator and AEA Staff Member.

Louise Battaglia, Phoenix. Executive Assistant, State of Arizona.

Gwen M. Bedford, Phoenix. Library Science, Research, and Aging Services.

Linda Bentheim, Phoenix. Director, Corporate Communications, St. Joseph's Hospital and Medical Center.

Barbara Ann Bermudez, Tucson. Data Management Administrator, Hughes Aircraft Company.

Suzanne Renee Bias, Phoenix. Senior Business Operations Manager, Arizona State University College of Fine Arts.

Armida Guerena Bittner, Globe. Gila County School Superintendent.

Pamela R. Blagrave, Showlow. Accountant & Consultant, Management Alternatives.

Denise Blommel, Scottsdale. Attorney, Stephens Watts Day & Brown.

Jacki L. Bowers, Phoenix. President, Bowers Worldwide Travel Service.

Patricia J. Bried, Scottsdale. Associate Director of Adult Education, Franciscan Renewal Center.

Carolyn Bristo, Phoenix. Management Assistant, City of Phoenix, Development Services Department.

Joyce W. Brockway, Sedona. Owner/Broker, Century 21 Preferred Properties, Century 21.

Filomena M. Brooks, Tucson. Educational Director, Young Explorers Schools.

Karen Burr, Phoenix. Self-Employed, Free-lance Writer/Editor, Burr & Burr Associates, Ltd.

Janice Chilton, Payson. State Democratic Vice Chair/County Democratic Chair, and Gila County Zoning Commissioner.

Shelley M. Cohn, Phoenix. Arts Administrator, Arizona Commission on the Arts.

Phillippa Maltese Consoli, Phoenix. Administrative Assistant, St. Joseph's Hospital and Medical Center.

June A. Cornelison, Sedona. Mayor, City of Sedona, and Private Investigator.

Cindy Cornelius, Phoenix. Marketing Director, Southwest [Phoenix/Tucson], Greiner, Inc., Engineers & Planners.

Aliki Coudroglou, Scottsdale. Professor, Arizona State University.

Loretta "Sam" DeLong, Tucson. Government Relations/Public Affairs Consultant, DeLong & Associates, Inc.

Jule C. Devoe, Douglas. Director, Douglas Public Library, City of Douglas.

Mary Dieterich, Tempe. Self-Employed Professional Tapestry Artist/Weaver.

Karen L. Disbrow, Tucson. Physical Therapist, Rehabilitation Associates, PC.

Helen S. Dusick, Phoenix. Personnel Division Manager, Maricopa County Personnel Department.

Patricia Eddings, Phoenix. Program Coordinator, Academic Enrichment Office, Arizona State University.

Agnes L. Edwards, Scottsdale. Real Estate Broker, Coldwell Banker.

Lorraine F. Elam, Glendale. Vice President of Administration and Benefits, Kerley Enterprises, Inc.

Janet G. Elsea, Phoenix. President, Communications Skills.

Joyce K. Elsner, Phoenix. Dean of Administrative Services, Glendale Community College.

Edith Nell Evans, Mesa. Special Assistant to Governor Mofford, State of Arizona.

Gloria Feldt, Phoenix. Executive Director, Planned Parenthood.

Betsi Flores, Tucson. Commercial Loan Officer, Valley National Bank.

Becky Foster, Kingman. Supervisor, Mohave County.

Leslie J. Foster, Scottsdale. Owner/Manager, Faciligroup.

L. Loreen Fox-Shipley, Glendale. Clinical and Counseling Psychologist.

Anne-Marie Furrey, Phoenix. Communications Manager, US West Communications.

Ilene Gordon, Scottsdale. Director, University of Arizona Rural Health Office, and Assistant Professor, University of Arizona College of Medicine.

Betty L. Groom, Flagstaff. Program Administrator, Coconino Career & Training Center.

Christine C. Iijima Hall, Phoenix. Assistant Vice Provost, Academic Affairs, ASU West.

Janice Hamlin, Mesa. Executive Director, Save the Family Foundation.

Janet Emilie Haning, Phoenix. Admissions Officer, University of Phoenix.

Naomi Harward, Tempe. Professor Emeritus, Arizona State University and Director, Undergraduate Social Welfare Program.

Susan L. Harwood, Gilbert. Manager, Organizational & Human Resources Development, Motorola, Inc.

Marilyn Evans Hawker, Mesa. Public Affairs and Special Events Firm Owner.

Mary Hayden-John, Tempe. Assistant to the Provost, ASU West Campus.

Mary Moll Hentges, Phoenix. CPA working as Audit Senior Manager, Ernst & Young.

Susan G. Hildebrand, Scottsdale. Director, Software Services, Bull HN Worldwide Info Systems.

Lera R. Holcomb, Phoenix. Management Assistant, City of Phoenix.

Gladys House, Scottsdale. EDP Systems Project Leader, State of Arizona.

Cathy Hufault, Oro Valley. Mayor, Oro Valley and Vice President, Executive Relocation.

Diane Hughes, Tempe. Manager, Public Affairs, Garrett Fluid Systems Division.

Carol Simon Kamin, Phoenix. Executive Director, Children's Action Alliance.

Ann Kennedy, Phoenix. Co-owner, Executive Director, American Institute.

Mary Kiewel, Tucson. Executive Sales Consultant, Coldwell Banker.

Laurel H. Kimball, Phoenix. Development Officer, Arizona State University.

Deborah Karr King, Phoenix. Community Volunteer.

Ellen Kirschbaum, Phoenix. Detention Support Administrator, Maricopa County Sheriff's Office.

A. Sue Kuhlman, Phoenix. Real Estate Appraiser MAI, Burke Hansen, Inc.

Judith A. Leary, Glendale. Certified Public Accountant, Self-Employed.

Camille Levee, Scottsdale. Membership Development Specialist, Arizona Cactus Pine Girl Scouts and Owner, Ace Vac & Sew.

Olive E. Linder, Sun City. Volunteer, Retired Teacher.

Sheryl Lindsay, Phoenix. Administrative Assistant, Larkins and Associates.

Carol Lockridge, Page. Manager & Escrow Officer, 1st American Title Insurance Agency of Coconino, Inc.

Maria "Angie" L.A. Lopez, Chandler. Administrative Secretary, Arizona House of Representatives.

Linda MacLeish-Jensen, Phoenix. Assistant Director, Employee Assistance Program, EAPlus and a Member of St. Lukes Health System.

Anna L. Martin, Yuma. Director, Adult Literacy Program, Yuma County Library District/Yuma Reading Council.

Nadine Mathis, Chandler. Owner, SUMMA Associates.

Barbara Mawhiney, Tempe. Director, Equal Opportunity/Affirmative Action, Arizona State University.

Mary J. McCormick, Yuma. Associate Director, Yuma Private Industry Council, Inc.

Ruth V. McGregor, Phoenix. Appellate Judge, Arizona Court of Appeals.

Joy Mee, Phoenix. Assistant Planning Director, City of Phoenix.

Karen Gill Meyer, Paradise Valley. Residential Realtor.

M. Elaine Morrissette, Kingman. Retired Co-Owner of Credit Bureau.

Ruth Anne Myers, Scottsdale. District Director, U.S. Immigration and Naturalization Service.

Linda Sue Nadolski, Phoenix. City Council Member, City of Phoenix.

Betty J. Newlon, Tucson. Head, Division of Educational and Professional Studies, University of Arizona.

Nettie Ball Obleton, Tempe. Behavioral Health Counselor, ASEPO Counseling & Consulting Services.

Carol Padwe, Scottsdale. Associate VP, Investments, Dean Witter Reynolds Inc.

Terri Palmberg, Mesa. Parks, Recreation, and Cultural Administration, City of Mesa.

Kathy Parker, Phoenix. Teams Engineer, Motorola.

Gael Parks, Phoenix. Supervisor, Deputy Adult Probation Officer, Maricopa County.

Alyce L. Pennington, Tucson. Attorney, Richards & Eisenstein.

Tammy J. Perkins, Phoenix. Senior Management Assistant, Intergovernmental Programs, City of Phoenix.

Robin Pettett, Phoenix. Sales, Systems Consultant, AT&T.

Donna Peyton, Glendale. Employee Relations Administrator, Allied-Signal.

Nancy Phillips, Scottsdale. Psychiatric Social Worker.

Pat A. Pratt, Flagstaff. Employment Counselor, Coconino County, Coconino Career & Training Center.

Sandra Rankin, Tempe. Program Manager, Children's Health Center, St. Joseph's Hospital and Medical Center.

Cindy Resnick, Tucson. State Representative - District 14, Arizona House of Representatives.

Katherine A. Rolle, Phoenix. Partner in Public Accounting Firm, Coopers & Lybrand.

Jean Rosenberg, Phoenix. Executive Director, Arizona Women's Education & Employment.

Bertha M. Ruby, Glendale. Counselor, Arizona State Prison.

Susanne F. Salem, Phoenix. Vice President and Partner, The Prisma Group, Inc.

Romona Saunders, Chandler. Civil Engineer, U.S. Department of Interior, Bureau of Reclamation.

Cynthia Sawyer, Phoenix. Deputy Sheriff Sergeant, Maricopa County Sheriff's Office.

Helen S. Schaefer, Tucson. Retired Teacher, Community Volunteer.

Dorothy A. Schubert, Mesa. Directors of Volunteers.

Mary A. Scott, Chandler. Grandmother.

Arlena E. Seneca, Phoenix. Educational Consultant.

Mary Anne Seymour, Tucson. Specification Writer, Hughes Aircraft Co.

Mary Margaret Smith, Gilbert. Assistant Administrator, Casa Blanca Clinic.

Carolyn Staggs, Tucson. Computer Services/Full-Time Student.

Helen Stern, Tempe. Manufacturer's Representative, G & M Manufacturing, Inc.

Mary C. Stevens, Phoenix. Attorney, Arizona State University.

Selma E. Targovnik, Paradise Valley. Physician, Doctors Targovnik, Ltd.

B. J. Tatro, Phoenix. Human Services Consultant, BJ Tatro Consulting.

Ramonia Thomas, Phoenix. Commercial Credit Representative, Arizona Public Service Co.

Judith C. Tingley, Phoenix. Psychologist.

Kimberlee Tolon, Phoenix. Full-Time Student.

Nancy Van der Voort, Prescott. Self-Employed.

Jane Wabnik, Phoenix. Education and Public Issues Consultant.

Sandra J. Werthman, Scottsdale. Marketing Director, Kitchell Contractors.

Barbara J. Wicks, Chino Valley. Postmaster, Chino Valley and Chino Valley Town Councilmember.

Vivienne F. Williams, Phoenix. Assistant CEO, Phoenix Camelback Hospital.

Diane Wilson, Tucson. Director, PHASE for Displaced Homemakers, University of Arizona and Arizona Department of Education.

Julia M. Wolfe, Phoenix. President and CEO, Phoenix Day Child Development Center.

Lin Wright, Tempe. Chair and Professor, Department of Theatre, Arizona State University.

Cynthia Yaeger, Tempe. Compliance Officer, National Labor Relations Board.

Julia Soto Zozaya, Phoenix. Owner and Manager, American International Diversified.

Patricia Zurga, Tempe. Assistant Comptroller, Arizona State University.

Glossary

Androgyny: A term for lifestyles that combine elements of masculine and feminine behavior but cannot be classified as either masculine or feminine. Androgyny is an attempt to create personhood without manhood and womanhood.

Connectedness Model: Developed by Robin West, this model challenges the traditional legal assumptions of human nature. The traditional legal perspective has defined people as separate, autonomous beings and has defined human rights in terms of maintenance of autonomy. West's model suggests that the traditional view represents a male view. She argues that women define their human nature in terms of connections with other people.

Core economy: The 500-800 largest multinational corporations which contribute over one-half of the U.S. Gross National Product. These firms tend to be the leaders in their industries, be highly bureaucratized, have complicated operating procedures, and have leadership structures that are difficult to enter.

Disparate Impact Doctrine: This doctrine, established in *Griggs v. Duke Power Co.* in 1971, prohibits employment practices having a discriminatory effect.

Disparate Treatment Doctrine: The provision of Title VII that prohibits employment practices motivated by discriminatory intent.

Dual career couple: Each spouse in this kind of relationship is highly trained, committed to career advancement, and receives financial benefits for her or his career activities.

Dual earners: A couple in which both members are employed out of economic necessity. Both do not necessarily have careers.

Dual Labor Market Theory: A theory that the economy contains two distinct labor markets, an internal market and an external market, each of which has its own system of determining prices and allocating labor. The internal market jobs tend to have high wages, good benefits, advancement potential, and job stability. The external market offers relatively low wages, few benefits, little advancement potential, and high job turnover.

External career: This sociological focus on career development examines the career paths in organizations, career stages recognized by employers, and the career types recognized in a society.

Feminist jurisprudence: Models of social justice developed to overcome male biases in the existing legal systems. These models focus on two main goals: expanding people's understanding of equality and expanding people's understanding of human nature.

Gender: Distinct from sex, gender refers to the roles and behavior patterns cultures expect men and women to play.

Gender culture: A generic term referring to the variety of ways in which people are shaped by socialized sex-role expectations.

Glass ceiling: This term describes a barrier many women feel they encounter in the work force that prevents them from rising to the top of their organizations. Although this barrier does not overtly appear in laws, company policies, or employment contracts, many women nevertheless report that they are denied the right to advance beyond this point.

Internal career: The psychological term for the self-development, motivation, enhancement of personal capital, and development of mentoring and anchor networks undertaken by an individual in pursuit of a career.

Latchkey children: These minors must spend a portion of their day unsupervised (usually the time period is the gap between the end of the school day and the end of the parents' work day) because day care is unavailable and/or unaffordable.

Mentor: A person who sponsors a student or protege and who uses her or his influence to highlight the protege's talents and skills.

Mommy track: Career tracks in work organizations that are designed to accommodate a careerist's commitment to home and family. Usually the track allows more flexibility for personal roles, but limits the level of organizational success.

Nonprofit sector economy: This sector functions in a similar manner to the public sector economy, but operates according to its own bureaucratic rules. Private organizations, which tend to rely heavily on volunteer labor, make up this sector.

Peripheral economy: The roughly 14,000 firms that contribute about one-fourth of the U.S. Gross National Product. This sector is highly competitive. The majority of the firms are small, labor intensive, and geographically dispersed. Although this sector offers opportunity to entrepreneurs, it also offers little job security.

Pink collar ghetto: This term refers to the tendency for women to be employed in clerical, secretarial, and administrative support positions in contrast to male laborers who are more likely to be blue collar workers.

Public sector economy: This sector contains government jobs. Along with the nonprofit sector, it accounts for about 25% of the U.S. economy.

Role model: A person who serves as a guide for another person as the second person develops her or his career or lifestyle.

Role overload: This problem occurs when a person has more social roles than he or she can reasonably fulfill.

Role strain: This problem occurs when one's social roles directly conflict with each other. For example, the expectation that a good mother places her children's needs above other needs directly conflicts with the expectation that a good worker places the needs of her or his employer above all other needs.

Second shift: This terms refers to the child-care and home-care responsibilities that are performed primarily by the wives in dual career and dual earning couples.

Segmented Labor Market Theory: This theory posits that the economy consists of three segments: the core, the periphery, and the public/nonprofit sectors. In each sector, career opportunities and barriers operate differently.

Sex role socialization: The process by which men and women learn the gender behavior expected in their culture.

Sex role spillover: Barbara Gutek developed this term to refer to the particular experience of women whose co-workers and employers consider the women's traditional sex roles be considered their primary work role. The result is that these women workers have been expected to perform as surrogate spouse, surrogate parent, or surrogate daughter roles in the workplace.

Social biology: A viewpoint suggesting that differences between the actions and attitudes of women and men can be explained by biological factors, such as reproductive capabilities, genetics, or physical structure.

Social cognition theories: Theories that claim that women and men identify with different "cognitive schema," or ways of viewing the world.

Social learning theories: These theories suggest that major social institutions, including the family, schools, media, and workplace, reward some behaviors and punish others. People learn how to act by learning to pursue rewarded behavior and to avoid punished behavior. These theories argue that men and women are taught to act differently.

Socialization: The process by which people learn the values, beliefs, and behaviors that are expected of them by the traditions of the culture in which they are raised.

Super woman syndrome: A term used to identify the effects of role overload and role strain that occur when women are simultaneously expected to fulfill traditional female and male roles.

Title VII of the Civil Rights Act of 1964: This law prohibits "discrimination on the basis of sex, race, color, religion, or national origin in any employment condition." Sex was included at the last minute by opponents of the Civil Rights Act who believed that an amendment for women's equality would kill support for the act.

Tokenism: Exists when a small number of women and minorities (less than 15%) are in an occupation or organization. The tokens typically are viewed as representing their entire race or gender.

Velvet ghetto: This term refers to career tracks and management positions that neither prepare women employees for, nor facilitate their movement to, higher levels of authority.

Suggested Readings

The literature relevant to understanding the role of women in the U.S. economy is diverse and large. The following list is selected from among the works cited in this book to provide the general reader with additional references for pursuing the topics highlighted in this volume. The list is not intended to be either comprehensive or inclusive.

Women, the Law, and the U.S. Economy

Amundsen, Kirsten. 1971. *The silenced majority.* Englewood Cliffs, NJ: Prentice-Hall.

Eichner, Maxine. 1988. Getting women work that isn't women's work: Challenging gender biases in the workplace under Title VII. *Yale Law Journal* 97(June): 1404.

Eisenstein, Zillah R. 1988. *The female body and the law.* Berkeley: University of California Press.

Erie, Steven P., Martin Rein, and Barbara Wiget. 1983. Women and the Reagan revolution: Thermidor for the social welfare economy. In *Families, politics, and public policy,* ed. Irene Diamond. New York: Longman.

Kelly, Rita Mae, and Jane Bayes, eds. 1988. *Comparable worth, pay equity, and public policy.* Westport, CT: Greenwood.

Kirp, David, Mark Yudof, and Marlene Franks. 1986. *Gender justice.* Chicago: University of Chicago Press.

MacKinnan, Catharine A. 1989. *Toward a feminist theory of the state.* Cambridge, MA: Harvard University Press.

McGlen, Nancy, and Karen O'Connor. 1983. *Women's rights: The struggle for equality in the nineteenth and twentieth centuries, Part II.* New York: Praeger.

Minow, Martha. 1987. The Supreme Court, 1986 term leading cases: Affirmative action—gender preferences. *Harvard Law Review* 101(1): 300-310.

Moller Okin, Susan. 1989. *Justice, gender, and the family.* New York: Basic Books.

National Academy of Sciences. 1981. *Women, wages, and work: Equal pay for work of equal value.* Washington, DC: National Academy of Sciences.

O'Connor, Sandra Day. 1990. Women and the Constitution: A bicentennial perspective. *Women & Politics* 10(Summer): 5-16.

Rhode, Deborah E. 1989. *Justice and gender: Sex discrimination and the law.* Cambridge, MA: Harvard University Press.

West, Robin. 1988. Jurisprudence and gender. *University of Chicago Law Review* 55 (Winter): 1-72.

Williams, W. 1982. The equality crisis: Some reflections on culture, courts, and feminism. *Women's Rights Law Reporter, 7.*

The Segmented Labor Market, Sex Segregation, and Women's Employment

Amsden, Alice H., ed. 1980. *The economics of women and work.* New York: St. Martin's.

Bayes, Jane. 1988. Occupational sex segregation and comparable worth. In *Comparable worth, pay equity, and public policy,* eds. Rita Mae Kelly and Jane Bayes, 15-47. Westport, CT: Greenwood.

Bergmann, Barbara R. 1987. *The economic emergence of women.* New York: Basic Books.

Blau, Francine D., and Marianne A. Ferber. 1966. *The economics of women, men, and work.* Englewood Cliffs, NJ: Prentice-Hall.

Blau, Francine D., and Marianne A. Ferber. 1987. Occupations and earnings of women workers. In *Working women: Past, present, future,* eds. K. S. Koziara, M. H. Moskow, and L. D. Tanner, 37-68. Washington, DC: BNA Books.

Brown, Clair, and Joseph A. Pechman, eds. 1987. *Gender in the workplace.* Washington, DC: Brookings Institution.

Doeringer, P. B., and M. H. Piore. 1971. *Internal labor markets and manpower analysis.* Lexington, MA: D.C. Heath.

Epstein, Cynthia Fuchs. 1988. *Deceptive distinctions: Sex, gender and the social order.* New Haven, CT: Yale University Press.

Evans, Sara M., and Barbara J. Nelson. 1989. *Wage justice: Comparable worth and the paradox of technocratic reform.* Chicago: University of Chicago Press.

Howe, Louise Kapp. 1977. *Pink collar workers.* New York: G.P. Putnam's Sons.

Huerta, Faye C., and T. A. Lane. 1981. Participation of women in centers of power. *Social Science Journal* April: 71-86.

Kelly, Rita Mae, and Jane Bayes, eds. 1988. *Comparable worth, pay equity, and public policy.* Westport, CT: Greenwood.

Piore, M. J. 1984. Notes for a theory of labor stratification. In *Conference on labor market segmentation,* eds. R.C. Edwards, M. Reich, and D.M. Gordon, 125-150. Lexington, MA: D.C. Heath.

Reskin, Barbara F., ed. 1984. *Sex segregation in the workplace: Trends, explanations, remedies,* Committee on Women's Employment and Related Social Issues, Commission on Behavioral and Social Sciences and Education, National Research Council. Washington, DC: National Academy Press.

Reskin, Barbara F., and Heidi Hartmann, eds. 1986. *Women's work, men's work: Sex segregation on the job.* Washington, DC: National Academy Press.

Scott, Joan. 1988. *Gender and the politics of history.* New York: Columbia University Press.

Stump, Roger W. 1986. Women clergy in the United States: A geographical analysis of religious change. *Social Science Quarterly* 67(June): 337-352.

Trieman, Donald J., and Heidi Hartmann. 1981. *Women, work, and wages: Equal pay for jobs of equal value.* Washington, DC: National Academy Press.

U.S. Commission on Civil Rights. 1984. *Comparable worth: Issues for the '80s.* Washington, DC: Commission on Civil Rights.

Vertz, Laura. 1987. Pay inequalities between women and men in state and local government: An examination of the political context of the comparable worth controversy. *Women & Politics* 7(Summer): 43-57.

Sex Roles, Gender Stereotypes, and Career Success

Almquist, E. M., and S. S. Angrist. 1971. Role model influences on college women's career aspirations. *Merrill-Palmer Quarterly* 17(3): 263-279.

Anderson, Margaret. 1988. *Thinking about women: Sociological perspectives on sex and gender.* New York: Macmillan.

Arthur, Michael B., Douglas T. Hall, and Barbara S. Lawrence, eds. 1989. *Handbook of career theory.* Cambridge, UK: Cambridge University Press.

Backhouse, Constance, and Leah Cohen. 1981. *Sexual harassment on the job.* Toronto: Prentice-Hall.

Basow, S. A. 1980. *Sex role stereotypes: Traditions and alternatives.* Monterey, CA: Brooks/Cole.

Brereton, T. F. 1977. The problems of race and sex in public agency staffs. *Public Administration Review* 37(5): 604-607.

Brown, Stephen M. 1979. Male versus female leaders: A comparison of empirical studies. *Sex Roles: A Journal of Research* 5(October): 595-661.

Bushardt, Stephen C., Aubrey Fowler, and Regina Caveny. 1987. Sex role behavior and leadership: An empirical investigation. *Leadership and Organizational Journal* 8(5): 13-16.

Cherpas, C. C. 1985. Dual-career families: Terminology, typologies, and work and family issues. *Journal of Counseling and Development* 63(10): 616-620.

Chodorow, Nancy. 1978. *The reproduction of mothering: Psychoanalysis and the sociology of gender.* Berkeley: University of California Press.

Cunningham, Mary Ann. 1984. *Power play.* New York: Simon & Schuster.

Deaux, Kay. 1976. *The behavior of men and women.* Monterey, CA: Brooks/Cole.

deBeauvoir, Simone. 1952. *The second sex,* trans. H.M. Parshley, New York Modern Library. New York: Vintage Books.

Deutchman, I. E. 1986. Socialization to power: Questions about women and politics. *Women & Politics* 5(4): 79-89.

Dobbins, G. H. 1986. Equity vs. equality: Sex differences in leadership. *Sex Roles* 15(9/10): 513-525.

Dziech, Billie Wright, and Linda Weiner. 1984. *The lecherous professor.* Boston: Beacon.

Echols, J. 1985. Sex differences in achievement patterns. In *Nebraska symposium on motivation, 1984: Psychology and gender,* ed. T. B. Sonderegger, 97-132. Lincoln: University of Nebraska Press.

Elder, Glenn H. 1969. Appearance and education in marriage mobility. *American Socio-logical Review* 34: 519-533.

Farganis, Sondra. 1986. *The social reconstruction of the feminine character.* Totowa, NJ: Rowman & Littlefield.

Farmer, H. S. 1985. Model of career and achievement motivation for women and men. *Journal of Counseling Psychology* 32: 363-390.

Fassinger, Ruth E. 1985. A causal model of college women's career choice. *Journal of Vocational Behavior* 27(August): 123-153.

Friedan, Betty. 1981. *The second stage.* New York: Summit Books.

Gilligan, Carol. 1982. *In a different voice: Psychological theory and women's develop-ment.* Cambridge, MA: Harvard University Press.

Greene, W. H., and A. O. Quester. 1982. Divorce risk and wives' labor supply behavior. *Social Science Quarterly* 63(1): 16-26.

Greenglass, Esther R., and Reva Devins. 1982. Factors related to marriage and career plans in unmarried women. *Sex Roles* 8: 57-72.

Gutek, Barbara A. 1985. *Sex and the workplace: The impact of sexual behavior and harassment on women, men, and organizations.* San Francisco: Jossey-Bass.

Gutek, Barbara A., and L. Larwood, eds. 1987. *Women's career development.* Newbury Park, CA: Sage.

Gutek, Barbara, and Ann H. Stromberg, eds. 1988. *Women and work, an annual review,* Vol. 3. Newbury Park, CA: Sage.

Hale, Mary M., and Rita Mae Kelly. 1989. *Gender, bureaucracy and democracy.* Westport, CT: Greenwood.

Herbert, Claire. 1989. *Talking of silence: The sexual harassment of school girls.* New York: Palmer.

Hertz, Rosanna. 1986. *More equal than others: Women and men in dual career marriages.* Berkeley: University of California Press.

Hess, B. H., and M. B. Sussman. 1984. *Women and the family: Two decades of change.* New York: Haworth.

Hochschild, Arlie. 1989. *The second shift.* New York: Viking.

Hyde, Janet Shibley. 1985. *Half the human experience: The psychology of women* 3rd ed. Lexington, MA: D.C. Heath.

Josselson, R. 1987. *Finding herself: Pathways to identity development in women.* San Francisco: Jossey-Bass.

Kanter, Rosabeth M. 1977. *Men and women of the corporation.* New York: Basic Books.

Kelly, Rita Mae, and Mary Boutilier. 1988. *The making of political women: A study of socialization and role conflict.* Chicago: Nelson-Hall.

Kimball, Gayle. 1988. *50-50 parenting.* Lexington, MA: D.C. Heath.

Lipman-Blumen, J. 1982. *Gender roles and power.* Englewood Cliffs, NJ: Prentice-Hall.

Maccoby, E. E., and C. N. Jacklin. 1974. *The psychology of sex differences.* Stanford, CA: Stanford University Press.

MacKinnon, C. A. 1979. *Sexual harassment of working women: A case of sex discrimi-nation.* New Haven, CT: Yale University Press.

Mainiero, Lisa A. 1989. *Office romance: Love, power, and sex in the workplace.* New York: Rawson of McMillan.

Mednick, M. T. S., S. S. Tangri, and L. W. Hoffman. 1975. *Women and achievement.* New York: John Wiley.

Mednick, Martha T. 1988. On the politics of psychological constructs. *American Psychol-ogist* 44(8): 1118-1123.

Pleck, Joseph. 1985. *Working wives/working husbands.* Beverly Hills, CA: Sage.

Reily, P. J. 1980. *Sexual harassment in the navy.* Unpublished master's thesis. U.S. Navy Post Graduate School, Monterey, CA.

Rix, Sara E., ed. 1988. *The American woman: 1988-89.* New York: W.W. Norton.

Sargent, Alice G. 1977. *Beyond sex roles* 2nd ed. St. Paul, MN: West.

Sekaran, Uma. 1986. *Dual-career families: Contemporary organizational and counseling issues.* San Francisco: Jossey-Bass.

Shaver, Phillip, and Clyde Hendrick, eds. 1987. *Sex and gender.* Beverly Hills, CA: Sage.

Signorielli, Nancy. 1989. Television and conceptions about sex roles: Maintaining conventionality and the status quo. *Sex Roles* 21(516): 341-361.

Stein, A. H., and M. M. Bailey. 1973. The socialization of achievement oriented females. *Psychological Bulletin* 5(51): 345-366.

Zellman, G. L. 1976. The role of structural factors in limiting women's institutional participation. *Journal of Social Issues* 32(3): 33-46.

Women, Work, and Management

Arthur, Michael B., Douglas T. Hall, and Barbara S. Lawrence, eds. 1989. *Handbook of career theory.* Cambridge, UK: Cambridge University Press.

Bilensky, Marilyn Loden. 1985. *Feminine leadership: Or how to succeed in business without being one of the boys.* New York: Time Books.

Carr-Ruffino, N. 1985. *The promotable woman.* Belmont, CA: Wadsworth.

Catalyst. 1986, April. *Female management style: Myth and reality.* New York: Catalyst.

Desjardins, Carolyn. 1989. Gender issues in community college leadership. *American Association of Women In Community and Junior College Journal* (June): 5-9.

Duerst-Lahti, Georgia, and Cathy Marie Johnson. 1990. Gender and style in bureaucracy. *Women & Politics* 10(4): 67-120.

Dye, Thomas, and Julie Strickland. 1982. Women at the top: A note on institutional leadership. *Social Science Quarterly* June: 333-341.

Ferguson, Kathy. 1988. *The feminist case against bureaucracy.* Philadelphia: Temple University Press.

Franklin, D., and J. Sweeney. 1988. Women and corporate power. In *Women, power, and policy: Toward the year 2000* 2nd ed, eds. E. Bonspanth and E. Stope. New York: Pergamon.

Fuchs, Victor R. *Women's quest for economic equality.* Cambridge, MA: Harvard University Press.

Gallese, L. R. 1985. *Women like us: What is happening to the women of the Harvard Business School, Class of 75—The women who had the first chance to make it to the top?* New York: William Morrow.

Gutek, B., A. H. Stromberg, and L. Larwood eds. 1988. *Women and work, an annual review,* Vol. 3. Newbury Park, CA: Sage.

Hale, Mary M., and Rita Mae Kelly. 1989. *Gender, bureaucracy, and democracy.* Westport, CT: Greenwood.

Hardesty, Sarah, and Nehama Jacobs. 1986. *Success and betrayal: The crisis of women in corporate America.* New York: Franklin Watts.

Hennig, Margaret, and Anne Jardim. 1977. *The managerial woman.* Garden City, NY: Anchor/Doubleday.

Josefowitz, Natasha. 1980. Management men and women: Closed vs. open doors. *Harvard Business Review* 58(October): 56-62.

Josefowitz, Natasha. 1980. *Paths to power: A woman's guide from first job to top executive.* Reading, MA: Addison-Wesley.

Kanter, Rosabeth M. 1977. *Men and women of the corporation.* New York: Basic Books.

Kelly, Rita Mae, Mary M. Hale, and Jayne Burgess. 1991. Gender and managerial/leadership styles: A comparison of Arizona public administrators, *Women & Politics* 11(2), 19-39.

Korn/Ferry international profile of women senior executives. 1982. New York: Korn/Ferry International.

Lipman-Blumen, J. 1982. *Gender roles and power.* Englewood Cliffs, NJ: Prentice-Hall.

Loden, Marilyn. 1985. *Feminine leadership, or, how to succeed in business without being one of the boys.* New York: Time Books.

Melia J., and P. Lyttle. 1986. *Why Jenny can't lead: Understanding the male dominant system.* Saguache, CO: Operational Politics.

Morrison, Ann M., Randall P. White, and Ellen Van Velson. 1987. *Breaking the glass ceiling.* Reading, MA: Addison-Wesley.

Morrison, Ann M., and Mary Ann Von Glinow. 1990. Women and minorities in management, *American Psychologist* 45(2): 200-208.

Powell, Gary N. 1988. *Men and women in management.* Newbury Park, CA: Sage.

Rosener, Judy B. 1990. Ways women lead. *Harvard Business Review* (November-December): 119-125.

Schein, Edgar H. 1987. Individuals and careers. In *Handbook of organizational behavior,* ed. Jay W. Lorsch, 155-171. Englewood Cliffs, NJ: Prentice-Hall.

Statham, Anne. 1985. Women managers: Leadership style, development, and misunderstandings. In *Women and work: Selected papers,* eds. W. Knezek, M. Barrett, and S. Collins. Arlington: University of Texas, Arlington.

Statham, Anne. 1987. The gender model revisited: Differences in the management styles of men and women. *Sex Roles* 16(7/8): 409-429.

Tucker, Sharon. 1985. Careers of men and women MBAs, 1950-1980. *Work and Occupations* 12(2): 166-185.

Wood, Marion M., and Susan T. Greenfield. 1976. Women managers and fear of success: A study in the field. *Sex Roles* 2(December): 375-387.

Strategies for Change

Bose, Christine, and Glenna Spitze, eds. 1987. *Ingredients for women's employment policy.* Albany: State University of New York Press.

Chafetz, Janet Saltzman. 1990. *Gender equity: An integrated theory of stability and change.* Newbury Park, CA: Sage.

Crocker, Jennifer, and Kathleen M. McGraw. 1984. What's good for the goose is not good for the gander. *American Behavioral Scientist* 27(3): 357-369.

Dinnerstein, Dorothy. 1983. *The mermaid and the minotaur.* New York: Harper & Row.

Gelb, Joyce, and Marian Lief Palley. 1982. *Women and public policies.* Princeton, NJ: Princeton University Press.

Hawkesworth, Mary E. 1990. *Beyond oppression: Feminist theory and political strategy.* New York: Continuum.

Larwood, Laurie, Barbara Gutek, and Urs E. Gattiker. 1984. Perspectives on institutional discrimination and resistance to change. *Groups and Organization Studies* 9(3): 333-352.

Littleton, Christine A. 1987. Restructuring sexual equality. *California Law Review* 75: 1279.

Littleton, Christine A. 1989. Feminist jurisprudence: The difference method makes. *Stanford Law Review* 41: 751-784.

MacKinnon, Catherine A. 1987. *Feminism unmodified*. Cambridge, MA: Harvard University Press.

Menkel-Meadow, Carrie. 1989. Excluded voices: New voices in the legal profession making new voices in the law. *University of Minnesota Law Review* 42: 19.

Michael, Carol M., and David M. Hunt. 1985. Women and organizations: A study of mentorship. In *Preparing professional women for the future: Resources for teachers and trainers,* ed. V. Jean Ramsey, 177-190. Ann Arbor: University of Michigan Press.

Noe, Raymond A. 1988. Women and mentoring: A review and research agenda. *Academy of Management Review* 13(1): 65-78.

Rhode, Deborah L. 1989. *Justice and gender: Sex discrimination and the law.* Cambridge, MA: Harvard University Press.

Sherry, Suzanna. 1986. Civic virtue and the feminine voice in constitutional adjudication. *Virginia Law Review* 72: 543.

Tarr-Whelan, Linda, and Lynne Crofton Isensee, eds. 1987. *The women's economic justice agenda: Ideas for the states.* Washington, DC: National Center for Policy Alternatives.

Tong, Rosemarie. 1989. *Feminist thought.* Boulder, CO: Westview Press.

West, Robin. 1988. Jurisprudence and gender. *University of Chicago Law Review* 55: 1, 4.

Wildman, Stephanie M. 1984. The legitimation of sex discrimination: A critical response to Supreme Court jurisprudence. *Oregon Law Review* 63: 265.

Women and the Arizona Economy

Brown, Carol Osman. 1979. Women executives—Phoenix' greatest resource. *Phoenix Metro Magazine* April, 82-87, ff.

Hale, Mary M., and Rita Mae Kelly, eds. 1989. *Gender, bureaucracy, and democracy: Careers and equal opportunity in the public sector.* Westport, CT: Greenwood.

Kelly, Rita Mae, ed. 1988. *Women and the Arizona political process.* Lanham, MD: University Press of America.

Monk, Janice, and Alice Schlegal, eds. 1986. *Women and the Arizona economy: The First Arizona Women's Townhall.* Tucson: University of Arizona, Southwest Institute for Research on Women.

Prentice, M. Christine. 1986. Women in the Arizona economy. In *Arizona's changing economy,* ed. Bernard Ronan, 249-262. Phoenix, AZ: Commerce Press.

Name Index

Subject Index

258

About the Author and Project Director

Rita Mae Kelly (Ph.D.) is Director and Chair of the School of Justice Studies and Professor of Justice Studies, Political Science, and Women's Studies at Arizona State University, Tempe. She holds a doctorate in political science from Indiana University. Dr. Kelly is the author of several books including *Community Control of Economic Development* and *The Making of Political Women*. She is editor of *Promoting Productivity in the Public Sector: Problems, Strategies, and Prospects*; *Gender and Socialization to Power and Politics*; *Comparable Worth, Pay Equity, and Public Policy*; *Women and the Arizona Political Process*; *Gender, Bureaucracy, and Democracy*; and is editor of the Praeger Book Series on women and politics (with Ruth B. Mandel) and a Sage series on public policy. Dr. Kelly is Past President of the Policy Studies Organization (1988-89), the Western Political Science Association (1988-89), and is editor of *Women & Politics*.

About the Other Contributors

Marcia Cech-Soucy (B.A.) is a master's degree candidate in the School of Justice Studies at Arizona State University. She earned her bachelor's degree in Women's Studies at ASU and serves on various university and community boards that address the needs of women.

Deborah De Paoli (B.A.) is currently a candidate for Juris Doctor at the Arizona State University College of Law. She earned her bachelor's degree in political science at UCLA. De Paoli has served on the Organizing Committee for the International Ecofeminist Conference, and currently works in the Arizona Attorney General's Office. She also is a Faculty Associate in the School of Justice Studies at Arizona State University.

Kimberly Fisher (B.A.) is a master's degree student in the School of Justice Studies at Arizona State University. She earned her bachelor's degree in political science with a minor in Women's Studies at ASU. Fisher's accolades include Phi Beta Kappa membership, two public speaking national championships, and Rhodes Scholarship finalist.

Phoebe Morgan Stambaugh (M.S.) is currently a doctoral candidate in the School of Justice Studies at Arizona State University. She earned her master's degree in the School of Justice Studies at ASU. She has presented papers at the annual meetings of the Western Political Science Association and the Fourth International Interdisciplinary Congress on Women. She has been an intern in the Arizona Governor's Office of Women's Services, a media image producer, and a public school instructor.